Trademark Acknowledgements

Wrox has endeavored to provide trademark information about all the companies and products mentioned in this book by the appropriate use of capitals. However, Wrox cannot guarantee the accuracy of this information.

Credits

Authors
S. Jeelani Basha
Romin Irani

Technical Reviewers
Steven J. Baker
Sanjeev N. Ramachandra
Eric Paul Schley
David Whitney
Dave Writz

Commisioning Editor
Benjamin Hickman

Technical Editors
Benjamin Hickman
Dan Maharry
Chanoch Wiggers

Managing Editor
Jan Kolasinski

Project Manager
Beckie Stones

Production Coordinators
Abbie Forletta
Sarah Hall

Proof Reader
Chris Smith

Cover Design
Natalie O'Donnell

About the Authors

S. Jeelani Basha

Jeelani works as a Senior Software Engineer at InSync Information Systems, Fremont, California. He has a Bachelor's in Electrical Engineering and is a Sun Certified Java2 Programmer. He has more than five years of experience using J2EE technology.

He has also co-authored two other titles for Wrox, *Professional J2EE EAI* and *Professional Java Web Services*. His current subject of interest is web services and is putting part of his efforts into making web services a viable solution for enterprise applications. Jeelani welcomes your comments at s_jeelani@yahoo.com.

Thanks to my lovely wife, Hasi, with out whose support and encouragement I would have never completed the chapters. Thanks to Wrox for giving me one more opportunity to write on web services.

Romin Irani

Romin Irani is a Senior Software Engineer with InSync Information Systems, Inc in Fremont, California. He graduated with a Bachelors degree in Computer Engineering from University of Bombay, India. He has around seven years of experience, starting out in the Microsoft world but now fully immersed into Java technologies. He welcomes your comments at romin@rocketmail.com.

I am most thankful to my wife Devyani, whose co-operation and love made this possible. For all the long nights and early mornings that I took to write the chapters, she was right behind me. And of course due credits to my parents, Khushru and Gulrukh for all that they have taught me in life.

AXIS

Table of Contents

v

Introduction

Introduction

The **A**pache e**X**tensible **I**nteraction **S**ystem (AXIS) is the latest implementation of SOAP for Java. In effect, it is version 3 of Apache SOAP, the de facto standard SOAP implementation used with Java. With Sun's official support for SOAP still working its way through the Java community process, AXIS looks set to become the most important SOAP implementation for Java.

AXIS is a complete ground-up reimplementation; it is designed to be flexible, modular, and unlike previous implementations, which were intended as a proof of concept, it has been designed with performance in mind. This modular approach will enable it to keep pace with future developments in the SOAP protocol. It also makes for a uniquely extensible message processing system. Message processing in AXIS is built on a series of modules (known as Handlers); adding custom functionality to AXIS is as simple as extending the basic handler class and then deploying to the AXIS engine.

Who Is This Book For?

This book is for professional Java developers looking to keep up with the latest implementation of SOAP for Java. If you just want to create and deploy AXIS-based clients for other people's web services, or develop your own web services, or implement your own modules to plug into AXIS this book will provide numerous relevant examples.

What Does This Book Cover?

This book covers AXIS from the point of view of web service and a web service client developers. We look at all the tools provide with the AXIS System, its architecture, how to extend it using custom handlers, and how to build real applications using it.

Chapter by chapter, here's what to expect:

❑ **Chapter 1 – Introduction to AXIS**
We start off by introducing AXIS, web services, and how they relate to each other; then we describe how to set up an AXIS SOAP server and deploy our first AXIS-based web service.

❑ **Chapter 2 – AXIS**
This chapter looks at AXIS from a user-centric view, describing the tools that are available for creating client-side stubs and server-side skeletons for AXIS web services. Once you have generated the appropriate stubs or skeletons a web service can be called just like any other Java class.

❑ **Chapter 3 – Architecture**

Before going any further we need to understand how AXIS actually works. Here we look at all of the components that make up the AXIS message processing system and how messages flow between them.

❑ **Chapter 4 – Custom Handlers in AXIS**

The basic AXIS system is built from a series of message handlers; extending AXIS simply requires you to write a new handler and then deploy it in the AXIS system. In this chapter we develop two custom handlers one for logging messages and one for logging performance.

❑ **Chapter 5 – Advanced AXIS Features**

In this chapter we demonstrate some of the more advanced features that are available when using AXIS, including: serializing custom data types, sending SOAP attachments, HTTP Authentication, SSL communication, and using asynchronous transport protocols.

❑ **Chapter 6 – Interoperability**

One of the key benefits offered by web services is that they should be able to interoperate with clients written for any SOAP implementation. In this chapter we discuss the issues that can prevent this and demonstrate some of examples of where it does work.

❑ **Chapter 7 – Future Directions for AXIS**

AXIS is still in beta and many new features should become available in future versions. In this chapter we look at what aims the AXIS team have set themselves and other things that may influence the future of AXIS.

❑ **Chapter 8 – Case Study**

In this chapter we develop a full case study using AXIS web services built around a supply-chain management system for a car manufacture and its dealers.

❑ **Appendix A –** AXIS TCP Monitor

❑ **Appendix B –** J2EE Integration

❑ **Appendix C –** JAX-RPC

What Do You Need?

Most of the code in this book was tested with the Java 2 Platform, Standard Edition SDK (JDK 1.4) and the Java 2 Platform, Standard Edition SDK 1.3. You can download the appropriate SDK for your platform from http://java.sun.com/j2se/1.4/download.html.

Servlet Container

In order to deploy the AXIS servlet you will need a web container that supports the Servlet 2.3 and the JSP 1.2 specifications. We used Jakarta Tomcat 4.0.3; the latest build of Tomcat is available from **http://jakarta.apache.org/tomcat**.

Apache AXIS

Apache AXIS, which can be downloaded from http://xml.apache.org.

Additional Software

There are a few pieces of software that are required for a particular example or chapter:

Database

The case study in Chapter 8 requires access to a database; we used MySQL 3.23, which is available to download from: http://www.mysql.com/downloads/index.html.

JMS server

In Chapter 5 we develop a custom handler for the Java Message System; hence we need a JMS server. We used BEA WebLogic 6.1; an evaluation edition can be downloaded from: http://commerce.bea.com/downloads/weblogic_server.jsp.

EJB Container

Appendix B demonstrates how to expose an EJB as a web service. To deploy the EJB will need an EJB container supporting version 2.0 of the EJB specification. We used JBOSS 2.4.4. This is available to download from http://www.jboss.org/binary.jsp.

Microsoft .NET Framework

Chapter 6 uses a client program written in C# to demonstrate interoperability; to compile and run the C# example you will need the .NET Framework SDK. This can be downloaded from http://msdn.microsoft.com/downloads/.

AXIS

1

Introduction to AXIS

The **A**pache e**X**tensible **I**nteraction **S**ystem, or AXIS for short, is an exciting new development in the field of web services A complete re-architecture and implementation of the hugely popular Apache SOAP project, it was designed and developed from the ground-up to be more modular, more flexible, and generally more efficient. It comes with several new exciting features, which we shall cover throughout the course of the book.

In this chapter, we will cover the following:

❑   A brief introduction to web services and the key technologies that help enable a web services system – SOAP, WSDL, and UDDI

❑   The key features of AXIS, comparing it to its previous incarnation – Apache SOAP

❑   The installation of AXIS

❑   Writing our first web Service in AXIS

One cannot overemphasize the fact that we need to install new software correctly, the first time around. More so, with a developing technology like AXIS, which is still at beta 1 stage as this book was sent to press (April 2002). One of the main aims of this chapter then will be to provide detailed instructions on installing AXIS and verifying that its installation was successful.

SOAP and Web Services

Recently, **web services** have been garnering all the attention in the computer industry. Many see them as the solution to all kinds of problems, ranging from application integration within the enterprise to executing business transactions across enterprises. In the next few sections, we shall concentrate on the basics of web services and the key technologies they depend on. Readers familiar with web services concepts and technologies like **SOAP**, **WSDL**, and **UDDI** might want to skip over to the next section, and go straight to *AXIS Beta 1 Features* where we will start our tour of AXIS.

Introducing SOAP

SOAP (**S**imple **O**bject **A**ccess **P**rotocol) is a lightweight XML-based protocol that supports **RPC** (Remote Procedure Calls) and **Messaging** over any network protocol but primarily over HTTP. Since it uses an XML-based protocol instead of a binary format, it is highly interoperable across platforms, programming languages, component models, etc. As it is based on message passing, SOAP can easily be implemented over asynchronous protocols such as SMTP and Java Messaging Services as well.

SOAP has several advantages when you compare it to its predecessor, the XML-RPC Protocol. XML-RPC is a simple protocol that allows remote method calls using XML as the encoding and HTTP as the transport protocol. SOAP builds upon this protocol by providing more support for complex data types and different transport protocols along with the ability to exactly specify how we want the message to be processed.

Introducing Web Services

A web service is a piece of software functionality that is accessible over a network and built on technologies that are independent of platform, programming language and component model. Web services are based on a **S**ervice-**O**riented **A**rchitecture (SOA) where software functionality is distributed as a set of services. In order for a service to exist within the SOA realm, there needs to be a common mechanism to describe, discover, and invoke services. In Figure 1, you'll see the different roles and the interactions between the roles in a Service-Oriented Architecture.

Figure 1

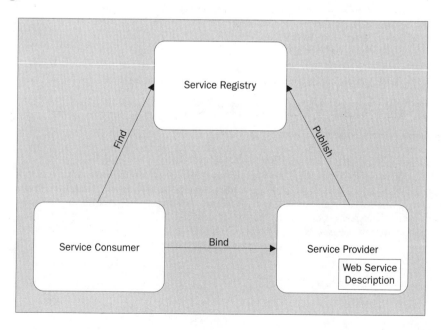

An SOA describes three basic roles:

❑ **Service Provider**
   The Service Provider is responsible for the implementation of the web service. One of the first tasks that a service provider needs to do is determine the functionality they want to expose as a web service. Often this functionality is already present in their existing systems. Once they have done that, they need to **describe** the interface to this functionality in a standard fashion. Finally, they need to **publish** this interface to a registry for service consumers to **find** (discover) their web service.

❑ **Service Registry**
   The Service Registry functions as a repository of web services. Service providers typically **publish** their web service definitions to this registry. So, service registries have facilities not only to allow service providers to **publish** their web services but also to act as a **repository** for potential service consumers to **find** (discover) these web services and provide them with the necessary information to help them **bind** and **invoke** the web service.

❑ **Service Consumer**
   The Service Consumer makes use of the web service created by the service provider. It retrieves all the necessary information for binding to the web service from the service registry, including the interface to the web service that the service provider has published. The interface gives it the details of the methods, parameters, and transport protocol necessary to make use of the service.

The SOA defined above is an abstract model but it does have several concrete manifestations. One of these is the interoperable **web services stack**, as defined by several companies like IBM, Microsoft, etc. This describes the technologies used to achieve the functions that we saw above: find, bind, and publish. A common web services stack, which employs platform- and vendor-neutral standards, is essential in order to achieve interoperability.

Figure 2 shows the web services stack and its related technologies.

Figure 2

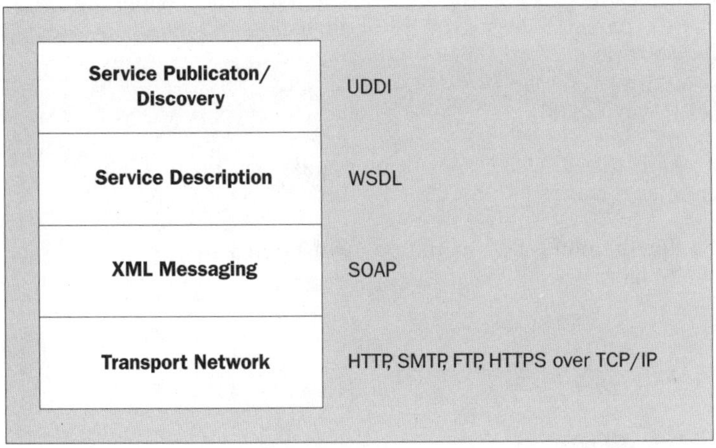

Service Publicaton/ Discovery	UDDI
Service Description	WSDL
XML Messaging	SOAP
Transport Network	HTTP, SMTP, FTP, HTTPS over TCP/IP

At the lowest level is the **transport layer** that is responsible for the communication between **endpoints** – communication ports that can send and receive messages. Web services technologies protect the investment in existing network technologies by utilizing some of the commonly available transport mechanisms that are already in widespread use, especially HTTP. It is important to note that we could use any transport protocol and are in no way bound to just HTTP. One level up, the **messaging layer** is responsible for the invocation of a web service by the service consumer. Here, the service consumer uses SOAP messages to call methods exposed by the web service and the service provider describes their web service interface in a standard fashion with **WSDL** (Web Services Description Language). Finally, at the top level is the **discovery layer**, implemented in **UDDI** (Universal Description and Discovery Interface).

Before we get to AXIS itself then, we'll quickly recap the three technologies at work in the web services stack:

❑ SOAP – a standard mechanism for invoking web services

❑ WSDL – a standard mechanism for describing web services

❑ UDDI – a standard mechanism for publishing and discovering web services

With an understanding of each of these, we'll be able to appreciate the advances that AXIS makes over previous versions of Apache SOAP.

SOAP

Version 1.0 of the Simple Object Access Protocol, or SOAP 1.0, was released in late 1999 and version 1.1, which incorporated the XML Schema DataTypes instead of the native type system that was used in SOAP 1.0, followed in early 2000. SOAP Version 1.1 has the most widespread support among web services platform vendors and toolkit implementations.

The current version of SOAP is version 1.2, working draft 3, and is divided into two documents: **Messaging Framework** and **Adjuncts**. The messaging framework paper discusses the SOAP envelope and the transport-binding framework. The adjuncts paper discusses the RPC convention and the encoding rules along with the description of an HTTP binding specification. You can get more details from http://www.w3.org/TR/soap12-part1 and http://www.w3.org/TR/soap12-part2.

AXIS completely supports the SOAP 1.1 specification and is closely following the SOAP 1.2 specification as it makes its way (slowly) through to recommendation.

To understand the different entities that would be involved in a basic SOAP system, have a look at Figure 3:

Figure 3

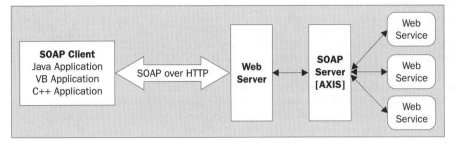

A SOAP client sends a SOAP message to a web service over HTTP. The message is intercepted by a web server that delegates the processing of the message to a SOAP server (also called a SOAP engine), which in turn invokes the appropriate web service. AXIS is a SOAP server, receiving calls from and sending responses as SOAP messages to SOAP clients.

SOAP Message

A SOAP Message is an XML document that consists of the following three parts as given below. At the highest level, it looks like this:

```
<SOAP-ENV:Envelope
  xmlns:SOAP-ENV="http://schemas.xmlsoap.org/soap/envelope"
  xmlns:xsd="http://www.w3.org/2001/XMLSchema"
  xmlns:xsi="http://www.w3.org/2001/XMLSchema-instance"
  SOAP-ENV:encodingStyle="http://schemas.xmlsoap.org/soap/encoding/">

  <SOAP-ENV:Header>
    ...
  </SOAP-ENV:Header>

  <SOAP-ENV:Body>
    ...
  </SOAP-ENV:Body>

</SOAP-ENV:Envelope>
```

We can see that a SOAP message consists of the following:

SOAP Envelope

The SOAP envelope is the mandatory top-level element of the SOAP message. It contains an optional <Header> element, which lets you specify any extra information about the message that is not the message itself, and a mandatory <Body> element that contains the actual payload of the SOAP message, be it a request from an endpoint or a response from a server. If you like, you can think of the <Envelope> element as similar to a postal envelope.

Within the `<Envelope>` element, you can specify namespaces and the encoding style of the message. If a SOAP application (client, server, etc.) receives a message with a namespace other than `http://schemas.xmlsoap.org /soap/envelope`, it must return a version error. Meanwhile, the `xmlns:xsd` namespace is used to reference elements and attributes to the XML Schema specification, and the `xmlns:xsi` namespace is used to reference elements and attributes to an instance of the XML Schema.

The `encodingStyle` attribute is used to specify to the recipient of a SOAP message which serialization format was used to encode a given element and its descendants. The SOAP specification gives this as `http://schemas.xmlsoap.org/soap/encoding`.

SOAP Header

The SOAP specification does not define how it will handle features like authentication, security, transactions, versioning, etc. However, to garner widespread acceptance of the protocol, applications are allowed to extend the protocol by adding information to the `<Header>` element. For example, you could use the `<Header>` element to add security information as shown below:

```
<SOAP-ENV:Header>
   <axis:security xmlns:axis="http://www.wrox.com/axis">
      <axis:loginid>0495-40359-35345309-9-935-349543</axis:loginid>
   </axis:security>
</SOAP-ENV:Header>
```

The `<Header>` element has two attributes; `mustUnderstand` and `actor` – both extremely important within the context of **SOAP intermediaries**. These are components that sit in the chain between the SOAP client and SOAP server, processing both the request flow and the response flow of the message. AXIS provides support for SOAP intermediaries by letting you introduce your own handlers that can intercept the request and/or response flows.

A `mustUnderstand` attribute indicates to the recipient of the SOAP message (an intermediary or endpoint) that the particular attribute must be understood, otherwise a SOAP fault needs to be thrown. If the `mustUnderstand` attribute value is set to 1, it must be recognize the `<Header>` element and process it. If it does not recognize the element, then it must report the exception as a SOAP Fault. If `mustUnderstand` is set to 0, the processing of this element is optional. An example of a `mustUnderstand` attribute is shown below in a sample scenario:

```
<SOAP-ENV:Header>
   <axis:transaction xmlns:axis="http://www.wrox.com/axis"
                 SOAP-ENV:mustUnderstand="1">
   <axis:transactionid>3534-121212</axis:transactionid>
   </axis:transaction>
</SOAP-ENV:Header>
```

An `actor` attribute, meanwhile, specifies the name of the SOAP intermediary that the `<Header>` element is meant for. If a SOAP intermediary receives a SOAP header in which it is specified as an actor, it must process it, unless `actor` is set to `http://schemas.xml-soap.org/soap/actor/next`, in which case the `<Header>` element is meant for the next intermediary in the chain. If this attribute is not present, the SOAP header is intended for the ultimate (final) recipient of the message.

For example, if we want to target a payment intermediary, we can do it as shown below:

```
<SOAP-ENV:Header>
   <axis:payment xmlns:axis="http://www.wrox.com/axis"
                 SOAP-ENV:actor="http://www.wrox.com/axis/payment">
     <customerid>CUSTOMER-123</customerid>
   </axis:payment>
</SOAP-ENV:Header>
```

SOAP Body

The `<Body>` element defines the payload of the message. You can think of the `<Body>` element as being similar to a letter inside the postal envelope. The element can be an RPC call or a message. It could also contain a **SOAP fault** in the case of errors. The SOAP specification describes how an RPC call is mapped into an XML structure.

For example, suppose we need to invoke, via SOAP, a method called `getPrice()` on the `SparePartPrice` object. The SOAP RPC serialization of this call will be as shown below:

```
<SOAP-ENV:Envelope ...>
   <SOAP-ENV:Header>...</SOAP-ENV:Header>
   <SOAP-ENV:Body>
      <ns1:getPrice xmlns:ns1="SparePartPrice">
         <sku xsi:type="xsd:string">SKU-123</sku>
      </ns1:getPrice>
   </SOAP-ENV:Body>
</SOAP-ENV:Envelope>
```

The first child element in the `<Body>` element identifies the `getPrice()` method on the object. The namespace `ns1` indicates which object. It also has child elements, which indicate the required number of parameters to invoke the `getPrice()` method.

Similarly, when we get the response, it will look something like this:

```
<SOAP-ENV:Envelope ...>
   <SOAP-ENV:Header>...</SOAP-ENV:Header>
   <SOAP-ENV:Body>
      <ns1:getPriceResponse xmlns:ns1="SparePartPrice">
         <getPriceResult xsi:type="xsd:float">10.99</getPriceResult>
      </ns1:getPriceResponse>
   </SOAP-ENV:Body>
</SOAP-ENV:Envelope>
```

At the same time, there is complete flexibility to use a message – a **document-based protocol** instead of the RPC mechanism described above. In the document-based protocol, you normally think in terms of sending the message to the SOAP server, the SOAP server then processing the message and returning you a response message. The key difference is that you are now dealing with an entire message rather than objects and methods and parameters. By using the messaging paradigm, you distance yourself more from the implementation on the server side. It is entirely dependent on the server to process your message, interpret the individual elements and then invoke the appropriate implementation on the backend. In short, the <Body> element will contain the entire XML document that will be interpreted by the recipient and processed accordingly. The document-based protocol is especially important when dealing with electronic transactions based on standards like ebXML, RosettaNet, etc. where entire XML documents contain details about the transaction.

For example, a document-based protocol might have a request as shown below:

```
<SOAP-ENV:Envelope ...>
<SOAP-ENV:Header>...</SOAP-ENV:Header>
   <SOAP-ENV:Body>
      ...[XML Document as Request] e.g. ebXML Payload / RosettaNet
         Payload
   </SOAP-ENV:Body>
</SOAP-ENV:Envelope>
```

In addition, the response is similar:

```
<SOAP-ENV:Envelope ...>
   <SOAP-ENV:Header>...</SOAP-ENV:Header>
   <SOAP-ENV:Body>
   ...[XML Document as Response]
   </SOAP-ENV:Body>
</SOAP-ENV:Envelope>
```

SOAP Transport Protocol Bindings

As we saw earlier, SOAP is independent of the internet protocol you choose to send SOAP messages over. However, the SOAP specification only defines bindings for HTTP POST requests. Therefore the HTTP binding specifies the relationship between parts of the SOAP message and the various HTTP headers. Those most commonly found in a SOAP request are Content-Type, Content-Length, and a custom header SOAPAction. The actual SOAP message is passed as the body of the HTTP request or response.

Let's take a quick look at this under the guise of a simple SOAP transaction that invokes the getPrice() method on the SparePartPrice object we've seen previously. getPrice() takes a single parameter as input – the part number (SKU) – and returns a value indicating the price of the part. Here's the SOAP request:

```
POST /axis/services HTTP/1.0
Content-Length: 445
Host: localhost
```

```
Content-Type: text/xml; charset=utf-8
SOAPAction: ""

<?xml version="1.0" encoding="UTF-8"?>
<SOAP-ENV:Envelope
   SOAP-ENV:encodingStyle="http://schemas.xmlsoap.org/soap/encoding/"
   xmlns:SOAP-ENV="http://schemas.xmlsoap.org/soap/envelope/"
   xmlns:xsd="http://www.w3.org/2001/XMLSchema"
   xmlns:xsi="http://www.w3.org/2001/XMLSchema-instance">
   <SOAP-ENV:Body>
      <ns1:getPrice xmlns:ns1="SparePartPrice">
         <sku xsi:type="xsd:string">SKU-123</sku>
      </ns1:getPrice>
   </SOAP-ENV:Body>
</SOAP-ENV:Envelope>
```

The SOAPAction HTTP header helps the server identify the request as a SOAP request and specifies the intent of the message. Basically, it is a **URI**. By the intent of the SOAP message, we mean providing the Server enough information to help it route the SOAP message to the correct recipient for processing.

▶▶ **A URI (Uniform Resource Identifier) is a string that identifies a unique resource. URIs are categorized into URNs and URLs. A URN (Uniform Resource Name) is a location-independent string for the resource and its general form is *urn:namespace-identifier:namespace-specific-string*. A URL (Uniform Resource Locator) provides details on how exactly to access this resource. It has the form *protocol-name://server-name/resource-path***

A SOAPAction value of " " means that the intent of the request is provided by the **HTTP request URI**. An empty value for SOAPAction means that the intent is not specified. The first child of the <Body> element along with its namespace could also indicate the intent of the SOAP message. In fact, AXIS ignores the SOAPAction header and instead relies on this approach: the first child of the <Body> element and its namespace. In the above example, the <getPrice> element indicates that the method name is getPrice() on the object identified by the namespace ns1 – SparePartPrice. The SOAP Server will then use the appropriate handlers to invoke the getPrice() method on the SparePartPrice object.

Similarly the SOAP Response maps on to the HTTP response as shown below:

```
HTTP/1.1 200 OK
Content-Type: text/xml; charset=utf-8
Content-Length: 480
Date: Mon, 11 Feb 2002 12:10:32 GMT
Server: Apache Tomcat/4.0.3 (HTTP/1.1 Connector)
```

```
<?xml version="1.0" encoding="UTF-8"?>
<SOAP-ENV:Envelope
        SOAP-ENV:encodingStyle="http://schemas.xmlsoap.org/soap/encoding/"
        xmlns:SOAP-ENV="http://schemas.xmlsoap.org/soap/envelope/"
        xmlns:xsd="http://www.w3.org/2001/XMLSchema"
        xmlns:xsi="http://www.w3.org/2001/XMLSchema-instance">
  <SOAP-ENV:Body>
    <ns1:getPriceResponse xmlns:ns1="SparePartPrice">
     <getPriceResult xsi:type="xsd:float">10.99</getPriceResult>
    </ns1:getPriceResponse>
  </SOAP-ENV:Body>
</SOAP-ENV:Envelope>
```

The HTTP binding follows the HTTP standard in dealing with status codes. We know from HTTP that a response status code of 200 means that the request was processed successfully. Similarly, a status code of 500 means that there was an internal server error and a SOAP Fault is included in the response. Note that ideally, we would expect that Content-type to be text/xml but while returning errors in a web application it is common practice to return it as text/html.

SOAP Data Encoding Rules

SOAP Data Encoding specifies how to serialize the data for transmission via the XML payload. SOAP uses the XML Schema encoding standard found at http://schemas.xmlsoap.org/soap/encoding.

To define the specific rules for encoding your data, you can use the xsi:type mechanism as shown below. xsi:type is used to indicate the data type of the parameter. SOAP specifies a number of built-in simple types that can be specified using the xsi:type attribute. For example a xsi:type="xsd:string" indicates that it is a string. The xsi namespace references the XML Schema standard.

```
POST /ea-axis/services HTTP/1.0
Content-Length: 445
Host: localhost
Content-Type: text/xml; charset=utf-8
SOAPAction: ""

<?xml version="1.0" encoding="UTF-8"?>
<SOAP-ENV:Envelope
        SOAP-ENV:encodingStyle=
"http://schemas.xmlsoap.org/soap/encoding/"
        xmlns:SOAP-ENV=
"http://schemas.xmlsoap.org/soap/envelope/"
        xmlns:xsd="http://www.w3.org/2001/XMLSchema"
        xmlns:xsi="http://www.w3.org/2001/XMLSchema-instance">
  <SOAP-ENV:Body>
    <ns1:getPrice xmlns:ns1="SparePartPrice">
     <sku xsi:type="xsd:string">SKU-123</sku>
```

```
        </ns1:getPrice>
    </SOAP-ENV:Body>
</SOAP-ENV:Envelope>
```

The benefit of using the xsi:type mechanism is that we can define a SOAP document that is self-describing in both its structure and the data types. AXIS uses the xsi:type mechanism.

SOAP Fault Handling

The SOAP specification also states that all errors should be reported as SOAP <Fault> elements. The <Body> element of a SOAP response message can contain the <Fault> element as shown below:

```
<SOAP-ENV:Body>
  <Fault>
    <faultcode>...</faultcode>
    <faultactor>    </faultactor>
    <faultstring>    </faultstring>
    <detail>    </detail>
  </Fault>
</SOAP-ENV:Body>
```

❏ <faultcode/> – Used to indicate the source of the fault. It can take the following values:

FaultCode	Description
VersionMismatch	A VersionMismatch indicates that the recipient of the message did not understand the namespace attribute element of the <Envelope> element.
MustUnderstand	MustUnderstand indicates that the recipient of the element child of the <Header> element had a MustUnderstand attribute but the recipient did not understand that attribute .
Client	Client indicates that the SOAP message did not contain all the necessary information needed for the recipient to process it. A possible reason for this could be that some information was missing in the <Body> element or that the message was incorrectly formed. It is generally an indication that the message should not be resent without change.
Server	Server indicates that the recipient of the message was not able to process the message due to some server-side problem. In all probability, the fault was not due to the message contents.

❏ <faultactor/> – This element is used to identify the service that caused the fault.

❏ <faultstring> – This provides a more detailed description of the problem.

❏ <detail/> – Provides more application specific information. It must be present if the <Body> element could not be processed.

WSDL

As you may have guessed, Web Services Description Language (WSDL) is a grammar for describing web services. With it, we can describe the purpose of the web service: what it does, the methods that can be invoked, the parameters that need to be passed to the methods, the parameter types, the binding protocol to use, and so on. In short, given a WSDL document about a web service, you should be in a position to invoke the functionality of the web service.

A WSDL document is an XML document, structured as shown in Figure 4:

Figure 4

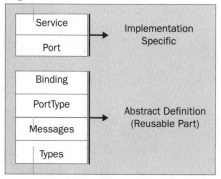

It's easiest to view a WSDL document as consisting of two parts: first, an abstract definition of the web service – the data types, methods, etc. – and second, details of the binding to the transport protocol that that particular service and SOAP server implementation are using.

Let us briefly describe the different elements:

- **Type** – A `<type>` element represents the data types used: float, integer, string, etc. WSDL uses the XML Schema specification for data type encoding.

- **Message** – Each `<message>` element represents a parameter of a service invocation. An operation in WSDL terminology is the method signature – the relationship between the input and output messages.

- **PortType** – A `<portType>` is a collection of operations (i.e. methods) exposed by the service. A `<portType>` has a collection of messages – it is similar in concept to a class in Java. Just as a class has methods, a `<portType>` contains messages (methods).

- **Binding** – Binding is used to specify two things. The transport protocol which will be used (SOAP can be used over HTTP, SMTP, or possibly any other transport) and the style of request (`rpc` and `document` are the two styles).

- **Service** – A `<service>` element is the actual implementation-specific detail. It will reference a `<Binding>` element and associate it with a `<port>` element, which contains the address of the endpoint: a HTTP URL, etc.

We will continue with the same example of a `SparePartPrice` object that has a single method called `getPrice()`. The `getPrice()` method takes a single input parameter, a string identifying the spare part number, and it returns back a float indicating its price. The WSDL document for the same is shown below:

```
<?xml version="1.0" encoding="UTF-8"?>
```

The root element is the `<definitions>` element and it defines all the appropriate namespaces:

```
<wsdl:definitions
  targetNamespace=
    http://localhost:8080/ea-axis/services/SparePartPrice"
  xmlns="http://schemas.xmlsoap.org/wsdl/"
  xmlns:SOAP-ENC="http://schemas.xmlsoap.org/soap/encoding/"
  xmlns:impl=
    "http://localhost:8080/ea-axis/services/SparePartPrice-impl"
  xmlns:intf="http://localhost:8080/ea-axis/services/SparePartPrice"
  xmlns:wsdl="http://schemas.xmlsoap.org/wsdl/"
  xmlns:wsdlsoap="http://schemas.xmlsoap.org/wsdl/soap/"
  xmlns:xsd="http://www.w3.org/2001/XMLSchema">
```

The `<message>` elements define the input parameter (`getPriceRequest`) and the output parameter (`getPriceResponse`). Note the appropriate data types.

```
<wsdl:message name="getPriceResponse">
  <wsdl:part name="return" type="xsd:float"/>
</wsdl:message>

<wsdl:message name="getPriceRequest">
  <wsdl:part name="in0" type="xsd:string"/>
</wsdl:message>
```

The name attribute of the `<portType>` element identifies the object – `SparePartPrice` and its **operations** (methods). Note the signature of the method: the input is a `getPriceRequest()` message that takes a string, and the output is a `getPriceResponse()` that gives a float result.

```
<wsdl:portType name="SparePartPrice">
  <wsdl:operation name="getPrice" parameterOrder="in0">
    <wsdl:input message="intf:getPriceRequest"/>
    <wsdl:output message="intf:getPriceResponse"/>
  </wsdl:operation>
</wsdl:portType>
```

The `<binding>` element maps the `<portType>` element (`SparePartPrice`) to a specific protocol. In this case, it maps it to the SOAP binding.

```
<wsdl:binding name="SparePartPriceSoapBinding"
  type="intf:SparePartPrice">
```

```
    <wsdlsoap:binding style="rpc"
      transport="http://schemas.xmlsoap.org/soap/http"/>
    <wsdl:operation name="getPrice">
      <wsdlsoap:operation soapAction="" style="rpc"/>
      <wsdl:input>
        <wsdlsoap:body
          encodingStyle="http://schemas.xmlsoap.org/soap/encoding/"
          namespace=
            "http://localhost:8080/ea-axis/services/SparePartPrice"
          use="encoded"
        />
      </wsdl:input>
      <wsdl:output>
        <wsdlsoap:body
          encodingStyle="http://schemas.xmlsoap.org/soap/encoding/"
          namespace=
            "http://localhost:8080/ea-axis/services/SparePartPrice"
          use="encoded"
        />
      </wsdl:output>
    </wsdl:operation>
  </wsdl:binding>
```

Finally, the <service> element maps the binding to a <port> element – a physical address or endpoint over which the web service is accessible.

```
<wsdl:service name="SparePartPriceService">
  <wsdl:port binding="intf:SparePartPriceSoapBinding"
             name="SparePartPrice">
    <wsdlsoap:address location=
      "http://localhost:8080/ea-axis/services/SparePartPrice"/>
  </wsdl:port>
</wsdl:service>
</wsdl:definitions>
```

The current version of WSDL is 1.1 and the specification can be obtained from http://www.w3.org/TR/wsdl. AXIS provides support for the WSDL 1.1 standard. It contains utilities that allow you to generate WSDL files from Java class files and vice-versa. We shall see more of AXIS's support for WSDL in Chapter 2, where we will focus on a user-centric view of AXIS.

UDDI

The last remaining part in the web services puzzle is Universal Description and Discovery Interface (UDDI). In a Service-Oriented Architecture, it is important that clients are able to find web services. In order for them to find these services, it is also important that there be a mechanism for the creators of web services to publish information about them, UDDI provides a central repository where both web service publishers and clients can come together. UDDI functionality can be broken down into two parts:

Publication

The publication part of the UDDI API allows an organization to provide details about itself and its web services to a registry service. The UDDI specification defines a structure for this business information to be written to, as shown in Figure 5.

Figure 5

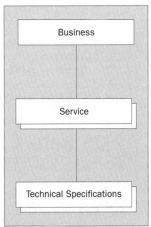

The `<Business>` element on top contains information about the business in general – address, contract information, business classification code, etc. It contains one or more `<Service>` elements that capture the different web services that this business provides such as credit-checking services, or inventory services. Each `<Service>` element will contain one or more technical specification, which contains details about the service; usually a WSDL document. A `<Service>` element can also be categorized as belonging to a particular type of service; for example, a credit-checking service.

Discovery

The discovery part of the UDDI API allows you to search through a UDDI registry for the businesses that have published their details. The discovery process might involve anything from just browsing through a particular category of business to finally selecting a business and downloading its technical specifications (WSDL document) to determine the technical details of invoking the web services that the business has to offer.

The current version of UDDI is version 2.0 and the specification is available from http://www.uddi.org.

From Apache SOAP to AXIS

And so we come to AXIS itself – the next generation of the Apache SOAP project, a Java-based, open source implementation of the SOAP 1.1 and SOAP with Attachments specification from the Apache Group (http://xml.apache.org/soap/). Currently at version 2.2, Apache SOAP has been widely hailed as an excellent SOAP implementation for deploying Java-based web services, but it has several limitations:

❑ It has no support for WSDL

❑ It has extremely poor support for layered architectures and SOAP intermediaries

❑ The default RPC provider in Apache SOAP does not provide access to any headers in the SOAP envelope

❑ It does not implement the `mustUnderstand` attribute

❑ Apache SOAP does not function unless every typed value is explicitly typed in the envelope using the `xsi:type` attribute

❑ It does not use the SOAPAction HTTP header

❑ The current implementation has limited support for non-HTTP-based transport protocols

❑ The Apache SOAP implementation uses DOM (Document Object Model) as its parsing mechanism, which is slower in comparison to SAX (Simple API for XML)

❑ It does not fully implement all three sections of the XML Schema specification

The Apache AXIS team therefore decided that to really take the Apache SOAP implementation to the next generation while also keeping extensibility in mind – AXIS will be extensible by plugging in configurable components – re-architecting the whole thing was the right way to go. The development of AXIS started in January 2001 and the first beta was released on December 14, 2001.

AXIS Beta 1 Features

AXIS beta 1, then, has the following features:

❑ **Full Support for SOAP Version 1.1 and the Upcoming XML Protocol (SOAP Version 1.2):** The current version of AXIS supports the SOAP version 1.1 specification. The upcoming SOAP 1.2 protocol is being tracked to ensure full compliance with it.

AXIS supports SOAP elements like <Envelope>, <Header>, and <Body>. It supports the mustUnderstand attribute, and SOAP <Fault> elements, and it provides preliminary support for SOAP messages with attachments. However, the SOAP actor feature is not yet implemented.

❑ **Flexible Messaging Framework:** AXIS provides a great mechanism for introducing your own extensions into the SOAP engine. The extension types that it supports include handlers, chains, serializers, and deserializers. A **handler** is an object that is capable of processing the request flow, response flow, and fault flow. You can combine handlers into groupings known as chains and then control the order of the handlers in the chains via a flexible deployment mechanism.

❑ **Flexible Deployment System:** Currently AXIS provides a flexible mechanism to deploy a wide range of components with minimal effort. It supports drop-in service deployment – you can take your Java source file, rename it as a .jws (Java Web Service) file and place that in a directory that AXIS can find. In addition, it currently provides a Web Service Deployment Descriptor (WSDD) file that can configure a wide variety of components: handler objects, chains, services, serializers, de-serializers, etc.

- ❑ **Flexible Transport Framework:** A transport object contains details about the particular network protocol such as HTTP, SMTP, FTP, etc. AXIS provides a transport framework that helps you create your own pluggable transport senders and transport listeners. By default it provides transport senders and listeners for SOAP over various protocols like HTTP, SMTP, FTP, etc. Work is currently in progress to provide a wide range of transport senders and listeners including JMS support.

- ❑ **Speed:** AXIS offers much greater performance in comparison to Apache SOAP since it uses the SAX API as compared to the DOM API. It is a known fact that the SAX API is much faster than its DOM equivalent because it is an event-based API and does not need to load the entire XML document into memory.

- ❑ **Data Encoding Support:** AXIS currently supports SOAP encoding as present in Apache SOAP 2.2. It provides automatic serialization/deserialization for a wide variety of data types as per the XML Schema specification. It also provides a relatively easy mechanism to write your own serializer/deserializer. It has support for automatic serialization/deserialization of Java Beans. It provides automatic two-way conversions between Java "List" collections and SOAP arrays. Currently support is being built for partially transmitted arrays and multidimensional arrays.

- ❑ **Full support for WSDL:** AXIS provides full support for the WSDL specification. It supports the ability to obtain the WSDL document for a service at run time. It also provides excellent tools like Java2WSDL that generates a WSDL document from the existing Java classes that make up a web service. The WSDL2Java utility can be used to generate both stubs and skeletons from the WSDL document.

- ❑ **Built-in Providers:** A provider in AXIS is responsible for implementing the actual back-end logic of invoking the service. AXIS comes in with built-in providers that handle both RPC and message-oriented transactions. In addition to these providers, development is going on to add support for EJB, COM, etc.

- ❑ **Improved Logging Features:** AXIS uses the Log4J API (http://jakarta.apache.org/log4j) for logging and debugging information. The API is highly configurable and allows flexible logging according to message priority, message type. It also allows flexible formatting of the log messages.

- ❑ **Standalone version of HTTP Server:** AXIS comes with a standalone version of a single-threaded HTTP server for processing SOAP Requests. It only supports HTTP basic authentication, however, because there is no standard for security to which SOAP implementations should adhere and interoperability is key when working with SOAP.

- ❑ **Security Support:** AXIS supports basic user authentication via a security provider. Currently, work is in progress to support transport-level and SOAP-level security. AXIS also provides an interface for security providers that allows easier integration into existing security providers especially the security providers with J2EE Application Servers.

- ❑ **Error and Fault Handling:** Currently work is in progress to define an extensible Java Exception mapping to a SOAP Fault and vice versa from a SOAP Fault Mapping to Java Exceptions.

For a list of AXIS features that are currently being worked on and what we can expect in future versions of AXIS, please refer to Chapter 7.

Installing AXIS

In this section, we'll work through an installation of AXIS beta 1 on a Java-free machine. Once we've tested that everything is working, we'll develop our first web service, Hello AXIS and see it run. We'll keep the deployment of the Hello AXIS service as simple as possible in this chapter and go into more detail in the chapters that follow.

Software Requirements

We will refer to the root directory for your system as <root-directory> from here on in. On a windows system this might be C:\, on Unix it might be /usr/local/bin.

There are three pieces of software readily available on the Internet that you need to download and install as follows:

❑ **Java Development Kit version 1.4.0**
We will be using **version 1.4.0** of the JDK to run AXIS in this book. Please follow the links to the correct download for your operating system from http://java.sun.com/j2se/ and install it in <root-directory>\j2sdk1.4.0.

❑ **Jakarta Tomcat version 4.0.3**
Jakarta Tomcat is the Java servlet engine we'll be using throughout the book. You can find its installers for download at http://jakarta.apache.org/builds/jakarta-tomcat-4.0/release/v4.0.3. Find and download the correct binary installer (Note: don't download the 'LE' light version) or RPM for your system and install it in <root-directory>\jakarta-tomcat. Included in this version of Tomcat are two very important pieces of the AXIS puzzle that previously had to be downloaded separately.

❑ **Xerces XML Parser**
The AXIS Engine needs a XML parser to process SOAP messages. The Xerces XML parser (xerces.jar) can be found in the \common\lib directory of the Tomcat 4.0.3 installation.

❑ **Java Activation Framework**
Similarly, AXIS needs the Java Activation Framework library available to enable support for Attachments. It (activation.jar) can be found in the \common\lib directory of the Tomcat 4.0.3 installation.

❑ **AXIS version Beta1**
Finally, we need to download AXIS itself. At this stage of its development, AXIS is an archive of the java files needed, which simply needs to be expanded into the correct directory. The beta 1 archives can be found at http://xml.apache.org/axis/dist/beta1/ and should be expanded into <root-directory>\xml-axis-beta1. With this done, you should find the following sub-directories have been created and populated:

- ❏ \docs

  This directory contains the documentation for AXIS. It has several useful documents including one on installation, a developers guide, and an architecture guide.

- ❏ \lib

  This directory contains the core JAR Files that are needed by AXIS. In beta 1, these are `axis.jar`, `clutil.jar`, `commons-logging.jar`, `log4j-core.jar`, `tt-bytecode.jar`, `jaxrpc.jar`, and `wsdl4j.jar`.

- ❏ \samples

  This directory contains the source code for several samples that you could deploy and see in action.

- ❏ \webapps

  Here you'll find a subdirectory `axis` containing the web application that you need to install in your servlet engine (Tomcat in our case). It contains the `web.xml` descriptor, which in turn holds the AXIS servlet mapping that will handle all your SOAP requests.

With these three pieces of software now installed on your machine, we need to set up a few environment variables and copy a few files to get them all working together. Note that in the next steps, you should replace <root-directory> with the actual path as appropriate. For example, `<root-directory>\j2sdk1.4.0` might become `c:\j2sdk1.4.0`.

1. Create the environment variable `JAVA_HOME` with the value `<root-directory>\j2sdk1.4.0`.

2. Create the environment variable `CATALINA_HOME` with the value of `<root-directory>\jakarta-tomcat`.

3. Create an environment variable `AXIS_HOME` with the value of `<root-directory>\xml-axis-beta1`.

4. Copy the `axis` directory from `<AXIS_HOME>\webapps` into the `<CATALINA_HOME>\webapps` directory.

5. Create the environment variable `AXIS_DEPLOYHOME` with a value of `<CATALINA_HOME>\webapps\axis`.

6. Make sure that the following JAR files from `<AXIS_HOME>\lib` are present in `<AXIS_DEPLOYHOME> \WEB-INF\lib`:
    `axis.jar`, `clutil.jar`, `log4j-core.jar`, `wsdl4j.jar`, `jaxrpc.jar`, `tt-bytecode.jar`, and `commons-logging.jar`.

7. Copy the same JAR files into `<CATALINA_HOME>\common\lib` directory. (This is to circumvent a bug in the classloader of Tomcat 4.0.3.)

We also need to set up a development directory for the web services we'll be using AXIS for:

8. Create your development directory – for example, `<root-directory>\wrox-axis` – and create the environment variable `AXIS_DEVHOME`, which points to this.

Whenever we develop any source code, we will develop it in `AXIS_DEVHOME` directory. When we have to deploy the code in the AXIS engine, we will need to copy it to the `AXIS_DEPLOYHOME\WEB-INF\classes` directory. Make sure to retain the package structure exactly as it is in the `AXIS_DEVHOME` directory.

9. Create the environment variable CLASSPATH and give it the following value. If this variable already exists, add the following value to the end of the current value. (Note: This has been spread across several lines for clarity but should all be on one line with no spaces in it.)

```
.;%JAVA_HOME%\bin;%AXIS_DEVHOME%;%AXIS_HOME%\lib\axis.jar;
%AXIS_HOME%\lib\jaxrpc.jar;%AXIS_HOME%\lib\clutil.jar;
%AXIS_HOME%\lib\wsdl4j.jar;%AXIS_HOME%\lib\log4j-core.jar;
%AXIS_HOME%\lib\commons-logging.jar;
%AXIS_HOME%\lib\tt-bytecode.jar;
%CATALINA_HOME%\common\lib\xerces.jar;
%CATALINA_HOME%\common\lib\activation.jar
```

Verifying the Basic Setup

All being well, AXIS is now installed and set up. However, not wishing to tempt fate, let's run a quick check to ensure that everything is indeed good to go.

Start Tomcat (by selecting **Apache Tomcat 4.0 | Start Tomcat** from the start menu if you are using windows). By default, the Tomcat Server is configured to run on port 8080. Start your browser and navigate to http://localhost:880\axis. You should see the following:

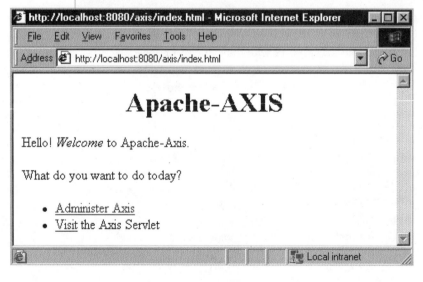

Click on **Visit the Axis Servlet**. You should see something similar to the following screen, which indicates that the AXIS Servlet was found:

Our First AXIS Web Service

With any luck your AXIS installation is working fine. There were quite a few
configuration details to take care of, but the moment of reckoning is finally here –
we shall create our first web service to be deployed in the AXIS engine. Rather
than break from tradition, we shall create a Hello World web service. The aim here
will be to demonstrate how easy it is to deploy a simple web service in AXIS. In
the chapters that follow, we'll go into more detail and explore the true capabilities
of the AXIS engine.

Hello World

The Hello World web service has a single method named
`getHelloWorldMessage()`. This method takes a parameter called `name` and
returns a string with the Hello World greeting. For example if we pass "AXIS" as the
value of the `name` parameter, the string returned will be "Hello World to AXIS".

The source code for the Hello World web service is shown below.

HelloWorld Web Service (HelloWorld.java)

```
// HelloWorld.java

public class HelloWorld {

  public HelloWorld() {
  }
```

```
public String getHelloWorldMessage(String name) {
   return "Hello World to " + name;
  }
}
```

As you can see, the `HelloWorld` class is very simple. It just defines an empty constructor and the `getHelloWorldMessage()` method that generates the Hello World message. Unlike a more traditional Hello World example, however, if we want to see our message we need to deploy the web service and create a client.

Deploying Hello World Web Service

Copy the `HelloWorld.java` file to `<AXIS_DEPLOYHOME>` and rename it as `HelloWorld.jws`. (JWS stands for Java Web Service.) AXIS comes with a built-in JWS handler that will process the request for a JWS file appropriately. This is known as **drop-in deployment** in the AXIS system. You will not need to write a deployment descriptor, or do any configuration at all. Even though this is an ideal mechanism, we shall see in the later chapters why this is not always sufficient. However, for the purposes of our simple example, this mechanism is fine.

HelloWorld Web Service Client (HelloWorldClient.java)

Our client program to the above HelloWorld web service is a little more complicated and we shall decipher it in detail. It makes use of the AXIS client-side APIs.

```
//HelloWorldClient.java

import java.net.URL;
import org.apache.axis.client.Service;
import org.apache.axis.client.Call;
import org.apache.axis.encoding.XMLType;
import javax.xml.rpc.ParameterMode;

public class HelloWorldClient {

  public HelloWorldClient() {}

  public static void main (String args[]) {
    try {
```

The endpoint URL variable defined below specifies the actual location of the web service. In essence, it serves as the URI for the web service. Remember that in the previous section, we deployed our web service by placing the `HelloWorld.jws` file in `<AXIS_DEPLOYHOME>` – the file is present in `<root-directory>\jakarta-tomcat\webapps\axis\WEB-INF\Helloworld.jws`.

```
      // EndPoint URL for the HelloWorld  Web Service
      String endpointURL =
        "http://localhost:8080/axis/HelloWorld.jws";
```

The `methodName` variable holds the name of the method that we wish to invoke. In our case, this is the `getHelloWorldMessage()` method.

```
String methodName = "getHelloWorldMessage";
```

The first step in establishing contact with the web service is to create a `Service` object present in the `org.apache.axis.client` package.

```
Service service = new Service();
```

Then using this `Service` object, we need to create a `Call` object present in the `org.apache.axis.client` package. Imagine a `Service` object as having a number of methods, each of which is encapsulated by a `Call`.

```
Call call = (Call) service.createCall();
```

Now, that we have created the `Call` object, we need to fill it with appropriate information: the service location, which method of the service you want to call, the parameters for each method, the input parameter data types and the data type of the result.

```
//Set the endPoint URL
call.setTargetEndpointAddress(new java.net.URL(endpointURL));
//Set the methodname to invoke - getHelloWorldMessage
call.setOperationName(methodName);
```

We saw that the `getHelloWorldMessage` takes a single input parameter, which is of type `String` and returns a `String` type that contains the greeting. You can define input parameters by calling the `addParameter()` method on the `call` object. The `addParameter()` method takes three parameters: a user-defined name of the parameter, the parameter data type (in our case this is a `String`) and whether the parameter is an input parameter, output parameter, or input/output parameter.

The `setReturnType()` method in the `Call` object is used to set the return type of the method. In our case, this is a `String`.

```
call.addParameter("name", XMLType.XSD_STRING,
                  ParameterMode.PARAM_MODE_IN);

call.setReturnType(XMLType.XSD_STRING);
```

Finally we call the `invoke` method on the `Call` object.

```
/*Setup the Parameters i.e. the name to be passed as input
   parameter to the HelloWorld Web Service*/

String result = (String) call.invoke( new Object[] { "AXIS" } );
//Print out the result
System.out.println(result);
}
```

```
    catch (Exception e) {
      System.err.println(e.toString());
    }
  }
}
```

Executing the Hello World Web Service Client

To test our Hello World web service, we need to execute the
`HelloWorldClient.java` file. First make sure that Tomcat is running on your
machine on port 8080 (default port). Save the `HelloWorldClient.java` source
file into the `<AXIS_DEVHOME>`/wroxaxis/chapter1 directory, then compile the
client source as shown below and then run the program. Notice that you will get
the message "Hello World to AXIS" back from our Hello World web service.

```
wrox-axis> javac wroxaxis/chapter1/HelloWorldClient.java
wrox-axis> java wroxaxis.chapter1.HelloWorldClient
Hello World to AXIS
wrox-axis>
```

Shown below are the SOAP Request and SOAP Response over the HTTP protocol:

SOAP Request

The first few lines are the HTTP part of the request. They indicate that we have
done an HTTP POST to the URL shown below, its content length, and content
type. A `SOAPAction` value of `""` indicates that the intent of the request is
specified by the URL itself – /axis/HelloWorld.jws. Finally, we have the XML
content whose top-level element is the SOAP Envelope.

```
POST /axis/HelloWorld.jws HTTP/1.0
Content-Length: 492
Host: localhost
Content-Type: text/xml; charset=utf-8
SOAPAction: ""

<?xml version="1.0" encoding="UTF-8"?>
<SOAP-ENV:Envelope
  SOAP-ENV:encodingStyle="http://schemas.xmlsoap.org/soap/encoding/"
  xmlns:SOAP-ENV="http://schemas.xmlsoap.org/soap/envelope/"
  xmlns:xsd="http://www.w3.org/2001/XMLSchema"
  xmlns:xsi="http://www.w3.org/2001/XMLSchema-instance"
  xmlns:SOAP-ENC="http://schemas.xmlsoap.org/soap/encoding/">
  <SOAP-ENV:Body>
   <getHelloWorldMessage>
    <name xsi:type="xsd:string">AXIS</name>
   </getHelloWorldMessage>
  </SOAP-ENV:Body>
</SOAP-ENV:Envelope>
```

SOAP Response

The SOAP Response binding to HTTP is shown below. A response code of 200 indicates that everything is fine. The HTTP header fields like content type, length, etc. follow this. Finally it is followed by the XML content containing the SOAP Response.

```
HTTP/1.1 200 OK
Content-Type: text/xml; charset=utf-8
Content-Length: 508
Date: Sat, 16 Mar 2002 04:01:50 GMT
Server: Apache Tomcat/4.0.3 (HTTP/1.1 Connector)

<?xml version="1.0" encoding="UTF-8"?>
<SOAP-ENV:Envelope
xmlns:SOAP-ENV="http://schemas.xmlsoap.org/soap/envelope/"
xmlns:xsd="http://www.w3.org/2001/XMLSchema"
xmlns:xsi="http://www.w3.org/2001/XMLSchema-instance">
<SOAP-ENV:Body>
  <getHelloWorldMessageResponse SOAP-ENV:encodingStyle=
"http://schemas.xmlsoap.org/soap/encoding/">
  <getHelloWorldMessageResult xsi:type="xsd:string">
Hello World to AXIS</getHelloWorldMessageResult>
  </getHelloWorldMessageResponse>
 </SOAP-ENV:Body>
</SOAP-ENV:Envelope>
```

Summary

The aim of this introductory chapter was to get your first footsteps down the AXIS web services road onto solid ground. We've looked at:

❑   The key technologies – SOAP, WSDL, and UDDI – that web services rely on to work and which AXIS implements to the very latest standards

❑   The feature set of AXIS beta 1 and the improvement that it already makes over Apache SOAP 2.2

❑   How to install and correctly configure AXIS on your test server

❑   The development and deployment of a simple web service with AXIS

There has been a lot of hype surrounding web services. Even now, there is no doubt about the benefits that web services can offer to organizations from both a business and a technical perspective. They give an organization the ability to reduce costs of internal integration, deliver changing business functionality in a flexible and non-obtrusive manner, help in easier maintenance and upgrade of solutions, etc. In order to achieve that, it is essential that the organization select a flexible and extensible web services platform on which to build its solutions. AXIS provides the right balance of flexibility and extensibility thanks to its open-standards-based architecture and adherence to the latest protocol specifications.

In the next chapter, we will look at AXIS from a user-centric view without getting into too many details about its architecture. We shall look at the variety of tools that Apache AXIS provides and extend on the right start that we have made so far with the Hello World example.

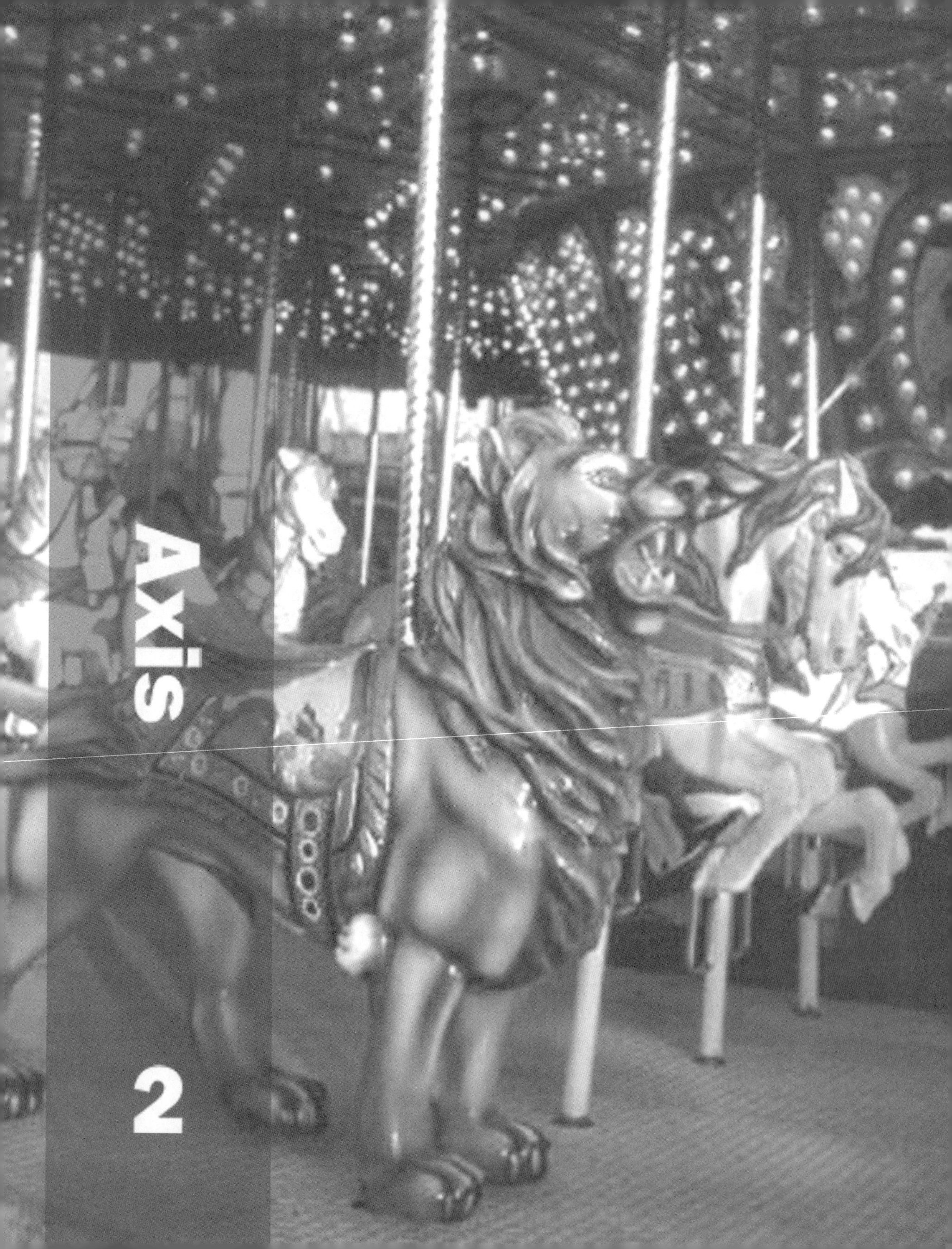
Axis
2

Getting Started with AXIS

2

In the previous chapter, we introduced AXIS and its features. We also deployed our first web service, HelloWorld, in AXIS. We'll continue now by taking a user-centric view of AXIS. In this chapter, we will:

❑ Cover the AXIS web service Deployment Descriptor (WSDD) and discuss how to deploy an RPC-based web service (SparePartPrice) using the WSDD. In the process we will also take a look at the Administration Utility (Admin) available in AXIS.

❑ Explore the AXIS Client API a little further, particularly method parameter types and method return types.

❑ Discuss the WSDL utilities supplied with AXIS.

❑ Generate Service Client Stubs and Server-side Skeletons using the AXIS tools **Java2WSDL** and **WSDL2Java.**

❑ Develop a message-based web service, a Purchase Order web service, and in the process learn to deploy a message-based web service using the WSDD.

❑ Discuss how to undeploy a web service in AXIS.

The emphasis throughout this chapter will be on using AXIS rather than developing some complex web service, so we shall keep our web services as simple as possible throughout this chapter and concentrate instead on using the tools. Note that we will not be delving into architectural pieces of AXIS. Keep in mind that this chapter is more geared towards the question "How can I do ABC using AXIS?" and so on. Chapter 3 will cover the nuts and bolts of the AXIS architecture and machinery behind the scenes to make it happen.

The AXIS Web Service Deployment Descriptor (WSDD)

In the previous chapter, we saw how easy it was to perform a drop-in deployment of a Java web service. All we had to do was rename our HelloWorld.java file to HelloWorld.jws and place it in Tomcat's webapps\axis directory. However, JWS-based deployment has a major limitation in that you need the source code of the file (.java) in order to do it. In some scenarios, this might not be possible and all you'll have will be the compiled (.class) files or a .jar file containing the necessary files. For example:

❑ You might just not have the .java files with you. For example you got a Java library packaged as a .jar.

❑ Different development teams might have built their own components and done their own versioning, etc. So all you would get from the team is a .jar or a .class file.

❑ You might want to expose existing applications as web services, which could have several sub-systems, etc.

AXIS provides a much more powerful alternative to JWS deployment in the form of the **Web Services Deployment Descriptor** (WSDD). This is an XML-based configuration file that captures everything you need to configure in AXIS. Indeed, its contents describe a variety of AXIS-deployable objects ranging from a simple web service to web service request/response handlers, transport handlers, and global web service request/response handlers. In addition to the above, it is also used to specify any bean mappings, serializers/deserializers, etc. that you may need.

So, in short, the WSDD is not just another alternative to JWS-based deployment to be used because you don't have the source code. By defining an all-encompassing XML grammar for configuration, the WSDD can fit all kinds of needs from a simple configuration to a complex chain of handlers. Nor is it just a legacy feature from Apache SOAP 2.2, which also had deployment descriptors. Those in AXIS are much richer in nature.

We'll take a step-by-step approach to looking at WSDD rather than throwing everything you can possibly configure in a WSDD at you right now. In the next section, we'll look at the elements of a simple WSDD and then, in Chapter 3, explore the WSDD and its different objects in much more detail. We'll also introduce additional details in later chapters as becomes appropriate.

Writing a Simple WSDD

For now then, we shall cover the basic elements in a WSDD for deploying a simple Java web service. The general structure for providing configuration details in a WSDD is shown below:

```
<deployment xmlns="http://xml.apache.org/axis/wsdd/"
  xmlns:java="http://xml.apache.org/axis/wsdd/providers/java">
  xmlns:xsi="http://www.w3.org/2000/10/XMLSchema-instance">
  <service name="Web Service Name" provider="ProviderType">
    <parameter name="className" value="Java Class Name"/>
    <parameter name="allowedMethods" value="method names"/>
  </service>
</deployment>
```

The root element, <deployment>, is used to indicate to the AXIS engine that this is a deployment (as opposed to an undeployment, which we'll see later). It defines three namespaces:

❑ The **default** namespace, http://xml.apache.org/axis/wsdd, which applies to all the elements defined in the WSDD

❑ The **java providers** namespace, http://xml.apache.org/axis/wsdd/providers/java, which we'll look at later

❑ The **XML Schema instance** namespace (xsi).

The main element we're interested in is the `<service>` element that states we are dealing with a web service. It has two mandatory attributes:

❑ **name** – is used to provide a unique name for the service. It is basically a URN (Unique Resource Name).

❑ **provider** – in AXIS, a provider (also known as a pivot handler) is responsible for invoking your web service class. AXIS provides two default provider types: an RPC-based provider, `java:RPC`, and a message-based provider, `java:MSG`. So, depending on the kind of web service that you write, you will have to select one of them. Note that, AXIS also has an additional EJB Provider, which we shall cover in Chapter 6. There is support currently being built for other providers like COM Provider, etc.

Last but not least in the WSDD, we have `<parameter>` elements. These are name-value pairs used to provide more information about your service, especially the java class name and the methods exposed in the class. Referring back to our example WSDD, the `<service>` element has two child `<parameter>` elements:

❑ **className** – The fully qualified class name for the web service. For example, `wroxaxis.chapter2.SparePartPriceService`.

❑ **allowedMethods** – A whitespace-delimited list of method names in the above class that can be invoked by a client of this web service. In this fashion, if there are certain methods that are private to the class, then you should not mention them in this list.

That's all there is to a very basic WSDD. The aim here was to introduce you to their structure so you can follow those we create for the example web services we build in the rest of this chapter. In Chapter 3, we'll look in much more detail at the handlers and other objects you can add to your descriptor.

The rest of this chapter is devoted to building two web services, one for each of the default providers with which AXIS may invoke your web service, and also the differences between the two types. To begin with, we'll write a simple RPC-based web service, and later, one which is message-based.

An RPC-based Web Service

Our sample RPC-based web service, `SparePartPrice`, has a single method that returns the price of an item given its part number (SKU). The input parameter is a `String`, which identifies the unique part number, and its return value a `float`, which gives the price of that item.

Note that since our focus is on AXIS and how we work with it, we won't develop anything particularly fancy in the web service itself. That is, there is no database access, no XML manipulation, etc, and exception handling in AXIS is covered later in Chapter 4. We shall simply be returning a constant value for the price irrespective of the part number. We trust that you, as competent Java developers, will be able to substitute this service for the business functionality you want to expose as a web service.

The source code for the `SparePartPrice` web service is shown below. The single method is called `getPrice()` and returns a constant value of `10.99` as a float.

```
//SparePartPrice.java

package wroxaxis.chapter2;

public class SparePartPrice {

    /** Creates new SparePartPriceService */
    public SparePartPrice() {
    }

    public float getPrice(String PartSKU) {
        return (float)10.99;
    }
}
```

Remember that in Chapter 1, we laid out how to set up the development environment for this book. Recall that we created the environment variable AXIS_DEVHOME, which points to the <root-directory>\wrox-axis directory on our machine. Save the above file SparePartPrice.java in %AXIS_DEVHOME%\wroxaxis\chapter2, so that we preserve the package structure. (Yes, that's <root-directory>\wrox-axis\wroxaxis\chapter2 – *Ed*.) We shall be following a similar mechanism for the rest of the chapters.

Compile the SparePartPrice.java file by giving the following command:

chapter2> **javac SparePartPrice.java**

You should now have a SparePartPrice.class file present in %AXIS_DEVHOME%\wroxaxis\chapter2 directory.

A WSDD for SpartPartPrice

If you'd like to deploy SparePartPrice as a drop-in to check it works go ahead, but we'll go ahead and use the WSDD file below instead to demonstrate this alternative deployment. First, we have the standard <deployment> element with its namespaces set correctly. Then all we need do is define the <service> element. Its name attribute should be unique to it but for clarity we've used SparePartPrice rather a GUID or other unique identifier of some sort. Since this is an RPC-based web service, the provider attribute has a value of "java:RPC". Finally, we define the two <parameter> elements, where we specify the className and the allowedMethods appropriately as shown below:

```
<deployment
    xmlns="http://xml.apache.org/axis/wsdd/"
    xmlns:java="http://xml.apache.org/axis/wsdd/providers/java">
    xmlns:xsi="http://www.w3.org/2000/10/XMLSchema-instance">
```

```
    <service name="SparePartPrice" provider="java:RPC">
      <parameter name="className"
                  value="wroxaxis.chapter2.SparePartPrice"/>
      <parameter name="allowedMethods" value="getPrice"/>
    </service>
</deployment>
```

We will save the above WSDD file (SparePartPriceServiceDeploy.wsdd) in the %AXIS_DEVHOME%\wroxaxis\chapter2 directory. Note that you can select any filename for the WSDD that you want.

AXIS Deployment Process

So far, we have written our web service, compiled it successfully, and created a WSDD for deploying it in AXIS. Now we'll look at the deployment process in AXIS to understand how it processes our WSDD files, and what configuration changes it makes. The overall deployment process is shown in Figure 1.

Figure 1

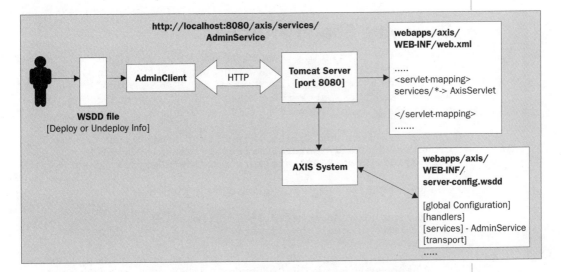

It is important to understand the process from two angles: the client and the server. The client–side is what you, as a user should be concerned with. The server-side is where AXIS lies. On the client–side, you will predominantly use the AdminClient Java class (org.apache.axis.client.AdminClient) for the following tasks:

❑ Deploying AXIS objects like Service, Handler, Provider, Transport, etc. that are specified using the WSDD file

❑ Undeploying AXIS objects using an undeploy WSDD file (we shall take a look at undeployment towards the end of this chapter)

❑ Retrieving a list of AXIS objects (web services, bean mappings, request/response handlers, etc.) configured in a particular instance of the AXIS Engine

Calls to the `AdminClient` from the command-line takes the following shape:

```
> AdminClient xml-files | list -l AdminServiceURL
```

where *xml-files* is a list of one or more WSDD descriptor files separated by spaces or, alternatively, the argument **"list"**. This latter option will give you a list of all the AXIS objects currently configured in AXIS. The *AdminServiceURL* meanwhile is the URL for the `AdminService`, which is what the `AdminClient` talks to as shown in the figure above. Typically, the AXIS `AdminService` is accessible at http://localhost:8080/axis/services/ AdminService.

The admin service is basically a message-based service that takes the `.wsdd` configuration files as input and interprets them accordingly to deploy or undeploy AXIS objects, list AXIS objects, etc. Depending on whether it is a deploy or undeploy WSDD file, it adds or removes entries in the `server-config.wsdd` file present in the `%AXIS_DEPLOYHOME%\WEB-INF` directory. If the file doesn't exist, the admin service will create it when next invoked.

Deploying SparePartPrice

Let's make use of the `AdminClient` utility and deploy the `SparePartPrice` web service. First, make sure that Tomcat is running on port 8080 (default port) and then navigate in a console window to `%AXIS_DEVHOME%\wroxaxis\chapter2`, where we saved the `SparePartPriceServiceDeploy.wsdd` file. Now you can run the `AdminClient` following the syntax seen earlier:

```
wrox-axis> java org.apache.axis.client.AdminClient
wroxaxis/chapter2/SparePartPriceServiceDeploy.wsdd-l
http://localhost:8080/axis/services/AdminService
```

You will see the following output in the console window:

```
Processing file SparePartPriceServiceDeploy.wsdd
<Admin>Done processing</Admin>
```

This means that the service has been deployed successfully. But how do we know that it has been deployed? This is where we use `AdminClient`'s `list` option:

```
wrox-axis> java org.apache.axis.client.AdminClient list-l
http://localhost:8080/axis/services/AdminService
```

This will give us a listing of all the AXIS objects deployed in your AXIS instance. Somewhere in the answer output in response to our query, you should see the following segment containing information about our `SparePartPrice` web service.

```
<service name="SparePartPrice" provider="java:RPC">
  <parameter name="allowedMethods" value="getPrice"/>
  <parameter name="className"
value="wroxaxis.chapter2.SparePartPrice"/>
</service>
```

Alternately, you can also go to the server-config.wsdd file present in the
%AXIS_DEPLOYHOME%\WEB-INF directory and find the same entry there.

Finally, remember to copy the SparePartPrice.class file from the
%AXIS_DEVHOME%\wroxaxis\chapter2 directory to the
%AXIS_DEPLOYHOME%\WEB-INF\classes\wroxaxis\chapter2 directory. With
that done, we've finished deploying our service using the WSDD file and the
AdminClient.

Creating a Client for SparePartPrice

All that remains is to write a client that makes use of our service. This one works
in a similar fashion to the one we saw in Chapter 1 but with some essential
differences as highlighted:

```
//SparePartPriceServiceClient.java
package wroxaxis.chapter2;

import java.net.URL;
import org.apache.axis.client.Service;
import org.apache.axis.client.Call;
import org.apache.axis.encoding.XMLType;
import javax.xml.rpc.ParameterMode;
import javax.xml.rpc.namespace.QName;

public class SparePartPriceServiceClient {

  // Creates new HelloWorldClient
  public SparePartPriceServiceClient() {
  }

  public static void main (String args[]) {
    try {
      // EndPoint URL for the SparePartPrice web service.
      String endpointURL =
        "http://localhost:8080/axis/services/SparePartPrice";
      // Method Name to invoke for the SparePartPrice web
      //service
      String methodName  = "getPrice";
      // Create the Service call
      Service service = new Service();
```

```
        Call call = (Call) service.createCall();
        call.setTargetEndpointAddress(new java.net.URL(endpointURL));
call.setOperationName(new
        QName("SparePartPrice",methodName));
        call.addParameter("sku",XMLType.XSD_STRING,
                        ParameterMode.PARAM_MODE_IN);
        call.setReturnType(XMLType.XSD_FLOAT);
        //Setup the Parameters i.e. the Part SKU to be passed as input
        //parameter to the SparePartPrice web service
        Object[] params = new Object[] {"SKU-123"};

        //Invoke the SparePartPrice web service
        Float price = (Float) call.invoke(params);
        //Print out the result
        System.out.println("The price is $" + price.floatValue());
        }
    catch (Exception e) {
        System.out.println(e.toString());
    }
  }
}
```

Save the SparePartPriceServiceClient.java in
%AXIS_DEVHOME%\wroxaxis\chapter2 then open a console window and
navigate to %AXIS_DEVHOME%. Compile SparePartPriceServiceClient.java
and run it as shown below:

```
wrox-axis> javac
wroxaxis/chapter2/SparePartPriceServiceClient.java
wrox-axis> java wroxaxis.chapter2.SparePartPriceServiceClient
The price is $10.99
```

To understand how the client code works, we need to look at the SOAP request
over HTTP, which is shown below:

```
POST /axis/services/SparePartService HTTP/1.0
Content-Length: 445
Host: localhost
Content-Type: text/xml; charset=utf-8
SOAPAction: ""

<?xml version="1.0" encoding="UTF-8"?>
<SOAP-ENV:Envelope
    SOAP-ENV:encodingStyle=
"http://schemas.xmlsoap.org/soap/encoding/"
    xmlns:SOAP-ENV="http://schemas.xmlsoap.org/soap/envelope/"
    xmlns:xsd="http://www.w3.org/2001/XMLSchema"
    xmlns:xsi="http://www.w3.org/2001/XMLSchema-instance">

  <SOAP-ENV:Body>
```

```
    <ns1:getPrice xmlns:ns1="SparePartPrice">
     <sku xsi:type="xsd:string">SKU-123</sku>
    </ns1:getPrice>
   </SOAP-ENV:Body>
</SOAP-ENV:Envelope>
```

The SOAPAction is "" so the intent of the SOAP request is specified by the POST URL — /axis/services/ SparePartService. The SparePartService half is the unique name we gave to our service in the WSDD file but how does /axis/services/ translate? The answer lies in the web.xml file you'll find in your %AXIS_DEPLOYHOME%\WEB-INF directory. Open it and you'll find that the /services/* pattern is mapped to the AxisService servlet. This explains our endPointURL in the client code. Always remember that the way to identify your deployed service in AXIS is by the following URL:

http://*<hostname>:<portname>/<axiswebapp>*/services/*<servicename>*

Into the SOAP message itself, we can see that the <Body> element contains a single child whose parameters are the object (web service) we want to use and the name of the method we want to invoke on it. The code in the client responsible for this is the call to setOperationName().

call.setOperationName(new QName("SparePartPrice",methodName));

The qualified name (QName) it takes as a parameter is constructed with two of its own parameters: a namespace, which in this case is the name of the object (SparePartPrice) we want to make use of, and the local name of the method we want to invoke on the object (getPrice()). Note that this object name needs to match the value you gave the name attribute of the <service> element in the SparePartPriceServiceDeploy.wsdd file.

When the client is run then, the call to setOperationName() resolves into the following piece of the SOAP request.

<ns1:getPrice xmlns:ns1="SparePartPrice">

When AXIS receives the request, it determines from the above fragment what the object is: SparePartPrice. It looks up this information from the server-config.wsdd file and determines the provider for it. Since it is the default RPCProvider present in AXIS, it hands off control to the RPCProvider. The RPCProvider then determines the class that needs to be instantiated and invoked from the <service> element: wroxaxis.chapter2.SparePartPrice.

Parameter Types and Return Types

Looking at both the client programs we have written so far, you can see that we have mentioned the data types of both the input parameters and results. Since we had to pass a String value as a data type and obtain a float value (price) as a result, we had used the following code:

```
call.addParameter("sku",XMLType.XSD_STRING,
                        ParameterMode.PARAM_MODE_IN);
call.setReturnType(XMLType.XSD_FLOAT);
```

So, basically the addParameter indicated to the AXIS client code that the input type is a String (using the XML Schema definition). Similarly, we used the setReturnType method to indicate that the output was a float value. The consequence of these calls results in the following SOAP fragments (we are showing only the relevant parts):

SOAP Request

```
<SOAP-ENV:Body>
    <ns1:getPrice xmlns:ns1="SparePartPrice">
     <sku xsi:type="xsd:string">SKU-123</sku>
    </ns1:getPrice>
</SOAP-ENV:Body>
```

In the SOAP request above, you will notice the parameter name (sku) that we passed as the element name has its xsi-type set to "xsd:string", which corresponds to org.apache.axis.encoding. XMLType.XSD_STRING. In other words, AXIS took care of the correct data encoding for us.

SOAP Response

```
<SOAP-ENV:Body>
    <ns1:getPriceResponse xmlns:ns1="SparePartPrice">
     <getPriceResult xsi:type="xsd:float">10.99</getPriceResult>
    </ns1:getPriceResponse>
 </SOAP-ENV:Body>
```

Similarly, in the SOAP response, we used setReturnType to explicitly state that our return type is a float and AXIS does the data encoding correctly for us.

Now then, what would happen, if we don't use the methods addParameter() and setReturnType() on the Call object – we do not explicitly state any data encoding instructions for the input parameters or the result? Shown below is the modified client SparePartPriceServiceClient1.java. The only difference between this code and SparePartPriceServiceClient.java is that we have eliminated the addParameter() and setReturnType() methods.

```java
//SparePartPriceServiceClient1.java
package wroxaxis.chapter2;

import java.net.URL;
import org.apache.axis.client.Service;
import org.apache.axis.client.Call;
import org.apache.axis.encoding.XMLType;
import javax.xml.rpc.namespace.QName;

public class SparePartPriceServiceClient1 {

  public SparePartPriceServiceClient1() {}

  public static void main (String args[]) {
    try {
      String endpointURL =
        "http://localhost:8080/axis/services/SparePartService";
```

```
        String methodName  = "getPrice";

        // Create the Service call
        Service service = new Service();
        Call call = (Call) service.createCall();
        call.setTargetEndpointAddress(new java.net.URL(endpointURL));
        call.setOperationName(new QName("SparePartPrice",methodName));

        //Setup the Parameters i.e. the Part SKU to be passed as input
        //parameter to the SparePartPrice web service
        Object[] params = new Object[] {"SKU-123"};

        //Invoke the SparePartPrice web service
        Float price = (Float) call.invoke(params);

        //Print out the result
        System.out.println("The price is $" + price.floatValue());
    }
    catch (Exception e) {
        System.err.println(e.toString());
    }
  }
}
```

Compile and run the above program. If you look at the SOAP request and SOAP response for this program, you will get the following (again only the relevant sections from the <BODY> element are shown). For details on how to trace the SOAP request/response, refer to Appendix A, which describes TCPMonitor, a tracing utility that comes along with AXIS.

```
<SOAP-ENV:Body>
  <ns1:getPrice xmlns:ns1="SparePartPrice">
    <arg0 xsi:type="xsd:string">SKU-123</arg0>
  </ns1:getPrice>
</SOAP-ENV:Body>


<SOAP-ENV:Body>
  <ns1:getPriceResponse xmlns:ns1="SparePartPrice">
    <getPriceResult xsi:type="xsd:float">10.99</getPriceResult>
  </ns1:getPriceResponse>
</SOAP-ENV:Body>
```

The only difference in the SOAP Request that you will notice is that instead of the sku parameter name, since we didn't specify one now, AXIS supplied a default element name of arg0. The xsi:type is still set correctly because AXIS interprets the params[] object and the data types in it. It comes out with a most appropriate XML Schema encoding type for your data. Similarly, because you have typecast the result explicitly to a float object, it set the xsi:type correctly in the SOAP response too. So, AXIS does a lot of things behind the scenes for you.

> *We definitely recommend it as a "Best Practice" to set the request and response parameter data types correctly instead of letting AXIS make that decision for you.*

WSDL Support in AXIS

AXIS includes some potentially good support for the Web Services Description Language (**WSDL**). For example, we'll use our `SparePartPrice` web service to demonstrate how easy it is to retrieve the WSDL for a deployed web service from AXIS.

Make sure that Tomcat server is running and that you have deployed the `SparePartPrice` web service as covered in the previous few sections of this chapter. Now navigate to http://localhost:8080/axis/services/SparePartPrice?wsdl in your browser and you'll see the WSDL displayed in the browser as shown below:

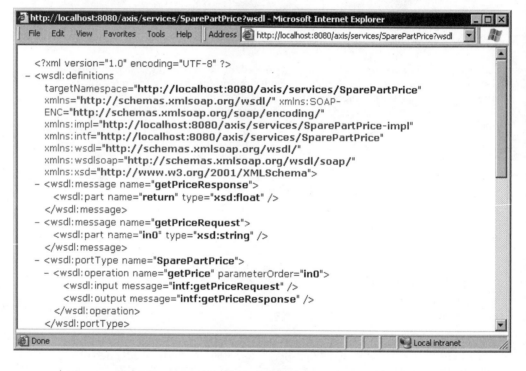

The template URL to retrieve the WSDL definition for a deployed web service in AXIS is thus:

http://<hostname>:<portname>/<axiswebapp>/services/<servicename>?wsdl

So, it translates to http://localhost:8080/axis/services/SparePartService?wsdl in our case. Note that the **?wsdl** option to generate WSDL files applies to *.JWS files as well. For example, to retrieve the WSDL file for the HelloWorld.jws service, which we deployed in %AXIS_DEPLOYHOME% back in Chapter 1, we'll need to browse to http://localhost:8080/axis/HelloWorld.jws?wsdl. Try this URL in your browser and you'll get the WSDL file for the same.

Apart from **?wsdl**, AXIS provides two powerful tools called Java2WSDL and WSDL2Java to work with Java classes and WSDL files.

Java2WSDL

The **?wsdl** option is useful if you have deployed your service in a servlet-based environment as we have, but what if you have Java classes from which you want to generate a WSDL file? AXIS provides a utility that tackles this issue called Java2WSDL (or org.apache.axis.wsdl.Java2WSDL to be precise). As the name suggests, it takes your java classes and produces a WSDL representation for them.

Java2WSDL can take quite a few input arguments as you can see if you call it in a console window with no arguments at all. Indeed, you'll get a list back of all the possible flags that you can use and their purpose.

```
> java org.apache.axis.wsdl.Java2WSDL

Java2WSDL emitter
Usage: java org.apache.axis.wsdl.Java2WSDL [options] class-of-
portType
Options:
        -h, --help
                print this message and exit
        -o, --output <argument>
                output Wsdl filename
        -l, --location <argument>
                service location url
        -s, --service <argument>
                service name (obtained from --location if not
                                specified)
        -n, --namespace <argument>
                target namespace
...
```

We won't look at all nineteen possible options as we'd be here all day, but feel free to experiment and try them all out. Our aim in this section is just to use Java2WSDL to generate a WSDL file given that we have already written the code for our web service – SparePartPrice.java. In this case, we only need to use four flags:

```
> java org.apache.axis.wsdl.Java2WSDL
        -o <WSDLfilename>
        -l "<serviceURL>"
```

```
-n "<TargetNamespace>"
-p "<PackageName>" "<Namespace>"
<Java Interface or Java Class Name>
```

where:

❑ -o is the name of the WSDL file to generate

❑ -l is the URL for the web service

❑ -n is the target namespace for the WSDL file. As discussed before, we can use the unique name we gave to the web service here.

❑ -p provides a mapping from Java package to namespace to ensure that all the classes within the specified package will be mapped to the namespace.

So let's go ahead and generate a WSDL file based on our `SparePartPrice` web service class file using Java2WSDL. First, make sure that Tomcat is running and that `SparePartPrice` has been deployed in AXIS. Then open a console window, navigate to your `%AXIS_DEVHOME%` directory, and make the following call:

```
wrox-axis> java org.apache.axis.wsdl.Java2WSDL -o
SparePartPrice.wsdl -l
"http://localhost:8080/axis/services/SparePartPrice"  -n
"SparePartPrice" -p"wroxaxis.chapter2"
"SparePartPrice" wroxaxis.chapter2.SparePartPrice
```

The `SparePartPrice.wsdl` file containing the WSDL for the service will be generated and saved in the `%AXIS_DEVHOME%` directory.

Make sure that you don't have any space immediately after the "-p" option in the Java2WSDL utility. Java2WSDL does not like it for some reason. However, there is no problem with having a space immediately after "-l" or "-n" option.

WSDL2Java

So far, we've seen how to create and deploy web services in AXIS and how to write clients that make use of them. We've also seen that writing the clients requires a careful sequencing of method calls (first create the `Service` object, then the `Call` object, then set the input parameters, result types, etc.) in order to generate the SOAP requests correctly. Wouldn't it be great if there was a utility that could generate all this client code for us? Fortunately, there is. The `WSDL2Java` (`org.apache.axis.wsdl.WSDL2Java`) program is meant for just that.

It's comes in handy in other situations as well. What if someone just gives you the WSDL file for their web service or if you visit one of the many sites like (http://www.salcentral.com or http://www.xmethods.com) that provide URLs to the WSDL files for various web services hosted in their web services directory? You definitely need a program that will take a URL pointer to a WSDL file and generate the Java client stubs for you to speed up their development.

The WSDL2Java utility not only generates the client stubs for you given a WSDL interface file, but also helps you generate the server-side skeleton code against a given WSDL file. Imagine a scenario where you are writing a web service from scratch. You would probably start with defining the WSDL interface first. Once you have that, you would like to generate skeleton code so that all you have to do is fill in the actual logic for your service to function as intended. The skeleton code will contain not only the correct wrapper classes to help you fill out pieces of the web service code, but it will also contain the WSDD files for deploying and undeploying your web service.

So, in summary, the `WSDL2Java` utility can be used for two purposes:

❑ Given a WSDL file, generate client stubs that contain all the plumbing code necessary to invoke the web service

❑ Give a WSDL file, generate server-side skeleton code along with WSDD files to deploy and undeploy the web service in AXIS

Let's look at each of the above tasks and in the process get familiar with `WSDL2Java`. Do not worry too much about the different arguments to `WSDL2Java`, we will cover them appropriately as need for our tasks.

Generating Client Stubs with WSDL2Java

Let's start with a definition. A **client stub**, with respect to web services, is a Java class that has the same interface as that of a web service. It provides us with the ability to call the web service as though it was a local object. In this section, we'll be using `WSDL2Java` to generate the client stubs for our `SparePartPrice` web service.

The first thing that we'll need then is the WSDL file for `SparePartPrice`. We could use either of the two approaches that we covered a little earlier, namely the `?wsdl` mechanism or the `Java2WSDL` utility. Recall though, that we used the latter technique to generate `SparePartPrice.wsdl` in the `%AXIS_DEVHOME%` directory earlier, so we'll make use of that. With the WSDL file to hand, we can run `WSDL2Java` with the following call from `%AXIS_DEVHOME%`:

```
wrox-axis> java org.apache.axis.wsdl.WSDL2Java -o
%AXIS_DEVHOME%-p wroxaxis.chapter2.stubs SparePartPrice.wsdl
```

where:

❑ `-o` is the output directory, where we want the client stub classes to get generated.

❑ `-p` is the package name. Specifying the package name will mean that the client stub classes will get generated in `<output-directory><package-name>`. In our case, this will be `%AXIS_DEVHOME%\wroxaxis\chapter2\stubs`.

Alternatively, instead of first obtaining the WSDL file and saving it as `SparePartPrice.wsdl`, we can direct WSDL2Java to retrieve it straight from AXIS online as follows:

```
wrox-axis> java org.apache.axis.wsdl.WSDL2Java -o
%AXIS_DEVHOME%-p wroxaxis.chapter2.stubs
```

http://localhost:8080/axis/services/SparePartPrice?wsdl

Whichever way you choose to follow, `WSDL2Java` will produce four files in
`%AXIS_DEVHOME%\wroxaxis\chapter2\stubs`.

```
SparePartPrice.java
SparePartPriceService.java
SparePartPriceServiceLocator.java
SparePartPriceSoapBindingStub.java
```

Instead of going through the code for each of file, it's more beneficial to see how
the set of java classes that have just been generated in those files relate to each
other. This will help us later when we use these classes to invoke the
`SparePartPrice` web service. Figure 2 shows the UML class diagram outlining
this relationship.

Figure 2

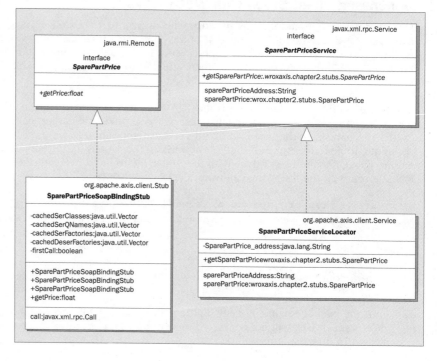

The first class to look at is the `SparePartPrice` interface class in the top left corner. It basically extends the `java.rmi.Remote` interface and has a single method, `getPrice()`, as we have seen before.

Next is the `SparePartPriceService` interface, which extends the `javax.xml.rpc.Service` method. The `SparePartPriceService` class basically acts as a **factory** for an instance of the client stub. You will notice a method called `getSparePartPrice()`, which returns the `SparePartPrice` interface. A concrete implementation of this class called `SparePartPriceServiceLocator` is generated as well and the implemented `getSparePartPrice()` method returns a concrete implementation of the client stub: the `SparePartPriceSoapBindingStub` class.

The `SparePartPriceSoapBindingStub` class is the actual client stub. If you go through the entire source, you will find that the `getPrice()` method actually retrieves a `Service` object, creates a `Call` object and then invokes the `SparePartPrice` web service that we have deployed in AXIS.

Using The Client Stubs

Using the client stub we've now generated to invoke the `SparePartPrice` web service is very simple. The UML Sequence diagram shown in figure 3 explains how to use the client stub generated classes.

Figure 3

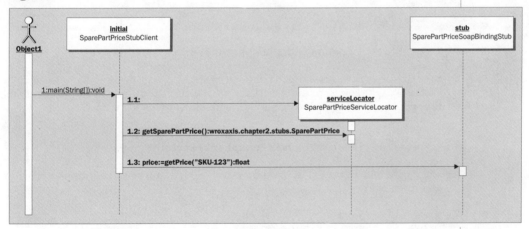

The sequence is as follows:

❑ Our first goal is to get a handle on the `javax.xml.rpc.Service` concrete object. So, we create an instance of the `SparePartPriceServiceLocator` class.

❑ Then we call the `getSparePartPrice()` method on this instance. This will give us a concrete implementation of the `SparePartPrice` remote interface; an instance of the `SparePartPriceSoapBindingStub` class.

❑ Finally, we invoke the getPrice() method on the SparePartPriceSoapBindingStub class instance returned from the previous call.

The code for our new client program is shown below. Contrast the simplicity and abstraction of this code with the client code that we have been writing so far.

```java
//SparePartPriceStubClient.java

package wroxaxis.chapter2.stubs;

public class SparePartPriceStubClient {

  public static void main (String args[]) throws Exception {

    SparePartPriceServiceLocator serviceLocator =
      new SparePartPriceServiceLocator();

    SparePartPriceSoapBindingStub stub  =
      (SparePartPriceSoapBindingStub)
      serviceLocator.getSparePartPrice();

  float price = stub.getPrice("SKU-123");
  System.out.println("The price is : $" + price);
  }
}
```

To run the above program, do the following steps:

Save SparePartPriceStubClient.java in %AXIS_DEVHOME%\wroxaxis\chapter2\stubs. Then compile all the client stub files generated by WSDL2Java and our stub client by giving the following command:

wrox-axis> **javac wroxaxis/chapter2/stubs/*.java**

Make sure that Tomcat is running on port 8080 (default port) and run the program as shown below:

wrox-axis> **java wroxaxis.chapter2.stubs.SparePartPriceStubClient**
The price is : $10.99

Success. The client stubs that we've generated with WSDL2Java work as we had hoped.

Generating Server-side Skeleton Code with WSDL2Java

The second use for WSDL2Java is to generate server-side skeleton code along with the WSDD files to deploy and undeploy the web service in AXIS, given the service's WSDL file. Let's take a look at that now.

Let's create a counterpart service for the SparePartPrice web service we've used so far. The SparePartDescription web service then also has only one method called getDescription(), which takes a String parameter identifying the part and returns a description for that part as a String.

The WSDL file for the service, SparePartDescription.wsdl is shown below. It begins, as always with various namespace declarations.

```
<?xml version="1.0" encoding="UTF-8"?>
<wsdl:definitions
  targetNamespace=
  "http://localhost:8080/axis/services/SparePartDescription"
  xmlns="http://schemas.xmlsoap.org/wsdl/"
  xmlns:SOAP-ENC="http://schemas.xmlsoap.org/soap/encoding/"
  xmlns:impl=
  "http://localhost:8080/axis/services/SparePartDescription-impl"
  xmlns:intf=
  "http://localhost:8080/axis/services/SparePartDescription"
  xmlns:wsdl="http://schemas.xmlsoap.org/wsdl/"
  xmlns:wsdlsoap="http://schemas.xmlsoap.org/wsdl/soap/"
  xmlns:xsd="http://www.w3.org/2001/XMLSchema">
```

The getDescription() method takes an input parameter of type String (identifying the part) and returns a String value containing the description of the part. Accordingly, we have two message elements, getDescriptionRequest and getDescriptionResponse, to declare.

```
<wsdl:message name="getDescriptionRequest">
  <wsdl:part name="in0" type="xsd:string"/>
</wsdl:message>
<wsdl:message name="getDescriptionResponse">
  <wsdl:part name="return" type="xsd:string"/>
</wsdl:message>
```

The <portType> element, which is similar to a class concept in Java, has one operation: getDescription as shown below.

```
<wsdl:portType name="SparePartDescription">
  <wsdl:operation name="getDescription" parameterOrder="in0">
    <wsdl:input message="intf:getDescriptionRequest"/>
    <wsdl:output message="intf:getDescriptionResponse"/>
  </wsdl:operation>
</wsdl:portType>
```

The binding element maps the portType to a specific protocol. In this case, we map it to the SOAP protocol.

```
<wsdl:binding name="SparePartDescriptionSoapBinding"
              type="intf:SparePartDescription">
   <wsdlsoap:binding style="rpc"
                     transport="http://schemas.xmlsoap.org/soap/http"/>
   <wsdl:operation name="getDescription">
      <wsdlsoap:operation soapAction="" style="rpc"/>
      <wsdl:input>
         <wsdlsoap:body
         encodingStyle="http://schemas.xmlsoap.org/soap/encoding/" namespace=
         "http://localhost:8080/axis/services/SparePartDescription"
            use="encoded"/>
      </wsdl:input>
      <wsdl:output>
         <wsdlsoap:body encodingStyle=
         "http://schemas.xmlsoap.org/soap/encoding/" namespace=
         "http://localhost:8080/axis/services/SparePartDescription"
            use="encoded"/>
      </wsdl:output>
   </wsdl:operation>
</wsdl:binding>
```

Finally, we have the `service` element, which maps the binding to the endpoint `http://localhost:8080/axis/services/SparePartDescription`.

```
<wsdl:service name="SparePartDescriptionService">
   <wsdl:port binding="intf:SparePartDescriptionSoapBinding"
              name="SparePartDescription">
      <wsdlsoap:address location="http://localhost:8080/axis/
      services/SparePartDescription"/>
   </wsdl:port>
</wsdl:service>
</wsdl:definitions>
```

Save `SparePartDescription.wsdl` in `%AXIS_DEVHOME%` and make the following call to `WSDL2Java`.

```
wrox-axis> java org.apache.axis.wsdl.WSDL2Java -o %AXIS_DEVHOME%
   -p wroxaxis.chapter2.skeleton -s
wroxais/chapter2/SparePartDescription.wsdl
```

The only changes are the addition of the option **-s**, which indicates that the skeleton code also needs to be generated, and the change of the package name to `wroxaxis.chapter2.skeleton`, so that we do not mix up our code with the `wroxaxis.chapter2.stubs` code that we generated in the previous section. Note that the generate skeleton option generates not only the Java source files for the server-side deployment along with the WSDD files for deployment/undeployment, but also the source code for the client stubs that we saw in the previous section. Thus it actually generates a complete end-to-end set of source files.

Server-side Skeleton Classes

The server-side skeleton classes provide a default implementation, i.e. skeleton, for the web service described by your WSDL file. The principle is again to separate out the business logic from the binding details.

Take a look at the 3 classes shown below which comprises the Spare Part Description web service. The class diagram for the same is shown below:

Figure 4

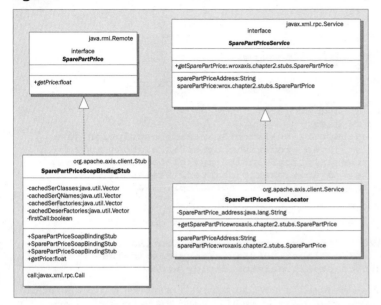

At the top, we have the Java Remote Interface `SparePartDescription`, which defines the `getDescription()` method. Then you have two concrete implementations of this interface: a `SoapBindingSkeleton`, which takes care of all the binding details i.e. (SOAP binding) and the `SoapBindingImpl` class, which contains the actual logic for the `getDescription()` method. You can put your code in the `getDescription()` method of the `SoapBindingImpl` class.

Client-side Stub Classes

The client stub classes are also generated to help ease your task in writing a client to invoke the Spare Part Description Service. The set of classes shown below follow a similar pattern to that we saw before and we will not go into the description of it here.

Figure 5

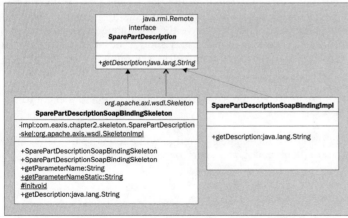

In addition to the above files, `deploy.wsdd` and `undeploy.wsdd` are also generated; these help you deploy the service and/or undeploy the Spare Part Description web service.

Deploying this Service

To deploy this service, you will need to do the following:

❑ Compile the server-side skeleton files:
```
wrox-axis> javac
wroxaxis\chapter2\skeleton\SparePartDescription.java
wrox-axis> javac wroxaxis\chapter2\skeleton\
SparePartDescriptionSoapBindingSkeleton.java
wrox-axis> javac wroxaxis\chapter2\skeleton\
SparePartDescriptionSoapBindingImpl.java
```

❑ Copy the `.class` files generated to the `%AXIS_DEPLOYHOME%\WEB-INF\classes\wroxaxis\chapter2\skeleton` directory.

❑ ```
wrox-axis> java org.apache.axis.client.AdminClient
-l http://localhost:8080/axis/services/AdminService
wroxaxis\chapter2\skeleton\deploy.wsdd
```

We leave it as an exercise to the reader to write a client that invokes the client stub. Follow the sequence diagram shown for the `SparePartPriceService` client program that used the client stubs generated from `WSDL2Java`.

# Message-based Services

We saw earlier in this chapter that AXIS supports two kinds of web services by default: RPC-based and Message-based. So far, we've covered the RPC-based variety where client classes are always concerned with linking to specific pieces of remote code. That is, we are always concerned about a method, its parameters and the response from that method.

Message-based services on the other hand are concerned with the processing of data and not specific methods. Indeed, you will likely have more options on how message-based services should behave and process data than RPC-based services and they are thus generally more flexible than RPC-based services for this reason. A message-based service might take a request and process it by calling other objects, or using other code etc. They also have the advantage of inherently supporting asynchronous processing: a client may send a message, disconnect and not reconnect for an indefinite period of time before querying for the reply message.

To demonstrate, let's create a new message-based web service and a client to use it. Our plan of action will be to:

❑ Write a catalog publisher message service that will allow a spare parts supplier to update their catalog at a spare parts dealer site

❑ Deploy the service in AXIS

❑ Write a client for the service
```

This new service fits into the scenario we've been building our Spare Part services to so far: A fictitious warehouse stocks all these spare parts, maintaining an inventory of the parts supplied by different suppliers. Suppliers are responsible for maintaining the catalog at the warehouse on their own. To aid them in this task, the warehouse owners decide to write a message-based service called **CatalogPublisher**, which will take an XML document containing the catalog details from each supplier and update their inventory. Each supplier will regularly create this catalog XML document and invoke `CatalogPublisher` whenever they want to update their catalog entries at the central warehouse.

Of course, in order to keep `CatalogPublisher` simple and focus on AXIS, we won't actually develop the sophisticated code at the backend to have the service work as advertised. Instead, we will simply return another XML document containing the number of items in the catalog that were updates and the date of processing as a response.

Figure 6 shows the interaction between suppliers, service and warehouse at a highlevel.

Figure 6

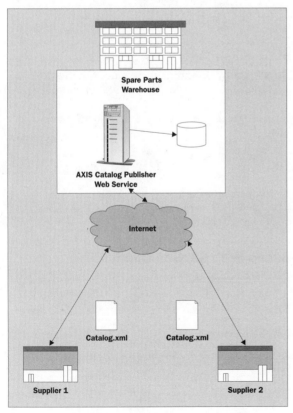

Listed below is a sample `catalog.xml` file that each supplier provides to the `CatalogPublisher` web service. It is pretty straightforward, containing a `<DOCUMENTINFO>` element, a `<SUPPLIERDETAILS>` element and the `<PRODUCTLIST>` element that contains a list of `<PRODUCT>` elements that this supplier provides to the warehouse.

```
<CATALOG xmlns="http://www.wrox.com/axis/catalog">
  <DOCUMENTINFO>
    <DATE>02/15/2002</DATE>
  </DOCUMENTINFO>
  <SUPPLIERDETAILS>
    <SUPPLIERID>12345-56789</SUPPLIERID>
    <SUPPLIERCONTACTEMAIL>support@supplier.com</SUPPLIERCONTACTEMAIL>
  </SUPPLIERDETAILS>
  <PRODUCTLIST>
    <PRODUCT>
      <SUPPLIER-PRODUCTSKU>SKU-1</SUPPLIER-PRODUCTSKU>
      <PRODUCTDESC>Spark Plug</PRODUCTDESC>
      <PRODUCTPRICE>10.99</PRODUCTPRICE>
      <PRODUCTUOM>Each</PRODUCTUOM>
    </PRODUCT>
    <PRODUCT>
      <SUPPLIER-PRODUCTSKU>SKU-2</SUPPLIER-PRODUCTSKU>
      <PRODUCTDESC>Wiper</PRODUCTDESC>
      <PRODUCTPRICE>2.99</PRODUCTPRICE>
      <PRODUCTUOM>Each</PRODUCTUOM>
    </PRODUCT>
  </PRODUCTLIST>
</CATALOG>
```

The response XML document that `CatalogPublisher` would return given the above `catalog.xml` file is shown below. It returns the count of the `PRODUCT` items that were present in the input XML and a `DATERECEIVED` element.

```
<CU:CATALOGUPDATE xmlns:CU="http://www.wrox.com/axis/catalogupdate">
  <ITEMCOUNT>2</ITEMCOUNT>
  <DATERECEIVED>02/16/2002</DATERECEIVED>
</CU:CATALOGUPDATE>
```

With the basics set up and the format of the XML files to be sent and received, it's time to write the service `CatalogPublisherService.java` and its client, `CatalogPublisherServiceClient.java`.

Writing the Message-based Web Service Client

It's slightly easier to follow the SOAP conversation between a message-based service and its client if we build the client first, so let's do that. The steps in writing a message-based web service client in AXIS are as follows:

❑ Create a `Call` object from the service object

❑ Invoke the `setTargetEndpointAddress` on the `Call` object to set the endpoint URL of the service

- ❑ Build an `Array` of `org.apache.axis.message.SOAPBodyElement` objects. When the SOAP request is generated, the SOAP Body element will contain the actual XML payload.

- ❑ Call the `invoke()` method on the `Call` object, passing the array of `SOAPBodyElement` objects built in the previous step. The return type will be a `Vector` of `SOAPBodyElement` objects, which you can typecast to an `org.apache.axis.message.SOAPBodyElement` object and get a DOM representation of the XML data.

You may see a similiarity between the first two steps here and those taken in an RPC-based service client, but after that the similarity ends. The source code is shown below:

```
// CatalogPublisherServiceClient.java

package wroxaxis.chapter2.messaging;

import org.w3c.dom.Element;
import org.apache.axis.client.Service;
import org.apache.axis.client.Call;
import org.apache.axis.message.SOAPBodyElement;
import org.apache.axis.utils.XMLUtils;

import java.io.File;
import java.io.FileInputStream;
import java.net.URL;
import java.util.Vector;

public class CatalogPublisherServiceClient {

  public static void main(String[] args) throws Exception {
```

First, we define the endpoint of the message-based web service in AXIS:

```
String endpointURL =
  "http://localhost:8080/axis/services/CatalogPublisherService";
```

Then build the `Service` and `Call` objects. Set the `TargetEndPointAddress` of the `Call` object.

```
Service service = new Service();
Call call = (Call) service.createCall();
call.setTargetEndpointAddress(new URL(endpointURL));
```

Next, define an `Array` of `SOAPBodyElement` objects. Since we have only one SOAP `<BODY>` element, the size is 1.

```
SOAPBodyElement[] reqSOAPBodyElements = new SOAPBodyElement[1];
```

Populate the SOAPBodyElement with the XML payload that you want to pass – in this case is in the catalog.xml file we created earlier. Conveniently, one of the constructors for the SOAPBodyElement class lets us pass a java.io.FileInputStream object to it and it builds the SOAP Body from the contents of the file. Be sure however to change the path to catalog.xml to wherever you have in fact saved it.

```
File catalogFile =
   new File("d:\\wroxaxis\\wroxaxis\\chapter2\\messaging\\catalog.xml");
FileInputStream fis = new FileInputStream(catalogFile);
reqSOAPBodyElements[0] =
   new SOAPBodyElement(XMLUtils.newDocument(fis).getDocumentElement());
```

Now we invoke the web service. The SOAPBodyElement array is passed as input to the invoke() method. The response is a Vector of SOAPBodyElement objects, which will contain the SOAP Body of the SOAP response message.

```
Vector resSOAPBodyElements =
   (Vector) call.invoke(reqSOAPBodyElements);
```

To retrieve an org.w3c.dom.Element object from the SOAPBodyElement, call the getAsDOM() method on it. From here, we make use of the org.apache.axis.utils.XMLUtils class, which contains several handy methods for manipulating XML; notably the static ElementToString() method, which converts an org.w3c.dom.Element object to a String.

```
SOAPBodyElement resSOAPBodyElement = null;
resSOAPBodyElement = (SOAPBodyElement) resSOAPBodyElements.get(0);
System.out.println(XMLUtils.ElementToString(
   resSOAPBodyElement.getAsDOM()));
   }
}
```

Once compiled and run, which we'll do later, the client generates the following SOAP Request to send over the wire to the server:

```
POST /axis/services/CatalogPublisherService HTTP/1.0
Content-Length: 1064
Host: localhost
Content-Type: text/xml; charset=utf-8
SOAPAction: ""

<?xml version="1.0" encoding="UTF-8"?>
<SOAP-ENV:Envelope
   xmlns:SOAP-ENV="http://schemas.xmlsoap.org/soap/envelope/"
   xmlns:xsd="http://www.w3.org/2001/XMLSchema"
   xmlns:xsi="http://www.w3.org/2001/XMLSchema-instance">
<SOAP-ENV:Body>
<CATALOG
xmlns="http://www.wrox.com/axis/catalog">
```

```
        <DOCUMENTINFO>
            <DATE>02/15/2002</DATE>
        </DOCUMENTINFO>
            .........
    </CATALOG>
  </SOAP-ENV:Body>
</SOAP-ENV:Envelope>
```

We'll look at the SOAP Response once we've built the `CatalogPublisher` web service itself, which is next on our agenda. Note that we're not paying any attention to error handling here. Again, this is simply to keep our focus on AXIS rather than the code it is serving. Chapter 4 looks in detail at exception handling in AXIS if you want to know more.

Writing the CatalogPublisher Web Service

One constant in implementing message-based services in AXIS is the signature for every method those services implement – they are all the same.

```
public Element[] methodname(MessageContext ctx, Vector elements)
```

where *ctx* is the `MessageContext` instance, which can be used to retrieve more information about the AXIS context and *elements* is a `Vector` that contains a collection of `<BODY>` elements (of type `org.w3c.dom.Element`) from the SOAP Message. The return value is always an `Array` of `org.w3c.dom.Element` objects, where each `Element` contains the XML Data that you wish to return.

The mechanism will become clear once we take a look at the code for the service:

```
// CatalogPublisherService.java
package wroxaxis.chapter2.messaging;


import javax.xml.parsers.DocumentBuilderFactory;
import javax.xml.parsers.DocumentBuilder;
import org.w3c.dom.Document;
import org.w3c.dom.Element;
import org.w3c.dom.NodeList;
import org.w3c.dom.Node;
import org.w3c.dom.Text;
import java.util.Vector;
import java.util.Date;
import java.text.SimpleDateFormat;
import org.apache.axis.MessageContext ;
import org.apache.axis.utils.XMLUtils;
import org.apache.axis.message.SOAPBodyElement;


import java.io.*;

public class CatalogPublisherService {
```

In keeping with all our services so far, the CatalogPublisher service has just a single method publishCatalog(). Note that the signature of the method conforms to the template that AXIS lays out.

```
public Element[] publishCatalog(MessageContext context,
  Vector soapBodyElements) throws Exception {
```

First, we need to retrieve the <Body> element in the SOAP request because that's where we'll find the message (in this case, the copy of catalog.xml) that was sent by the client. Since there is only one <Body> element, we pick that one up.

```
Element soapBody = (Element) soapBodyElements.get(0);
```

Now that we have the XML message, we need to analyse it. Remember that all we need to do in this simplified service is count the number of <PRODUCT> elements in the message and return that number, so we just retrieve the DOM NodeList for all <PRODUCT> elements and call the getLength() on the NodeList to make the count.

```
NodeList productList = soapBody.getElementsByTagName("PRODUCT");
//Get the count of <PRODUCT> elements in the NodeList
int productCount = productList.getLength();
```

If we were updating the warehouse's supplier catalog, this is where we would call it. To keep things simple of course, we don't call anything!

```
//Call back-end code
```

As discussed earlier, we want our response XML to take the form

```
<CATALOGUPDATE>
    <ITEMCOUNT>nnn</ITEMCOUNT>
    <DATERECEIVED>mm/dd/yyyy</DATERECEIVED>
</CATALOGUPDATE>
```

where <ITEMCOUNT> is the number of products that are present in the catalog.xml and <DATERECEIVED> is the date that this request was processed by this service. In order to build this response then, we use the DOM objects accordingly.

```
//Start Building Response Document
//Get a DocumentBuilder object
DocumentBuilderFactory factory =
  DocumentBuilderFactory.newInstance();
factory.setNamespaceAware(true);
DocumentBuilder builder = factory.newDocumentBuilder();
//Start creating the Response
//Creat a new DOM Document
Document responseDoc = builder.newDocument();
```

```
//Create the namespace aware root Element <CATALOGUPDATE>
Element resRoot = responseDoc.createElementNS(
"http://www.wrox.com/axis/catalogupdate","CATALOGUPDATE");
resRoot.setPrefix("CU");

//Create the ITEMCOUNT element
Element itemCount = responseDoc.createElement("ITEMCOUNT");
Text itemCountText = responseDoc.createTextNode(
   String.valueOf  (productCount));

//Create the DATE RECEIVED element
Element dateReceived = responseDoc.createElement("DATERECEIVED");
SimpleDateFormat fmt = new SimpleDateFormat("MM/dd/yyyy");
String date = fmt.format(new Date());
Text dateReceivedText = responseDoc.createTextNode(date);

//Append the child elements appropriately
resRoot.appendChild(itemCount);
itemCount.appendChild(itemCountText);
resRoot.appendChild(dateReceived);
dateReceived.appendChild(dateReceivedText);
```

Now we create an org.w3c.dom.Element array and assign the first element to the resRoot Element that contains the XML response and return it.

```
Element[] result = new Element[1];
result[0] = resRoot;
return(result);
  }
}
```

The SOAP Response returned is shown below:

```
HTTP/1.1 200 OK
Content-Type: text/xml; charset=utf-8
Content-Length: 426
Date: Sat, 16 Feb 2002 20:16:25 GMT
Server: Apache Tomcat/4.0.1 (HTTP/1.1 Connector)

<?xml version="1.0" encoding="UTF-8"?>
<SOAP-ENV:Envelope
        xmlns:SOAP-ENV=
"http://schemas.xmlsoap.org/soap/envelope/"
        xmlns:xsd="http://www.w3.org/2001/XMLSchema"
        xmlns:xsi="http://www.w3.org/2001/XMLSchema-instance">
```

```
<SOAP-ENV:Body>
    <ns1:CATALOGUPDATE xmlns:ns1="http://www.wrox.com/axis/catalogupdate">
        <ITEMCOUNT>2</ITEMCOUNT>
        <DATERECEIVED>02/16/2002</DATERECEIVED>
    </ns1:CATALOGUPDATE>
</SOAP-ENV:Body>
</SOAP-ENV:Envelope>
```

Deploying the CatalogPublisher Web Service

To deploy the CatalogPublisher service, we'll use a WSDD (CatalogPublisherServiceDeploy.wsdd) as we did for our RPC-based services. The main difference between this one and the others is the provider name. Since it is a message-based service, we need to specify java:MSG as the provider rather than java:RPC. The <parameter> elements for the <service> work the same as before with the className in this case set to wroxaxis.chapter2.messaging.CatalogPublisherService and the allowedMethods set to publishCatalog.

```
<deployment
        xmlns="http://xml.apache.org/axis/wsdd/"
        xmlns:java="http://xml.apache.org/axis/wsdd/providers/java"
        xmlns:xsi="http://www.w3.org/2000/10/XMLSchema-instance">
    <service name="CatalogPublisherService" provider="java:MSG">
        <parameter name="className"
        value="wroxaxis.chapter2.messaging.CatalogPublisherService"
        />
        <parameter name="allowedMethods" value="publishCatalog" />
    </service>
</deployment>
```

To deploy CatalogPublisher, we need to:

1. Make sure that Tomcat is running on port 8080 (default port)

2. Save CatalogPublisherService.java and CatalogPublisherServiceDeploy.wsdd in the %AXIS_DEVHOME\wroxaxis\chapter2\messaging directory.

3. Compile the CatalogPublisherService.java file by giving the following command:
   wrox-axis> **javac wroxaxis\chapter2\messaging\CatalogPublisherService.java**

4. Copy CatalogPublisherService.class to %AXIS_DEPLOYHOME%\WEB-INF\classes\wroxaxis\chapter2\messaging.

5. Use the AdminClient to deploy the service as follows:
   wrox-axis> **java org.apache.axis.client.AdminClient –l http://localhost:8080/axis/services/AdminService wroxaxis\chapter2\messaging\CatalogPublisherServiceDeploy.wsdd**

Last but not least, to make sure that `CatalogPublisher` does what we think it should, we need to run our client program and invoke it. Copy `CatalogPublisherServiceClient.java` to the `%AXIS_DEVHOME%\wroxaxis\` `chapter2\messaging` directory and compile it.

```
wrox-axis> javac
wroxaxis\chapter2\messaging\CatalogPublisherServiceClient.java
```

Then run the `CatalogPublisherServiceClient` as shown below:

```
wroxaxis> java
wroxaxis.chapter2.messaging.CatalogPublisherServiceClient
Received the following XML Response
-----------------------------------
<ns1:CATALOGUPDATE xmlns:ns1="http://
www.wrox.com/axis/catalogupdate">
   <ITEMCOUNT>2</ITEMCOUNT>
   <DATERECEIVED>04/18/2002</DATERECEIVED>
</ns1:CATALOGUPDATE>
```

We've tidied up the output to be a bit more readable here and the datestamp will of course reflect the date you're running the client, but otherwise, this is it. Well done.

Undeploying a Web Service in AXIS

Before we leave this chapter, there's only one loose end we have to tie up; we know how to deploy a web service to AXIS, but how do we undeploy one? Actually, it's not particularly difficult. Just as we provide a WSDD file with the `<deployment>` element and then use the `AdminClient` to deploy the service, we use a WSDD file with an `<undeployment>` element to undeploy the service. As you can see, it's a little different from the file to deploy a web service.

```
<undeployment xmlns="http://xml.apache.org/axis/wsdd/">
   <service name="servicename"/>
</undeployment>
```

As you may have guessed, *servicename* is the unique name given to the service that you wish to undeploy. For example, `CatalogPublisherService` or `SparePartPrice`. With the WSDD file created, the actual call to the AdminClient is not dissimilar to the ones we've made before.

```
> java org.apache.axis.client.AdminClient -l AdminserviceURL
undeployWSDDFile
```

To demonstrate, we'll undeploy our `CatalogPublisher` web service. First, we need to create `CatalogPublisherServiceUndeploy.wsdd` in `%AXIS_DEVHOME%\wroxaxis\chapter2\messaging`. It should not surprise you to see that this contains:

```
<undeployment xmlns="http://xml.apache.org/axis/wsdd/">
  <service name="CatalogPublisherService"/>
</undeployment>
```

With this achieved and Tomcat running, undeploying `CatalogPublisher` web service requires you only to open a console window, navigate to `%AXIS_DEVHOME%`, and make the following call to `AdminClient`.

wrox-axis> **java org.apache.axis.client.AdminClient**
-l http://localhost:8080/axis/services/AdminService
wroxaxis\chapter2\messaging\CatalogPublisherServiceUndeploy.wsdd

AdminClient will echo back to you that this has been done and if you run it again with the `list` option:

wrox-axis> **java org.apache.axis.client.AdminClient**
-l http://localhost:8080/axis/services/AdminService list

there will be no `<service>` entry for `CatalogPublisherService`. It has been successfully undeployed.

Summary

In this chapter, we have covered AXIS from a user-centric view. We took a look at the Web Service Deployment Descriptor (WSDD) – the configuration file used to deploy and undeploy a variety of AXIS configurable objects – and the `AdminClient` utility that uses WSDD files to do the deploying and undeploying. We also saw how to build both RPC-based and message-based web services for deployment on AXIS and their clients, and discovered that AXIS has two handy utilities, Java2WSDL and WSDL2Java, that can aid us in the more rapid development of our web services and their clients.

In the next chapter, we move on and look at the architecture of the AXIS message processing system.

axis

3

Architecture

The first two chapters introduced AXIS from a user-centric point of view explaining the fundamental features with simple examples. This chapter looks at the architecture and the main components involved in the system from a design-centric point of view. We will be focusing on the core components and the interaction between these components; since AXIS is basically a message-processing system, we'll also examine the path that messages take through both the client- and server-side systems.

Overview of the AXIS System

There are many SOAP implementations available; but its extensibility elevates AXIS above its predecessors. Flexibility has been a design goal since the start if the project and to achieve this AXIS has a modular design, where new functionality can be added simply by plugging in new modules. For example, to the basic configuration one might add:

- An SMTP or FTP message transport

- Application-specific serialisation and deserialisation

- Further service invocation mechanisms (CORBA, COM, etc.)

The core components of the AXIS System are:

- **AxisEngine** – this is the focal point of SOAP processing and acts as a controller for the other components.

- **MessageContext** – the `MessageContext` class is a wrapper for SOAP requests and responses; it provides context information about the message to the other components in the AXIS message-processing system.

- **Handlers** and **Chains** – handlers are the basic building blocks in the AXIS system. A handler takes a `MessageContext` and performs some action based on its contents then returns it to the calling code. A chain is a special handler that represents a sequence of other handlers.

- **Transports** – a transport component provides a mechanism for request messages get to the AXIS engine and for the return of response messages to a client.

- **Serializers and Deserializers** – these convert data from its native form into XML and vice versa.

- **Deployment and Configuration** – AXIS defines an XML-based deployment descriptor known as Web Service Deployment Descriptor (WSDD) that defines how a particular instance of AXIS behaves.

Introduction to AXIS Message Processing

As you can see from Figure 1, AXIS can exist on both the server and client side. As SOAP messages are all that is passed between each half of the system, it is perfectly possible that just one side of the system is based on AXIS and the other be based on some other SOAP implementation.

Figure 1

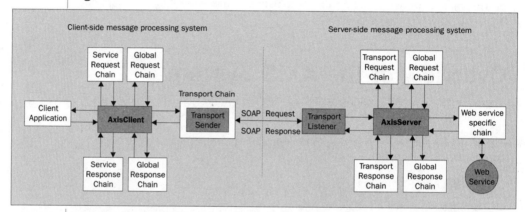

The hub of the system of on either side is an implementation of `org.apache.axis.AxisEngine`. In UML terminology, AXISEngine plays the role of an **actor** that interacts with the other message processing components like chains and handlers and coordinates the message flow through the system.

The AXIS message processing system uses an object of type `Message` for wrapping the SOAP request, response, and fault messages. These `Message` objects are put into `MessageContext` objects and then made available to all the components (chain, handler, etc.) of the message processing system through getter methods. A `MessageContext` object is basically a container for request, response, and fault messages that also provides context information like the transport protocol on which the message was received, references to an instance of `AxisEngine`, etc.

AXIS Engine

The abstract class, `AxisEngine` describes the AXIS message processing system in general. The `org.apache.axis.AxisEngine` abstract class provides implementations to helper methods for registering and deploying transport, handler, and chain components. AXIS provides the following implementations of `AxisEngine`:

❏ `AxisServer` – this acts as the `AxisEngine` for a server-side message processing system

❏ `AxisClient` – this acts as the `AxisEngine` for a client-side message processing system

The engine is also responsible for invoking all the chains in the order defined in the deployment descriptor and ensuring that the SOAP semantics are followed. For example, the engine makes sure that attributes like mustUnderstand are handled correctly.

Handlers, Chains, and Message flow

A handler provides a mechanism for processing message(s) that are contained in a MessageContext. Handlers enhance the basic functionality of the AXIS runtime system (AxisEngine) by providing additional message processing behavior and the AXIS Framework makes it easy to plug in application-specific handlers. For example, if we wanted to log all the requests and responses passing through the system we could simply plug in a suitable handler.

Clearly, the order in which handlers are invoked may change their effect. Therefore, handlers are grouped together using **Chains** (a special type of handler) into a single logical unit.

The AXIS engine invokes each chain by passing a SOAP message enclosed in a MessageContext object, then each handler is invoked sequentially to perform additional processing on the SOAP message. For example, Figure 2 shows the path of a message from the AXIS engine through a chain containing three handlers; finally control is returned to the AXIS engine, which could invoke other chains or return a response.

Figure 2

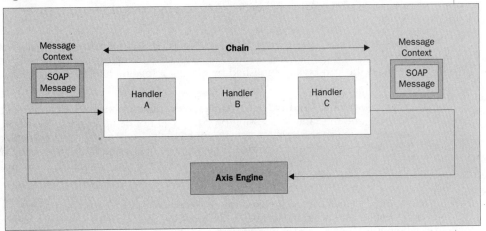

The sequence diagram overleaf shows that the handlers A, B, and C are invoked sequentially when the AXIS engine invokes the chain by calling its invoke() method, passing an object of type MessageContext. The chain invokes the handlers in turn by calling their invoke() methods.

Figure 3

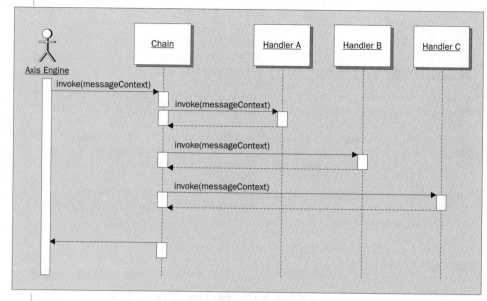

As you can see in Figure 1 the current version of AXIS contains three types of chain, which are invoked at different points in a message's passage through the system:

❑ **Transport Chains** – a transport-specific chain processes operations that are related to the transport protocol used to get the message to and from the AXIS engine.

❑ **Global Chains –** these provide a common processing functionality to all web services. For example, if it is required to log SOAP requests for of all web services this can be accomplished by placing a logging handler in a global chain.

❑ **Service-specific Chains** – each AXIS server can support many different web services and the same processing probably will not be appropriate for all of them. Service-specific chains contain functionality only useful for a particular service. For example, if a particular service requires some XSLT processing on the response message, this could be provided by adding a suitable handler in the service-specific chain.

Each of these chains can be invoked on either a request or a response message. Clearly, it might be desirable to invoke different handlers in each chain depending on whether a request or response message is being processed. AXIS uses the concept of flows to cope with this; when a chain is invoked on a request message only those handlers that are part of a chain's request flow are invoked, and for a response message only the response flow is invoked. It is also possible to define a fault flow for a chain to specify what should happen if a fault message is encountered.

Chains are discussed further in the section *Core AXIS Components*.

As AXIS implementations are divisible into client-side and server-side, it makes sense to deal with each separately.

Server-side Message Processing

The server-side message processing system receives a SOAP request, processes it, invokes the service, and returns (if required) a SOAP response. The message path is divided into the request flow that the message follows to a service and the response flow that any response message follows on the way back.

The following sequence diagram (Figure 4) shows the invocation of various chains in a server-side message processing system. The diagram does not cover the fault handling and assumes that all the chains process the message successfully. The fault handling is covered latter in the section *Fault Handling*.

Figure 4

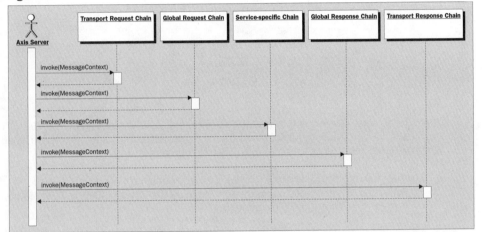

The flow of server-side message processing is also shown in the following diagram. The numbers from 1-11 indicate the flow of message in the message processing system.

Architecture

Figure 5

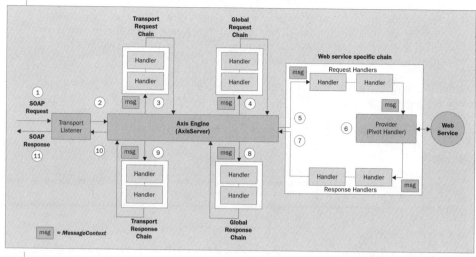

This diagram reflects the fact that the engine calls out to handlers, which are separate objects. Diagrams that put all the handlers "inside" the engine are also correct, however, because they reflect the fact that all the handlers are stored in an `EngineConfiguration` (`WSDDDeployment`) which is inside the engine.

1. The **Transport Listener** receives a SOAP request for a particular web service. The main job of a transport listener is to encapsulate the details of networking protocols. The transport listener:

    Packages the SOAP request into a `Message` object and puts that object into a `MessageContext` object.

    Then it sets the protocol-related properties on the `MessageContext`. For example, assuming the transport protocol is HTTP, the transport listener sets properties like the SOAP Action HTTP header, content type, content location etc. It also sets the `transportName` attribute so the correct transport chain is called.

2. The transport listener gets an instance of `AxisServer` and provides the necessary configuration information to it. In the current implementation of AXIS, the configuration information is contained in a Web Service Deployment Descriptor (WSDD) file (`server-config.wsdd`).

3. `AxisServer` then invokes the **Transport Request Chain** specified in the `Transport` object associated with that `transportName`. In the default, HTTP transport-based invocation, AXIS provides an URLMapper handler to map a URL to a `serviceHandler` field in the `MessageContext`. This field determines what service is eventually invoked. After invocation of all request handlers in the transport chain, the control is passed back to `AxisServer`.

4. Then `AxisServer` invokes the **Global Request Chain**. All handlers that are registered with the request flow of the global chain are invoked to process the message. A global request chain should contain handlers that provide some common functionality as this chain is invoked for all services, for example, if we want to log invocation for all services.

5. Then the **Service-Specific Chain** is invoked. First, all request handlers in the service specific chain are invoked and finally the MessageContext is passed to the provider.

6. A **Provider** (also known as **Pivot Handler** or **Dispatcher**) is responsible for actually invoking the service with the requested method. Any response is encapsulated in a Message object and added to the MessageContext. This is the key point in the message flow, where it passes from the request to the response flow. To indicate this has happened the MessageContext object's havePassedPivot property is set to true. The MessageContext, which now contains the request and the response message, is passed to the response handlers of the service-specific chain.

7. The service-specific response handlers processes the response message and then control is passed back to AxisServer.

8. AxisServer invokes the **Global Response Chain.**

9. The **Transport Response Chain** is invoked. The handlers in the transport chain are used to perform any processing of SOAP headers specific to the transport protocol used.

10. At this point, the invocation of all the chains is completed so AxisServer can pass control back to the transport listener.

11. The transport listener encapsulates the response Message object present in MessageContext into the correct format for the transport protocol being used and returns a SOAP response message to the client application over the appropriate protocol. For instance, the Transport Listener sets properties such as content type and content length for HTTP responses

Client-side Message Processing System

The client-side message processing system creates SOAP requests, sends them to a SOAP server and waits the response, if applicable. The numbers (from 1-9) in Figure 6 indicate the flow of message in the client message processing system.

Figure 6

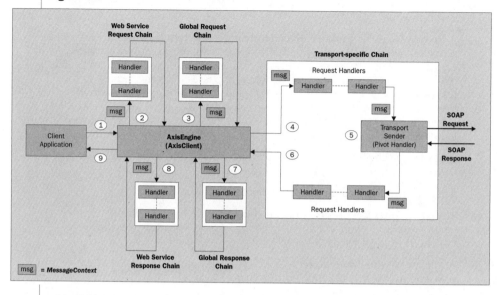

Lets look at each stage in detail:

1. To invoke AXIS a client application must first create a `Call` object
    (`org.apache.axis.client.Call`) using the `Service` class
    (`org.apache.axis.client.Service`). The `Call` object creates the request
    `Message` object and puts it into a `MessageContext` as a request message.
    Then `AxisClient` is invoked by passing the `MessageContext`. The current
    AXIS version uses a `client-config.wsdd` file to define the client-side
    configuration/deployment details.

2. `AxisClient` invokes the request handlers of the **Service-Specific Chain**.
    The request handlers are invoked sequentially and in the order defined in the
    deployment descriptor. For instance, you might want to log details like
    invocation time or how many times a particular user invoked the service for
    auditing purposes.

3. Then the **Global Request Chain** is invoked. If we have any processing
    common to all SOAP requests, we can do it with the handlers specified in the
    global request chain.

4. Then the request handlers in the **Transport-Specific Chain** are invoked,
    followed by the transport sender.

5. The **Transport Sender** plays the role of pivot handler on the client side. It is
    responsible for taking the SOAP request and sending it to a SOAP Server. AXIS
    provides a transport sender implementation for HTTP called
    `org.apache.axis.transport.http.HttpSender`; it takes the SOAP
    request message, opens a socket connection to the SOAP server, submits the
    request through HTTP POST, and waits for the response.

6. Once the response is received, the response message is encapsulated in a `Message` object and added to the `MessageContext`, and then the response handlers of the transport chain are invoked.

7. Again the **Global Response Chain** accomplishes any required processing such as logging.

8. Then the response handlers in the **Service-Specific Chain** are invoked if any service-specific processing on the SOAP response is required.

9. Finally, the response is sent back to the client application. There is no provider on the client side, since the service is being processed or provided by a "external or remote" node.

Other Message Patterns

While explaining how the server- and client-side AXIS systems work we have covered the Request/Response pattern that is usually used by HTTP-based web services. In this section, well look at the other message patterns that you can implement using an AXIS-based server:

1. One-way input message

2. One-way outbound message

One-way Input Message

In the one-way input message pattern, the flow of request message from client to server is similar to the request/response scenario. The main difference is in the behavior of provider. In this case, the provider does not wait for the response from the target web service but simply returns and the message processing is finished. Any response from the target web service is ignored. If any exception occurs at the target web service, then that exception/fault is either ignored or logged by using the service-specific or global chain, if any is defined. The fault or response is not sent back to the requestor; hence, the transport response chain is never invoked.

Figure 7

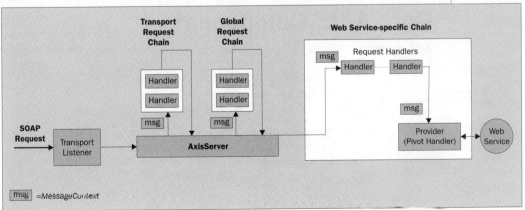

In some cases, a one-way web service is deployed with response and fault chains. For example, if we want to monitor the performance and response time, we could configure the server-side message system with timing handlers to indicate the responsiveness of processing.

One-way Outbound Message

In a one-way outbound message pattern, the client application sends the SOAP request to a SOAP server and proceeds with other processing without waiting for the response. It is possible that no response is expected or if one is, it may be received asynchronously through some other listener application. For example, if we use a message-oriented middleware-based transport handler, then the SOAP response may be received by a listener on the client side. The client application sends the message to the message server and proceeds with other processing. The listener receives the responses from the message server. This pattern is implemented by the Java messaging service-based example that we develop in Chapter 5.

Figure 8

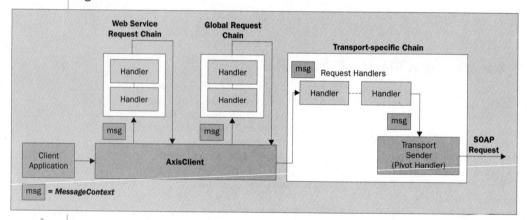

Core AXIS Components

Now we have discussed the overall message flow we can look at the individual components in detail.

Messages

The `org.apache.axis.Message` class represents the complete SOAP message including the SOAP part with zero or more attachments. The message can be a request message or a response message and a response message could actually be a fault message.

MessageContext

The flow of information in AXIS Framework is passed as `MessageContext` objects. The `MessageContext` can contain the following:

1. Request message – a `Message` object encapsulating a SOAP Request. This will be the outgoing message from a client or an incoming message to a server.

2. Response message – a `Message` object encapsulating a SOAP Response. This will be the incoming message to a client or the outgoing message from a server.

3. Service details – details such as target service name, the transport object on which the message is received, and the session associated with the current context etc.

4. Axis Engine and Mapping Registry – `MessageContext` keeps a reference to the AXIS engine for the current context. The Axis engine is an instance of `AxisServer` for a server-side message processing system and is an instance of `AxisClient` for a client-side message processing system. It also contains a reference to the `TypeMapping` registry that contains the mapping of qualified element names to objects that is required by serializers and deserializers.

5. Properties – `MessageContext` also contains other properties like user credentials (user ID and password), type of request message (for example: RPC/Document), etc.

The relation between `MessageContext` and `Message` is shown below. A `MessageContext` object may contain 0 to 2 `Message` objects that may be either a request message and/or a response message. AXIS defines an abstract class known as `Part` (`org.apache.axis.Part`) for representing Multiple Internet Message Extension (MIME) components. The `Part` class defines methods to add MIME Headers and setter and getter methods for Content Location, Content Type, and Content ID values.

Figure 9

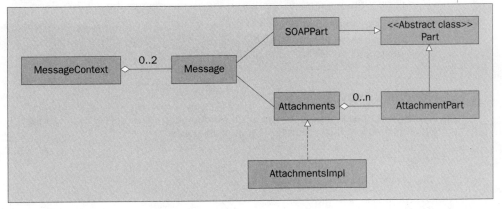

AXIS defines two implementation classes of `Part` known as `SOAPPart` and `Attachment`. We know that SOAP supports sending messages with attachments and AXIS represents these using the `Attachments` object. As shown in the diagram, an `Attachment` object may contain either zero or more (0..n) `AttachmentPart` objects. The `AttachmentPart` class represents the data contained in an attachment using the `javax.activation.DataHandler` defined in Java Activation Framework (JAF). This process is described further in Chapter 5 where we will be sending an image as an attachment.

Handlers

Handlers are invoked in sequence to process messages. A handler object in the flow may send a request, receive a response, or process a request to produce a response. A handler is responsible for some specific processing associated with a request, response, or fault flow. Typical examples of what you might use a handler for include:

1. Serialization/deserialization – to provide the serialization and deserialization required to turn binary data into XML and vice versa.

2. Encryption and decryption – a client application can use a handler to encrypt the SOAP request and the server can use a matching handler to decrypt it at the receiving side. We could also provide a handler to digitally sign a SOAP request and a handler to verify the signature at the receiving side.

3. Authentication and authorization – handlers can be used to provide authentication functionality. For instance, AXIS provides the handlers needed for HTTP BASIC authentication.

4. Logging and auditing – we can use handlers to provide a logging service. For example, we could provide a handler that processes the request flow to log the user details and other information like the usage count (number of times the service is used by the user) etc., in a file. This information could be used for billing if you were providing a fee-based web service. In Chapter 4, we will be writing a custom handler to log all the request messages.

5. XSLT – an XSLT handler could be provided to transform a message. An XSLT handler can be used to provide the content of `<SOAP:BODY>` in different formats such as HTML, XML, PDF, etc.

Handler Lifecycle

Figure 10 shows a state transition diagram depicting the lifecycle of a handler, which is controlled by the following four methods:

❑   `init()`

❑   `invoke(messageContext)`

❑   `onFault(messageContext)`

❑   `cleanup()`

Figure 10

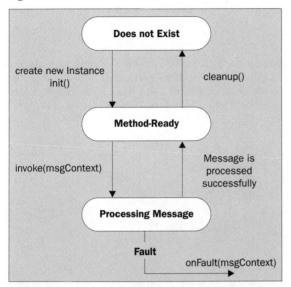

Initially the handler will be in the 'Does not Exist' state. The lifecycle of a handler starts when the AXIS runtime system creates a new instance of the handler class. Next, the init() method is called to enable the handler instance to initialize itself, setting the type mapping, initializing the configuration provider and so on. The ConfigurationProvider interface provides the configuration information for an AXIS engine. The implementation classes obtain the configuration information from some source (a file, string, etc.) and provide it to the AXIS engine.

Once the handler instance is created and initialized, it will be in a Ready State (Method-Ready) to process any request/response messages. The AXIS runtime system calls the invoke() method to process the message, which is shown as the 'Processing Message' state in the diagram. If the processing is successful, then the control is passed back to the AXIS engine, which then invokes the next handler in sequence. If the handler is the pivot handler, then it is responsible for invoking the service and receiving the response from the service. If a fault occurs during the processing of message, then the onFault() method will be called to undo the changes caused by invoke() method.

The AXIS engine calls the `cleanup()` method when the handler instance is no longer needed. The `cleanup()` method releases any resources that the handler instance was using and ends the life cycle of the instance again placing it in the 'Does Not Exist' state.

Figure 11 shows the relationship between various handlers. The `org.apache.axis.Handler` is the base interface and AXIS provides an abstract class known as `org.apache.axis.BasicHandler` with some setter and getter methods. Application-specific handlers can extend `BasicHandler` and provide specific implementation by overriding the inherited methods. It is worth noting that `AXISEngine`, the controller in the AXIS system, is itself a handler.

Figure 11

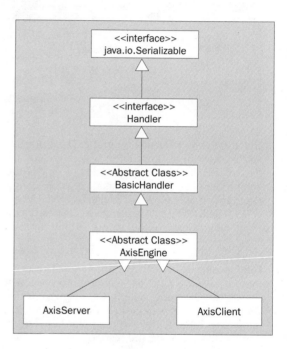

The following list shows some of the 21 handlers provided with the current beta 1 version of AXIS. AXIS also provides a default implementation of the handler interface known as `BasicHandler`, which implements simple property setter and getter methods, and provides a basic implementation for some of the handler methods. All the following handlers extend `BasicHandler` class.

❑ **DebugHandler** – this handler logs all the debugging messages in a log file.

❑ **EchoHandler** – this handler returns the same request message back to the client as response message. The request message is retrieved from the `MessageContext` and sent back as response message. This handler is provided (mainly) for checking interoperability issues.

❑ **ErrorHandler** – this handler is invoked during fault conditions and logs the AXIS Fault message.

- **HTTPAuthHandler** – this authenticates the credentials of the user trying to access a service with respect to a file called `user.lst` that contains a list of user names and passwords. This handler is used to implement HTTP BASIC authentication.

- **HTTPActionHandler** – this handler sets the target service property of `MessageContext` based on the contents of the `HTTPAction` header

- **JWSHandler** – in Chapter 1, we saw that simple web services can be deployed just by changing the file extension to `.jws` (Java Web Service). In such cases, the JWSHandler is used to set the target service name and JWS filename in the `MessageContext`, depending on the JWS configuration and the target URL.

- **JWSProcessor** – this handler is responsible for locating `.jws` (Java Web Service) files, copying them to `.java` files, and then compiling them so they are accessible as services.

- **LogHandler** – a handler used to log the invocation time and duration to a log file.

- **MD5AttachHandler** – this handler is responsible for processing MD5 attachments that are sent with the SOAP request. This handler uses the MD5 algorithm for creating a Message Digest (object of type `java.security.MessageDigest`) and encoding data.

- **SimpleAuthenticationHandler** – this handler is for authentication purposes. It checks the username and password with respect to the `users.lst` file.

- **SimpleAuthorizationHandler** – this checks the privileges of the user with respect to `perms.lst` file, which contains a list of user names and the services that they are able to access.

- **SimpleSessionHandler** – this handler is used for simple session management.

- **URLMapper** – a handler object that uses the extra path info of the request URI to map to a service name. For example, the URI `http://localhost:8080/axis/services/HelloService` is mapped to `HelloService`.

Chains

A chain is a handler; and the `Chain` class implements the `Handler` interface. As we saw earlier a chain contains a collection of handlers that are invoked sequentially and chains may be associated with request, response, and fault flows. For example, if we have two chains (chain A and chain B) in the request flow, then when the SOAP request is processed, chain A is invoked first and then chain B is invoked.

When an implementation of AXISEngine is invoked the `ConfigurationProvider` obtains all the configuration information from the deployment descriptor (WSDD) then loads all the chains, handlers, and services. A new handler can be added to a chain by providing a deployment descriptor and deploying it using the `AdminClient` utility class. When a new handler is added to an already executing chain, it will not be added to the chain directly, instead, a clone is created and then the handler is added to the cloned chain. Then the updated chain is made available for all the new SOAP requests; old version of the chain will be discarded once it is no longer being used to process any messages.

The TargetedChain Interface

The `org.apache.axis.TargetedChain` interface extends the basic `chain` interface; hence it can also contain a collection of handlers. A targeted chain is a special kind of chain that contains a request handler, a pivot handler, and a response handler.

Figure 12 shows a targeted chain with request handlers, a pivot handler, and response handlers. As we discussed earlier, it's at the pivot handler that a request message is emitted and any resulting response is received. When a response is received the pivot handler creates a `Message` object wrapping the response message and adds it to the `MessageContext`. The pivot handler also sets the `havePassedPivot` property to `true` to indicate to the AXIS engine that the `MessageContext` has passed through the pivot handler. The AXIS engine then invokes the response handlers defined in service, global, and transport chains. Each time a handler requests a message from `MessageContext`, the value of `havePassedPivot` is checked, if it is `true`, then the response message will be returned to the handler object.

Figure 12

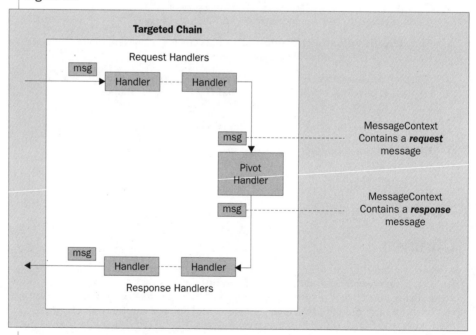

There are two types of pivot handler: a **transport sender**, for the client-side message processing system and a **provider**, for the server-side message processing system.

If we look at the class hierarchy diagram of a targeted chain (Figure 13) you can see that `TargetedChain` is an interface that extends the `Chain` interface by defining a pivot handler

Figure 13

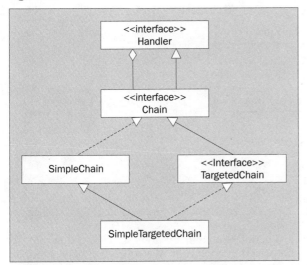

The org.apache.axis.SimpleTargetedChain class implements the
TargetedChain interface and extends the SimpleChain class. This could be the
transport chain at the client-side message processing system or the web service-
specific chain at the server-side message processing system.

Transports

We know that the SOAP specification is not based on a particular transport
protocol, though SOAP specification does define HTTP binding. It is quite possible
to use SOAP over different protocols such as SMTP, FTP, etc. Similarly, though
AXIS only comes with an implementation of SOAP over HTTP, it provides support
for other transports by allowing you to plug in your own transport handlers.

Figure 14 shows additional handlers plugged in to listen for SOAP requests over
HTTP, SMTP, and JMS. The diagram shows three types of clients (A, B, and C) that
communicate with the AXIS server using SOAP/HTTP, SOAP/SMTP and SOAP/JMS.
We could also have transport senders and transport listeners for any other relevant
protocol such as FTP or even a custom communication protocol, if needed.

Figure 14

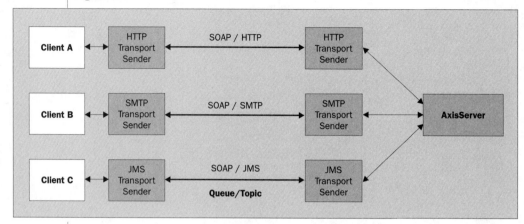

Since transport senders are just handlers, they need not just be placed in the transport chain; they could be placed in any chain. We could also have multiple transport senders for multicasting of messages. This means that the SOAP request message could be sent to various receivers using different transport mechanisms. This would be useful if the client application is required to send notifications to various receivers that are not accessible using just one protocol.

Transport Sender

The transport sender encapsulates details of networking protocols. This component is responsible for sending SOAP request messages to the transport layer of the network by obtaining the configuration properties from `MessageContext`. The `MessageContext` has an attribute called `transportName` that contains the name of the protocol so that the transport chain can invoke the correct transport sender.

AXIS provides a transport sender known as `org.apache.axis.transport.http.HTTPSender` for communicating over HTTP protocol. The `HTTPSender` sends the SOAP request as an HTTP request and receives the response as an HTTP response.

Transport Listener

The transport listener also encapsulates details of networking protocols. This component sits on the receiving end waiting to receive SOAP request messages; when one is received it prepares the incoming SOAP message for XML parsing.

A transport listener plays the role of receiver; it receives a SOAP request message and sends the SOAP response back to the client application. The transport listener could be a servlet, a JMS Listener application, or a mail server depending on what transport protocol is being used.

In the current implementation of AXIS, the server endpoint is deployed in a servlet container. The AXIS system comes with a servlet called `AxisServlet` that acts as the transport listener for SOAP requests over the HTTP protocol. The `org.apache.axis.transport.http.AxisServlet` receives the HTTP request to its `doPost()` method and creates a `Message` object by passing the input stream as shown below:

```
Message msg = new Message( request.getInputStream(),
                           false,
                           request.getHeader("Content-Type"),
                           request.getHeader("Content-Location");
```

The second parameter of type `Boolean` is `true` if the initial contents of the input stream contains just the SOAP body with no SOAP-ENV. It then creates a `MessageContext` and sets this `Message` object as the request message:

```
MessageContext msgContext = new MessageContext(axisengine);
msgContext.setRequestMessage(msg);
```

Apart from this, `AxisServlet` also sets other properties of `MessageContext` such as `transportName`, `securityProvider`, and the `Session` object. It then calls `AxisEngine`'s `invoke()` method, passing the `MessageContext` as input parameter. Any response it receives from the AXIS engine is sent as an HTTP response back to the client application.

Serializers and Deserializers

In this section, we will be discussing the components responsible for serialization (also known as marshaling or encoding) and deserialization (also known as unmarshaling or decoding).

The process of transforming a programming language-specific data type to a **stream** representation is called serialization and the component that handles serialization is known as a serializer. In AXIS, serializing a particular object involves opening a new XML element that represents the object, and then creating sub-elements for each of the object's members. The process of transforming the stream representation of an object back to its corresponding programming language-specific data type is called deserialization, in the context of AXIS and web services the stream will always be XML.

A serializer serializes a Java object to an XML representation based on the type of mapping defined between the corresponding Java type and the XML data type. The serializer uses the XML schema definition (XSD) for an XML schema instance (XSI) to generate the corresponding XML representation. Similarly the deserializer uses the type mapping defined between an XML data type and the corresponding Java type. AXIS is designed to use pluggable serializers and deserializers that support extensible mapping between XML data types and Java types. The serialization and deserialization framework defined in AXIS is based on Sun's Java API for XML-based Remote Procedure Call (JAX-RPC) specification. The JAX-RPC specification defines two base interfaces, `Serializer` and `Deserializer`, which are independent of any XML processing mechanism and XML representation. JAX-RPC implementations like AXIS extend these two interfaces to support development of serializers and deserializers based on a specific XML processing mechanism. The following class diagram shows the list of serializers provided by AXIS. All serializers implement the `org.apache.axis.encoding.Serializer` interface that in turn implements the JAX-RPC's `javax.xml.rpc.encoding.Serializer` interface. The relationship between AXIS and JAX-RPC is covered further in Appendix C.

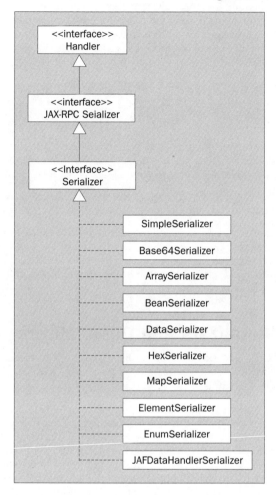

Figure 15

The class diagram (Figure 16) of deserializers, apart from the deserializer classes, shows two other interfaces, CallBack and SOAPHandler. The org.apche.axis.encoding.CallBack interface is provided to take care of the situations where a Java object that needs to be created has references to other Java objects that are yet to be deserialized. In such cases, the deserializer expects multiple values and cannot complete the deserialization until all values are received. The org.apache.axis.message.SOAPHandler is a helper class that overrides the SAX parsing functionality and uses the AXIS-specific deserialization context provided by the class (org.apache.axis.encoding. DeserializationContext).

Figure 16

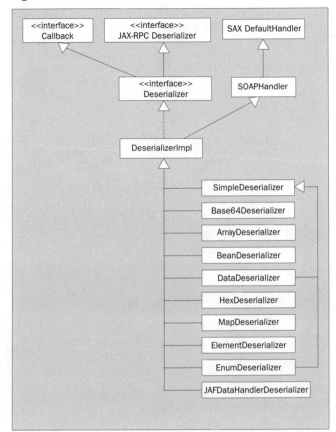

As we mentioned earlier, JAX-RPC and AXIS allow serializers and deserializers to be selected based on a particular XML processing mechanism like SAX or DOM. This is done using a factory pattern; in AXIS the serializer factory has a method called getSerializerAs(String mechanismType, which returns a serializer based on the specified XML processing mechanism type.

Type Mapping

Type mapping is simply specifying what data types in an XML schema, map to what Java class or primitive type so that objects can be correctly serialized or deserialized. A type mapping carries several pieces of information such as a URI describing the encoding style (for example http://schemas.xmlsoap.org/soap/encoding), a qualified name (QName) for the XML element, the Java class to be encoded from and decoded to, and the name of the serializer and deserializer Java classes.

The following class diagram shows that the `TypeMapping` (`org.apache.axis.encoding.TypeMapping`) interface provided by AXIS extends the `TypeMapping` (`javax.xml.rpc.encoding.TypeMapping`) interface defined in the JAX-RPC specification. The `TypeMapping` interface is the base interface for the representation of type mappings; it defines methods to register a new mapping with the serializer and deserializer, to get a list of supported namespaces, and to get an instance of serializer or deserializer for a particular mapping (Java type vs. QName) etc.

Figure 17

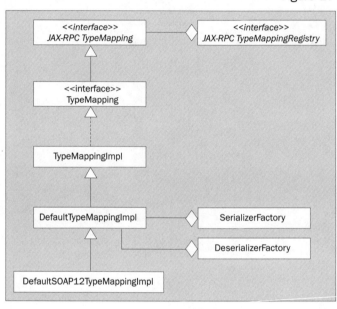

A default implementation is provided by AXIS in the class `org.apache.axis.encoding.DefaultTypeMappingImpl`, which contains a set of predefined type mappings for common data types found in SOAP messages.

TypeMappingRegistry

`TypeMappingRegistry` (`org.apache.axis.encoding.TypeMappingRegistry`) defines a registry for the type mappings (objects of type `org.apache.axis.encoding.TypeMapping`) for various encoding styles and XML schema namespaces (namespace URIs).

The `TypeMappingRegistry` provides a method, `register(TypeMapping, String [])`, to add a new `TypeMapping` instance to the registry; the array of strings represents the namespace URIs. We can also set the default `TypeMapping` instance for all encoding styles and XML namespaces supported by using the method `registerDefault(TypeMapping)`. Apart from this, `TypeMappingRegistry` also provides other utility methods to get the list of registered namespace URIs and the `TypeMapping` instance for a specified namespace URI.

Configuration of Type Mapping Registry

The JAX-RPC specification defines setter and getter methods in the `javax.xml.rpc.Service` interface as shown below:

```
package javax.xml.rpc.Service
Public interface Service {
...
  public void setTypeMappingRegistry(TypeMappingRegistry registry);
  public TypeMappingRegistry getTypeMappingRegistry();
...
}
```

By default, an AXIS `MessageContext` uses the same `TypeMappingRegistry` as the current instance of `AxisEngine`. AXIS provides a default registry implementation known as `TypeMappingRegistryImpl` for use by `AxisEngine`. Setter and getter methods are also provide in the `MessageContext` class for configuring the `TypeMappingRegistry`; these are useful if you need to dynamically change the type mapping while a message is being processed.

Fault Handling

If an exception occurs in the target web service it propagates back to the transport listener. The transport listener then converts the exception into an `AxisFault`. The `org.apache.axis.AxisFault` class can contain all the information that would go into a SOAP fault response message. `AxisFault` also contains methods to set the fault code, fault string, fault actor, and fault detail values.

When an exception occurs while a handler is processing the message, the handler catches its `onFault()` method and creates an instance of `AxisFault` to wrap the exception. Then handler throws the `AxisFault` back to the caller. The caller, which is a chain, catches the fault and throws it back to `AxisEngine`. If there is a fault chain defined for the service, then it is invoked and if there is any global fault chain is defined, this is also invoked. Finally, `AxisEngine` throws the fault back to the transport listener. The transport listener creates a SOAP Fault response and sends it back to the client application. Figure 18 illustrates a typical fault flow:

Figure 18

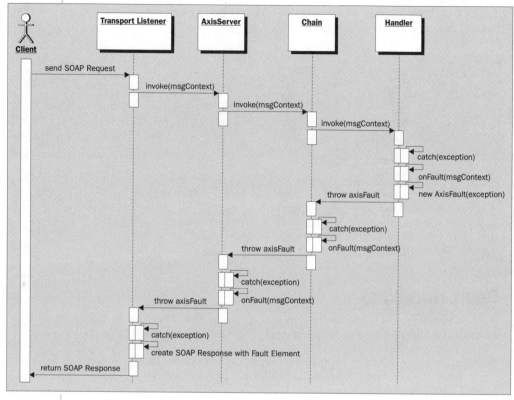

One deficiency with the AXIS fault handling mechanism is that you cannot map AXIS faults to specific Java exceptions, although this functionality may be available in later versions.

Provider Services

A provider is a handler responsible for locating and invoking the target web service and then receiving the response message, wrapping it in a `Message` object then adding that to the `MessageContext`. The next class diagram (Figure 19) shows the hierarchy of the all the providers currently available with AXIS.

Figure 19

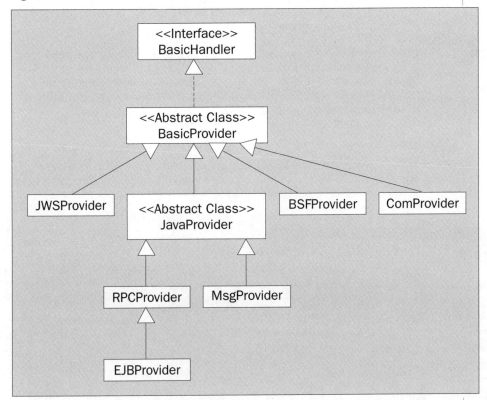

Although AXIS comes with the following providers, we can plug in a custom type provider if we need to access other types of service.

1. **JWSProvider** – The `org.apache.axis.providers.JWSProvider` is responsible for invoking services that are available as `.jws` files

2. **JavaProvider** – The `org.apache.axis.providers.java.JavaProvider` is responsible for invoking services that are implemented in Java

3. **BSFProvider** – The `org.apache.axis.providers.BSFProvider` is responsible for invoking services implemented using scripting language (Bean Scripting Framework)

4. **ComProvider** – The `org.apache.axis.providers.ComProvider` is responsible for invoking Microsoft's Component Object Model (COM)-based services.

   The `JavaProvider` is further subclassed based on the mechanism of invocation as listed below:

1. **RPCProvider** – The `org.apache.axis.providers.java.RPCProvider` is responsible for invoking RPC based web services.

2. **MsgProvider** – The `org.apache.axis.providers.java.MsgProvider` is responsible for invoking Message-based web services. For example, the provider for the Catalog Publisher web service that we have deployed in Chapter 2 is `MsgProvider`.

3. **EJBProvider** – The `org.apache.axis.providers.java.EJBProvider` is a sub class of `RPCProvider` and is responsible for invoking an EJB class deployed as a web service. In Appendix B, we will demonstrate using `EJBProvider` to invoke a stateless session bean, the only type of EJB that it currently supports.

Scope

A provider invokes a service based on the scope defined in the deployment descriptor. The AXIS system provides three levels of scope: `request`, `session`, and `application`. Though the WSDD file below shows `request` scope, it could be `session` or `application`:

```
<deployment name="SparePartPrice"
  xmlns="http://xml.apache.org/axis/wsdd/"
  xmlns:java="http://xml.apache.org/axis/wsdd/providers/java"
  xmlns:xsi="http://www.w3.org/2000/10/XMLSchema-instance">
  <service name="SparePartPrice" provider="java:RPC">
    <parameter name="className"
      value="wroxaxis.chapter2.SparePartPrice"/>
    <parameter name="allowedMethods" value="getPrice"/>
    <parameter name="scope" value="request"/>
  </service>
</deployment>
```

When a particular request to a service is dispatched to the provider (for example, `RPCProvider` or `MsgProvider`), it's the provider's job to invoke the service instance based on the scope. The invocation of service instance by provider in the three scenarios is as shown below:

Request Scope

When the scope is 'request' a new instance of the service is created for each request. The following steps describe the flow for request scope:

1. Get the current `MessageContext` using the `getCurrentMessageContext()` method

2. Get the service name from `MessageContext`

3. Create a new instance of service and invoke the service

Session Scope

A new instance of the service is created only once per session and will is used for all incoming request throughout the session. The following steps list the flow for request scope.

1. Get the current `MessageContext` using the `getCurrentMessageContext()` method.

2. Get the `Session` object from `MessageContext` using the `getSession()` method.

3. Get the service instance from the session object. If this is the first time that the service is invoked, then the session value doesn't contain the service instance. In this case, create a new service instance and add it to the `Session` object.

4. Return the service instance.

5. For all subsequent requests in the same session the same service instance is returned.

The following sequence diagram (Figure 20) shows the above scenario:

Figure 20

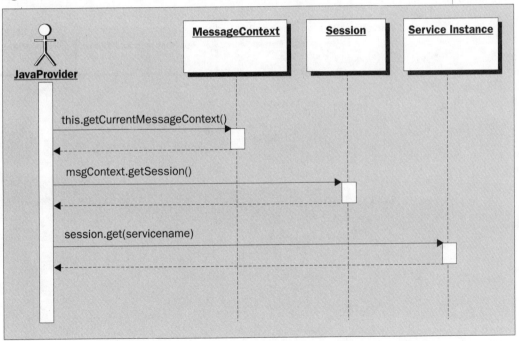

Application scope

When the scope is `application` a new instance of the service is created only once per server (`AxisServer`). That single instance will be used to process all incoming requests while the server is up and running. The following steps list the flow for request scope.

1. Get the current `MessageContext` using the `getCurrentMessageContext()` method

2. Get the AXIS engine (`AxisServer`) from `MessageContext` using the `getAxisEngine()` method

3. Get the `Session` object from `AxisEngine` using the `getApplicationSession()` method

4. Get the service instance from the session object

5. Return the service instance

6. For all subsequent requests to the service, return the same service instance

The following sequence diagram (Figure 21) shows the above scenario:

Figure 21

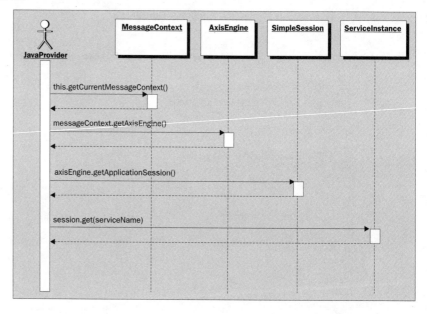

Configuration and Deployment

In this section, we'll look at the web service deployment descriptor (WSDD) used for deploying various components such as services, chains, and handlers to the AXIS engine. We will also discuss the administration utility classes actually used for deployment.

Web Service Deployment Descriptor (WSDD)

AXIS defines an XML-based deployment descriptor known as Web Service Deployment Descriptor (WSDD) to configure the properties of the AXIS engine (both `AxisClient` and `AxisServer`). The WSDD is the first step to facilitate easy plugging in of various application-specific handlers, chains, and transports. We'll call handlers, chains, and transports "**deployable items**" for the sake of convenience.

AXIS contains two WSDD files, `client-config.wsdd`, to configure deployable items for the client-side message processing system and `server-config.wsdd` to configure deployable items for the server-side message processing system.

The root element of WSDD is `<wsdd:deployment>` it contains the following sub-elements as shown in Figure 22. The prefix 'WSDD' refers to the target name space "http://xml.apache.org/axis/wsdd". In the diagram, question mark (?) stands for zero or one and asterisk (*) stands for zero or more elements.

Figure 22

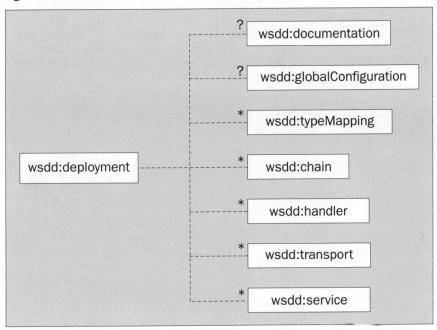

The sub elements of <wsdd:deployment>, have the following purpose:

1. **wsdd:documentation** – this is mainly for debugging and administration purposes; you can place any helpful descriptive information here.

2. **wsdd:globalConfiguaration** – as the name suggests, this section of WSDD describes the deployable items that are applicable to all services. The <wsdd:globalConfiguration> may contain global request, response, fault, and transport flows.

3. **wsdd:typeMapping** – this element describes the mapping between XML and a programming language-specific object. The <wsdd:typeMapping> element contains attributes like encodingStyle, qName and languageSpecificType for mapping of type names to the programming language-specific types and serializers and deserializers that are used for converting programming language-specific data types to XML and vice versa.

4. **wsdd:chain** – the <wsdd:chain> element defines a collection of handlers invoked sequentially as a unit. We can configure chains applicable to all services in global or transport-specific chains. As we saw earlier chains are generally associated with a flow. A flow defines sequential invocation of chains and handlers for a particular service.

5. **wsdd:handler** – the <wsdd:handler> element describes the deployment of an individual handler component. A handler contains a name attribute to describe the name, a type attribute to describe the programming language-specific object (the handler implementation class). It also contains optional parameter element with name and value attributes. The <wsdd:parameter> element can be used to describe any external resources like defining a log file to the logger handler etc.

6. **wsdd:transport** – the <wsdd:tranport> element describes the request, response and fault flows for a given transport mechanism.

7. **wsdd:service** – the <wsdd:service> element describes the service that needs to be deployed. A service is generally associated with a provider (either RPCProvider or MsgProvider). The service may define an optional fault flow and type mapping as shown:

Figure 23

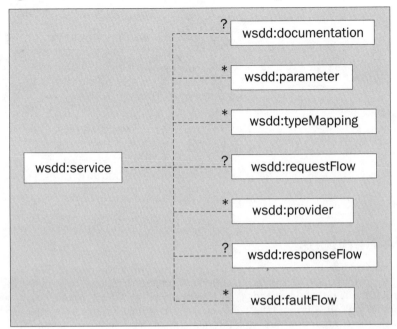

Flow

A flow defines a sequential invocation of deployable items and is categorized as a request flow, a response flow, or a fault flow and is represented as <wsdd:requestFlow>, <wsdd:responseFlow>, or <wsdd:faultFlow> respectively in the deployment descriptor. A request flow describes an inbound flow of a message to the AXIS engine. A response flow describes the outward flow of a message from AXIS and a fault flow represents the fault processing flow to be executed if a fault is thrown. The general structure of a flow can contain a chain or a handler plus the document and parameter elements. The 'Flow' element shown in Figure 24 represents any one of <wsdd:requestFlow>, <wsdd:responseFlow>, or <wsdd:faultFlow>.

Figure 24

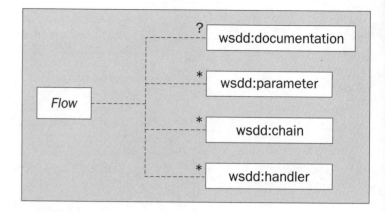

Admin Services

AXIS provides an administration system for configuring the AXIS engine. The configuration information of any deployable item (chains, handlers, transports, and services) that the AXIS engine needs could be provided in a deployment descriptor. Though the current beta version uses the WSDD format, we could very well provide the configuration information using a database, string, or some other custom implementation.

Providers

The beta implementation uses a provider known as org.apache.configuaration.FileProvider to enable an engine to be configured from a file containing the WSDD deployment descriptor.

If you look at Figure 25, the EngineConfiguration is the root interface. The implementations of this interface obtain configuration information and are responsible for this to the AXIS engine.

Figure 25

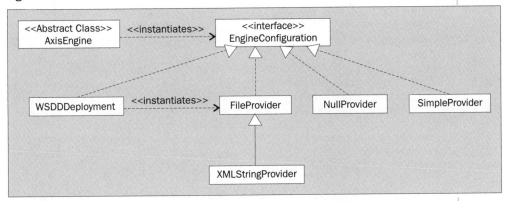

The root interface, EngineConfiguration, has methods to configure the AXIS system and store the configuration details. It also contains setter methods to get a deployable item as listed below:

❑ configureEngine(AxisEngine engine) – this method is used to configure the engine by reading all the configuration details like services, handlers, and chains from some source and configuring the engine. For example, in FileProvider, all the details are read from the WSDD file and loaded into memory.

❑ writeEngineConfig(AxisEngine engine) – this is used to save the configuration details. For example, FileProvider saves all the configuration information (the deployed services, handlers, chains, etc.) back to the WSDD file.

❑ getGlobalRequest() – an accessor method that returns the global request handler defined in the <requestFlow> element of <globalConfiguration>.

❑ getGlobalResponse() – similarly, this returned is the handler defined in the <responseFlow> element of<globalConfiguration>.

❑ getHandler(Qname) – this method returns an handler described in the WSDD file for a given qualified name.

❑ getService(Qname qname) – a method that returns the Service for the given QName from the pool of deployed services.

❑ getTrasnport(Qname qname) – this method returns the transport with respect to the QName.

There are four classes that provide implementations for EngineConfiguration:

FileProvider

As the name suggests, the `org.apache.axis.configuration.FileProvider` class is used to get and store configuration details from a file. In AXIS, the configuration information is provided in the deployment descriptor (WSDD).

In the current version, the AXIS system keeps the configuration information in memory by creating an object of type `org.apache.axis.configuration.wsdd.WSDDDeployment`, which contains the information fetched by `FileProvider`. Hence, for the client-side message processing system, the `WSDDDeployment` object is created by reading the configuration information from the `client-config.wsdd` and for the server-side message processing system, the `WSDDDeployment` object is created using `server-config.wsdd`.

WSDDDeployment

The `WSDDDeployment` creates an in-memory representation of handlers, transports, and services. For example, a handler is represented by `org.apache.axis.configuration.wsdd.WSDDHandler` and a chain is represented by `org.apache.axis.configuration.wsdd.WSDDChain`. Then all these objects are added to a `HashMap`-based registry. This handler can be use to programmatically configure the AXIS engine.

NullProvider

As the name suggests, `org.apache.axis.configuration.NullProvider` is a do-nothing provider. This class is used to create an AXIS engine with no configuration information as shown below:

```
AxisClient axisClient  = new AxisClient(new NullProvider());
```

SimpleProvider

AXIS comes with a provider class known as `org.apache.axis.configuration.SimpleProvider`, which enables `AxisEngine` to be configured dynamically. `SimpleProvider` contains `HashMap`-based registries of handlers, transports, and services. `SimpleProvider` defines methods for dynamically adding new handlers, transports, and services to the `HashMap` registries. `SimpleProvider` also optionally contains a reference to the default engine configuration that will be scanned for components not found in the `HashMap`-based registries. This class is very handy to programmatically deploy components at runtime.

The following code snippet shows adding a service known as `testService` dynamically to the AXIS system. The `deployService()` method adds the `testService` to the list of services present in the HashMap of `SimpleProvider`.

```
SOAPService testService = new SOAPService(new RPCProvider());
SimpleProvider provider = new SimpleProvider();
provider.deployService("MyTestService", testService);
```

The following code shows adding a new transport known as `testTransport` for communicating over the FTP protocol. The `deployTransport()` method adds the new transport to the list of transports present in the `HashMap` of `SimpleProvider`:

```
Transport testTransport = new FTPTransport();
provider.deployTransport("MyTransport", testTransport);
```

Then you can reconfigure the AXIS engine as shown below:

```
AxisEngine axisEngine = AxisEngine.getAxisEngine();
provider.configureEngine(axisEngine);
```

XMLStringProvider

The `XMLStringProvider` class is a helper class that accepts an XML deployment descriptor, as a `String` object. This class is very handy when we want to pass the deployment descriptor as a `String` object to configure AXIS engine. This class uses the `Admin` class to configure the engine from a string containing XML.

WSDDDeployment

When an AXIS engine is initialized, the WSDD file is read by `FileProvider` and an in-memory representation of the elements created. To facilitate this AXIS contains a family of WSDD classes.

The `WSDDTypeMappingContainer` is the common interface with functionality to contain `TypeMappings`.

As shown in Figure 26, `WSDDDeployment` implements `WSDDTypeMappingContainer` and `EngineConfiguration` interfaces and is the container for keeping all the deployed handlers, chains, transports, and type mappings. The `WSDDHandler`, `WSDDService`, `WSDDTransport`, and `WSDDTypeMapping` classes correspond to the class's handler, SOAP service, transport, and type mapping respectively.

Figure 26

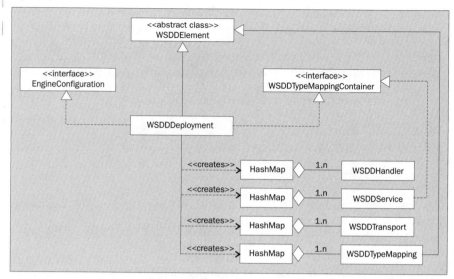

We have already discussed that a deployable item represents any component like handler, transport, chain, etc. The WSDDDeploytableItem is the counterpart of deployable item and has two subclasses known as WSDDTargetedChain, to represent a targeted chain, and WSDDHanlder.

The WSDDRequestFlow, WSDDResponseFlow, and WSDDFaultFlow represent the XML structures <requestFlow/>, <responseFlow/>, and <faultFlow/>.

Figure 27

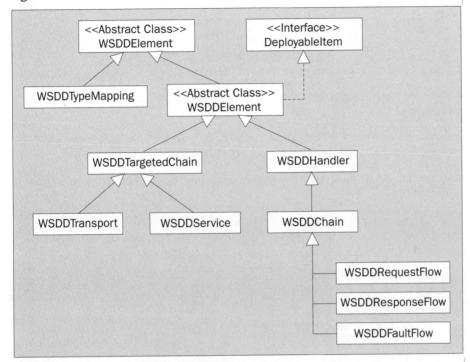

Admin Service and Admin Client

AXIS provides a utility service called org.apache.axis.utils.Admin to deploy
and undeploy handler, chain, service, transport, and type mapping objects. The
Admin class also provides a list functionality that can be used to get a list of all
the deployed components.

WSDD elements like <deployment>, <undeployment>, and <list> are mapped
to registerXXX(), undeployXXX(), and listConfig() respectively where
'XXX' is any one of Service, Handler, Transport, TypeMappings.

AXIS provides a utility class called org.apache.axis.client.AdminClient for
the client applications to access the Admin service for deployment/re-deployment,
undeployment, and list functionality. AdminClient constructs a Call object by
setting the target service URL to Admin Service
(http://localhost:8080/axis/services/AdminService). AdminClient
can be used both from the command line and programmatically.

Summary

We've now covered the core message processing system, the components involved, the services available, and the message patterns used. Let's quickly summarize the main concepts we have looked at:

1. The client- and-server side message systems have different, if related, massage flows.

2. The AXIS message processing system is made up of components: particularly handlers, chains, and targeted chains.

3. AXIS handles faults by wrapping them in an `AxisFault` object and propagating them back to the invoking chain and, via the AXIS engine, eventually to the transport listener.

4. AXIS can be configured by passing a deployment descriptor; by default the resulting state is persisted in a WSDD file.

In the next chapter we will put our knowledge of the architecture in to practice and develop some custom handlers, for logging messages and performing XSLT transformations.

axis

4

Custom Handlers in AXIS

In the last chapter, we covered the AXIS Architecture and are now in a better position to understand how AXIS works. The focus of this chapter will be to plug-in your custom functionality inside AXIS, in other words extending the default behavior of AXIS. Extensibility is one of the strong features of AXIS over other SOAP Engines. AXIS provides an elegant mechanism for extending its behavior via **Handlers**: objects that are capable of processing messages.

In this chapter, we will:

❑ Conduct a quick tour of Handlers: what they are, the various types of Handlers, and how they fit into the AXIS Architecture. We will also cover the classes that already implement some of the Handler functionality in AXIS and how to extend them to write our own custom Handlers.

❑ Discuss how to configure our own custom Handlers using the WSDD format.

❑ Write our first Request Handler in AXIS that will intercept SOAP Request messages in order to log a number of parameters that we are interested in.

❑ Write a couple of additional Handlers: a SOAP Request Handler and a SOAP Response Handler and use them in conjunction to determine the time it takes to make a call to our back-end service.

❑ Discuss different mechanisms for handling errors (faults) in our Handlers.

AXIS Handlers

In this section, we discuss in detail what the AXIS Handler and AXIS Chain are and how they fit into the AXIS Architecture. To recap from Chapter 3, a Handler provides a mechanism for the processing of Message(s) contained in the `MessageContext`. Handlers extend the functionality of the AXIS runtime system (`AxisEngine`) by providing additional processing behavior. A **Chain** in the AXIS System is itself a handler that contains a sequence of Handlers to be invoked on specified messages.

Why do we need to extend the behavior of AXIS via Handlers and Chains? The fact of the matter is that no system can be developed that can meet the needs of one and all. The same applies to AXIS. Take the examples that we have covered in the book so far, where we used the RPCProvider to invoke the back-end functionality present in a Java class. The AXIS Engine processes the SOAP Request and passes control to the RPCProvider, which invokes our Java class, and returns the SOAP Response.

This Simple Request/Response message processing is provided out of the box by AXIS. However, requirements vary from application to application. For example, what if we wanted to track every request to our Web Service and log that into a file. Suppose that we wish to track a particular SOAP Body Element, for example, the Price, in order to alert Sales Personnel by e-mail should the value exceed 10,000. For both these cases, we would need to intercept the Request Message. Similarly, we may wish to track the SOAP Response and note down the time it took to execute the service method.

The above scenarios stress the fact that it is not possible for the AXIS development team to provide solutions for every eventuality provided by production systems. However, by providing an architecture that allows developers to plug their custom functionality into the SOAP Request/Response, AXIS allows developers to extend its functionality. Your custom functionality can augment the mechanisms that AXIS provides through Handlers and Chains. In addition, many of these services should be provided in a way that is transparent to the service itself. For example, it should be possible to switch on and off both logging and performance metrics, and they should be implemented in a way that is transparent to the service invocation itself, and it should also be possible to otherwise customize the services according to the current business needs.

To best understand where Handlers fit into the AXIS Architecture, we have reproduced the diagram from the previous chapter that shows the flow of a message through the AXIS System from the serverside.

Figure 1

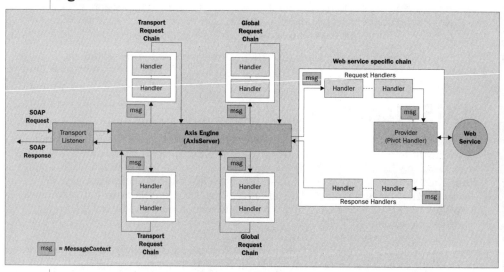

Let's see how the AXIS Engine deals with Handlers at run time. From the above diagram, the Transport Listener packages the SOAP Request into a `Message` object that is placed inside a `MessageContext` object. Once this is done, control is handed over to the Axis Engine along with the `MessageContext` object. The AXIS Engine first determines if there is a **Transport Request Chain**. If it exists, it will be invoked and the `MessageContext` object will be passed to it. The Transport Request Chain in turn will invoke all the Handlers present in the Transport Request Chain.

After the Transport Request Chain, the Axis Engine will determine if there is a **Global Request Chain** configured. If there is, it will invoke that Chain, which internally will result in the invocation of all the Handlers within it. Finally, the Axis Engine will invoke the **Web Service Request Chain**. The Web Service-specific Chain will contain a special type of Handler called the **Pivot Handler**, which is actually responsible for making the call to the Web Service. A Pivot can be thought of as the point where you actually make the request and get back a response. The RPCProvider and MsgProvider are Pivot Handlers provided by AXIS for handling of RPC-based Web Services and Message-based (Document) Web Services respectively.

Once the Pivot Handler has invoked the Web Service and obtained the result, the Axis Engine invokes the Chains in the reverse order as shown. That is, first the Web Service-specific Chain followed by the Global Response Chain and Transport Response Chain.

Let us now investigate Chains and Handlers in more detail. As we have seen so far, a Handler is an object that processes a message. A Chain is also a type of a Handler: it is basically a collection of Handlers where each handler is invoked in sequence. To understand how a message gets processed within a Chain, take a look at Figure 2 below.

Figure 2

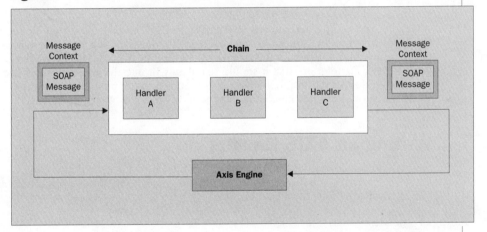

Figure 2 shows the AXIS Engine passing the MessageContext to the Chain. The MessageContext contains the Message, which contains the SOAP Message. The Chain in turn will call the invoke() method on each Handler, passing the MessageContext as a parameter to the invoke() method. Each Handler processes the message and returns control back to the Chain. So in the figure above, the Chain first invokes Handler A, passing it the MessageContext, Handler A processes the message, for example to log certain attributes of the message, send an e-mail, or perform XSL Transformation. It then returns control to the Chain. The Chain then invokes Handler B and finally Handler C.

The sequence diagram below describes this process visually:

Figure 3

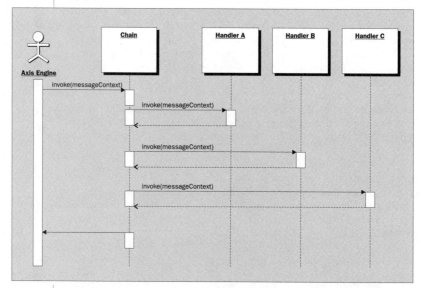

A Handler is thus an intermediary object: it is used to pre-process (in the Request Chain) or post-process (in the Response Chain) the message. In most cases, it will not have anything to do with the final destination – the Web Service. Key design goals for any Handler are that it should seamlessly fit into the Request/Response processing, do its task and then pass on the request to the next element in the Chain – it should not introduce any dependencies into the Web Service itself.

Writing an AXIS Handler

So, how do we go about writing our own handler in AXIS? AXIS defines an interface (`org.apache.axis.Handler`) that defines the methods for a Handler. The Lifecycle methods for a Handler are:

❑   `public void init()`

When the AXIS Engine creates an instance of the Handler, the `init()` method is called to allow the Handler to initialize itself.

❑   `public void invoke(MessageContext messageContext)`
`        throws org.apache.axis.AxisFault`

This is the main method where the Handler does its work. From the `messageContext` parameter, the Handler can retrieve the Request or Response Message and process it accordingly. This is really the heart of the Handler.

❑ `public void onFault(MessageContext messageContext)`
`throws org.apache.axis.AxisFault`

When an error (fault) occurs in the Chain, the AXIS engine will invoke the `onFault()` method of the Handler. In this method, the Handler should accordingly undo the changes as necessary, free resources, etc.

❑ `public void cleanup()`

When the instance of the Handler is no longer needed by AXIS, the `cleanup()` method is invoked.

In addition to the lifecycle methods, a Handler also contains a `Hashtable` of options (**name-value** pairs) that you can set and retrieve. The options could be configured during deployment via the WSDD definition of a Handler, which we shall cover in a moment.

In order to define a Handler, we simply implement the `org.apache.axis.Handler` interface. Alternatively, AXIS provides an abstract class, BasicHandler (`org.apache.axis.handlers.BasicHandler`), that provides a bare-bones implementation of all of the methods with the exception of the `invoke()` method that implements the specific Handler functionality.

So, writing a custom Handler in AXIS is as simple as extending the `org.apache.axis.handlers.BasicHandler` class and providing an implementation for the `invoke()` method. A skeleton class for a sample MyHandler is shown below:

```
import org.apache.axis.AxisFault;
import org.apache.axis.Handler;
import org.apache.axis.MessageContext;

import org.apache.axis.handlers.BasicHandler;

public class MyHandler extends BasicHandler {

  public void invoke(MessageContext messageContext)
        throws AxisFault {
    try {
      //Handler Code here
    }
    catch (Exception e) {
      throw AxisFault.makeFault(e);
    }
  }
}
```

Since the BasicHandler provides default implementations for the other Lifecycle methods (`init()`, `onFault()`, and `cleanup()`), we have only to provide the implementation for the `invoke()` method as shown above.

You should now be in a good position to understand how a Handler fits into the AXIS Architecture and what effort it would take to write an AXIS Handler. The kind of functionality that you would want to build into your Handler is obviously application-dependent. But fundamentally, it will involve processing the Request Message or Response Message and invoking some logic on it. Some examples of Handlers are:

❑ A **Logging Handler** that logs incoming requests to the Web Service.

❑ A **Billing Handler** that tracks the usage of a Web Service and logs the information needed for billing purposes.

❑ An **XSLT Transformer** in the Response Chain that will translate the data as per the target device requirements

❑ An **Authentication Handler** that will not allow the Request Message to go further if the Authentication fails for the request

But how do we specify to the AXIS Engine what handlers are present, their configuration details, etc.? That is the focus of the next section.

AXIS Handlers – WSDD Details

In this section, we will take a look at how we can configure our Handlers using the WSDD. In the process we will also cover a variety of configurations such as configuring Web Service Request Handlers, Response Handlers, Global Request Handlers, and so on.

WSDD – Looking into the Details

In Chapter 2, we took a first look at writing the WSDD (Web Service Deployment Descriptor). The WSDD as you saw, contained the details of the Web Service to deploy, its classes, the type of web service. (RPC/Message-based), and so on.

In Chapter 3, where we covered the AXIS Architecture, we went into further details about the WSDD. In this section, we will cover only the aspects of the WSDD that are useful for understand the Handler configuration including defining Handlers, Chains, RequestFlow, and ResponseFlow.

Let's first look at how to define a Handler element in WSDD. The syntax of a <handler> element in the WSDD is shown below:

```
<handler name="handlername" type="handlertype">
  <parameter name="param1name" value="param1value"/>
  <parameter name="param2name" value="param2value"/>
  ...
</handler>
```

The <handler> element has two attributes: a **name** for the handler, and the **type** of the handler. A Handler **type** can refer to the Java class that implements the handler, for example, java:wroxaxis.handlers.myhandler.

The `<handler>` element contains a collection of child `<parameter>` elements, which contain pairs of **name-value** attributes. A `<parameter>` can be used to provide configuration details for the handler. For example, if we have a handler that logs details into a file, we can specify the name of the log file attribute (`"logfilename"`) and its value (`"c:\\logfile.txt"`). The `<parameter>` elements are then made available through the `getOption()` method of the `org.apache.axis.handlers.BasicHandler` class.

An example of a Handler configuration is shown below. It defines a Handler called **MyLogHandler**, whose implementation is the Java class `wroxaxis.handlers.MyLogHandler`. The Handler takes a parameter named `logfilename`, whose value is `"c:\\logfile.txt"`:

```
<handler name="MyLogHandler"
         type="java:wroxaxis.handlers.MyLogHandler">
  <parameter name="logfilename" value="c:\\logfile.txt"/>
</handler>
```

Similarly, a **Chain,** which is a sequential collection of one or more Handlers, can be represented as follows:

```
<chain name="MyChain">
  <handler name="handlername" type="handlertype">
    <parameter name="param1name" value="param1value"/>

    . . .
  </handler>
  . . .
  <handler name="handlername" type="handlertype">
    <parameter name="param1name" value="param1value"/>

    . . .
  </handler>
  . . .
</chain>
```

Shown below is an example of a Chain, which consists of two handlers: `MyLogHandler` that we saw above and an `EmailHandler`, which sends an Email to the address specified in the `emailid` parameter:

```
<chain name="MyChain">
  <handler name="MyLogHandler"
           type="java:wroxaxis.handlers.MyLogHandler">
    <parameter name="logfilename" value="c:\\logfile.txt"/>
  </handler>
  <handler name="MyEmailHandler"
           type="java:wroxaxis.handlers.MyEmailHandler">
    <parameter name="emailid" value="axis@wrox.com"/>
  </handler>
</chain>
```

Handlers can be defined separately from a chain, which allows definitions to be reused between chains. The logger handler, for example, is certain to be reused across Web Services, and so should be defined independently of a specific chain. Another way of defining the above sample configuration is as shown below:

```
<handler name="MyLogHandler"
         type="java:wroxaxis.handlers.MyLogHandler">
  <parameter name="logfilename" value="c:\\logfile.txt"/>
</handler>
<handler name="MyEmailHandler"
         type="java:wroxaxis.handlers.MyEmailHandler">
  <parameter name="emailid" value="axis@wrox.com"/>
</handler>

<chain name="MyChain">
  <handler type="MyLogHandler"/>
  <handler type="MyEmailHandler"/>
</chain>
```

OK, so now we know how to define a Chain, we can go on to find how we can bind a particular Chain to a Request or Response, and how to define a Fault Processing Chain.

AXIS provides a configurable item in WSDD called a Flow to achieve the above tasks. A Flow defines the sequential invocation of handlers and handler chains for a particular service chain, global chain, or transport chain. AXIS supports three distinct types of Flows: Request flow, Response Flow, and Fault Flow. A Request flow describes inbound Messages. A Response Flow describes the outward flow of a Message, and a Fault Flow represents the fault processing flow to be executed in case of an AxisFault.

Request Flow, Response Flow, and Fault Flow are represented in the WSDD as `<requestFlow>`, `<responseFlow>`, and `<faultFlow>` respectively. Bearing in mind the two ways of defining chains above, the possible formats for a `<requestFlow>` element are shown below. Firstly, a Request Flow can be defined with the handlers defined inline:

```
<requestFlow>
  <handler name="handler1" type="java:...">
    <parameter name="..." value="..."/>
  </handler>
  ...
  <handler name="handler2" type="java:...">
    <parameter name="..." value="..."/>
  </handler>
</requestFlow>
```

Alternatively, the handlers can be defined separately and referenced in the Request Flow definition:

```
<handler name="handler1" type="java:...">
  <parameter name="..." value="..."/>
</handler>
...
<handler name="handler2" type="java:...">
  <parameter name="..." value="..."/>
```

```
</handler>
<requestFlow>
  <handler type="handler1"/>
  <handler type="handler2"/>
</requestFlow>
```

Finally, the Request Flow can refer to an existing defined chain as follows:

```
<requestFlow>
  <chain type="MyChain"/>
</requestFlow>
```

The `<responseFlow>` and `<faultFlow>` elements work in the same way. So basically a Flow is an enveloping element around the Chain, which indicates whether the Chain belongs to the **Request Flow**, a **Response Flow,** or a **Fault Flow**.

Any of these flows can then be present in a Transport Chain, Global Chain, and Web Service Chain, each represented by the following elements respectively:

❑   `<transport>`

❑   `<globalConfiguration>`

❑   `<service>`

AXIS Handlers – Sample Configuration

In order to reinforce the material we have covered so far, we will now look at how we can use the `<handler>`, `<requestFlow>`, `<responseFlow>` elements for a particular `<service>` in the WSDD file. In the example configurations below, we will use the `<service>` definition for the SparePartPrice service that we covered in Chapter 2. The `<service>` definition is shown below. The single method for this service, getSparePartPrice is specified, together with the implementing Java class, wroxaxis.chapter2.SparePartPrice:

```
<service name="SparePartPrice" provider="java:RPC">
  <parameter name="allowedMethods" value="getSparePartPrice"/>
  <parameter name="className"
             value="wroxaxis.chapter2.SparePartPrice"/>
</service>
```

A Service Request Handler

We want to track all the requests being made to the SparePartPrice service in a log file so we define a Handler to the SparePartPrice Request processing that logs some of the SOAP Request parameters. For the moment we are not concerned with the logic provided by the Handler implementation class itself, although it is provided in the source code as wroxaxis.handlers.RequestHandler. The log file name is specified by the `<parameter>` element.

We define the `<handler>` element providing the name of the handler, the Java class that implements the handler, and the log filename.

```
<deployment ...>

  <!—Service Request Handler -->
  <handler name="RequestHandler"
           type="java:wroxaxis.handlers.RequestHandler">
    <parameter name="logfilename" value="c:\\log\\request.log" />
  </handler>
```

We can now define a `<requestFlow>` element in the `SparePartPrice` `<service>` element. The `<requestFlow>` element consists of a sequence of child `<handler>` elements, which in this case points to the `RequestHandler` element defined above.

```
<service name="SparePartPrice" provider="java:RPC">
  <requestFlow>
    <handler type="RequestHandler"/>
  </requestFlow>
  <parameter name="allowedMethods" value="getSparePartPrice"/>
<parameter name="className"
           value="wroxaxis.chapter2.SparePartPrice"/>
  </service>
</deployment>
```

A Service Request and Service Response Handler

It is equally simple to add a Response Handler to the `SparePartPrice` service. All we need to do is define our new `<handler>` element, **ResponseHandler**, as shown below. In this example, an e-mail is sent to an address obtained from the `<parameter>` child element.

```
<deployment ..>
  <!—Service Request Handler -->
  <handler name="RequestHandler"
        type="java:wroxaxis.handlers.RequestHandler">
    <parameter name="logfilename" value="c:\\log\\request.log" />
  </handler>

  <!—Service Response Handler -->
  <handler name="ResponseHandler"
           type="java:wroxaxis.handlers.EmailHandler">
    <parameter name="emailid" value="axis@wrox.com" />
  </handler>
```

We now must add a `<responseFlow>` element to the `<service>` element. The `<responseFlow>` element is similar to the `<requestFlow>` element. It contains a collection of child `<handler>` elements that reference the `<handler>` elements that we defined above:

```
<service name="SparePartPrice" provider="java:RPC">
  <requestFlow>
    <handler type="RequestHandler"/>
  </requestFlow>
  <responseFlow>
```

```
        <handler type="ResponseHandler"/>
    </responseFlow>
    <parameter name="allowedMethods" value="getSparePartPrice"/>
    <parameter name="className"
               value="wroxaxis.chapter2.SparePartPrice"/>
  </service>
</deployment>
```

The configuration process is the same for Transport Chains and Global Service
Chain. Let us move now to writing and deploying our own Handlers.

SparePartInfo Web Service

The Handlers that we will cover in the next few sections will be written for a
sample Web Service that we will develop. To keep our discussion focused on the
Handlers, we will keep this Web Service simple. The Web Service is a
SparePartInfo Web Service, which works similarly to the SparePartPrice
service that we covered in Chapter 2. It has a single method called
getPartInfo(), which takes a String parameter identifying the SKU (Stock
Keeping Unit) number of the part. It returns a String value containing the part
information. To keep our implementation simple, we will be returning a hard-
coded string for the part information.

The next few files should be familiar to you now. First, we have the
SparePartInfo Web Service shown below:

```
// SparePartInfo.java
package wroxaxis.chapter4;

public class SparePartInfo {

  public SparePartInfo() {
  }

  public String getPartInfo(String PartSKU) throws Exception {
    return PartSKU + " - Part Info";
  }
}
```

Then we have the WSDD file for deploying this Web Service. It is straightforward;
consisting of a <service> element identifying the SparePartInfo service. It
contains <parameter> elements that state the classname and the
allowedMethods of this Web Service.

```
<!-- SPI-deploy.wsdd -->
<deployment name="SparePartInfo"
    xmlns="http://xml.apache.org/axis/wsdd/"
    xmlns:java="http://xml.apache.org/axis/wsdd/providers/java"
    xmlns:xsi="http://www.w3.org/2000/10/XMLSchema-instance">
  <service name="SparePartInfo" provider="java:RPC">
    <parameter name="className"
               value="wroxaxis.chapter4.SparePartInfo"/>
    <parameter name="allowedMethods" value="getPartInfo"/>
  </service>
</deployment>
```

The Java client program to invoke the SparePartInfo Service follows the same
pattern that we have seen for the clients before. You should be able to follow the
code easily now.

```java
// SparePartInfoServiceClient.java
package wroxaxis.chapter4;

import java.net.URL;

import org.apache.axis.client.Service;
import org.apache.axis.client.Call;
import org.apache.axis.encoding.XMLType;

import javax.xml.rpc.ParameterMode;
import javax.xml.rpc.namespace.QName;

public class SparePartInfoServiceClient {

  public SparePartInfoServiceClient() {}

  public static void main (String args[]) {
    try {

      // EndPoint URL for the SparePartInfo web service
      String endpntURL =
            "http://localhost:8080/axis/services/SparePartInfo";
      // Method Name to invoke for the SparePartInfo web service
      String methodName  = "getPartInfo";
      Service service = new Service();
      Call call = (Call) service.createCall();
      call.setTargetEndpointAddress(new java.net.URL(endpntURL));
      call.setOperationName(new
                        QName("SparePartInfo",methodName));
      call.addParameter("sku",XMLType.XSD_STRING,
                     ParameterMode.PARAM_MODE_IN);
      call.setReturnType(XMLType.XSD_FLOAT);

      //Pass the Part SKU as input parameter to the web service
      Object[] params = new Object[] {"SKU-123"};

      //Invoke the SparePartInfo web service
      String info = (String) call.invoke(params);

      System.out.println("Spare Part Information : " + info);
    }
    catch (Exception e) {
      System.err.println(e.toString());
    }
  }
}
```

Deploying and invoking the SparePartInfo Web Service

To deploy and invoke the SparePartInfo Web Service, follow the steps given below:

1. Create a directory named `%AXIS_DEVHOME%\wroxaxis\chapter4`. Copy the `SparePartInfo.java` and `SparePartInfoServiceClient.java` files to this directory, compile them and then copy the `SparePartInfo.class` file to the `%AXIS_DEPLOYHOME%\WEB-INF\classes\axis\chapter4` directory.
2. Copy `SPI-deploy.wsdd` to the `%AXIS_DEVHOME%\wroxaxis\chapter4` directory. Go to `%AXIS_DEVHOME%` and deploy the `SparePartInfo` Web Service by using the AXIS **AdminClient** and `SPI-deploy.wsdd` file as shown below, making sure that the various JAR files (most of which are in the AXIS lib directory) are available on the classpath:

    ```
    wroxaxis\chapter4> java org.apache.axis.client.AdminClient
    -l http://localhost:8080/axis/services/AdminService
    wroxaxis/chapter4/SPI-deploy.wsdd
    ```
3. Go to `%AXIS_DEVHOME%` directory and run the `SparePartInfoServiceClient` Java program as shown below. Again, the classpath should include the root of the client's package (in this case the AXIS home folder) and all of the relevant JARS. Verify the output with the output shown below.

    ```
    wrox-axis\chapter4>java
    wroxaxis.chapter4.SparePartInfoServiceClient
    Spare Part Information : SKU-123 - Part Info
    ```

Now that we have our `SparePartInfo` Web Service working, we will write our custom Handlers that will intercept the **Request/Response flows** to provide additional functionality. Let us move to our first custom Handler, the SOAP Request Logger, whose function it is to log some of the SOAP Request Message information into a log file.

SOAP Request Logger

In this section, we will write an AXIS Handler that will intercept the Request Message for the `SparePartInfo` Web Service. We will name this AXIS Handler: `AxisRequestLogger`. This handler will then retrieve some information from the SOAP Request and log that information into a file named `Request.log`. Readers should be able to expand on this section to provide a much more comprehensive logging mechanism.

Let us look at the SparePartInfo Web Service conceptually without any handlers:

Figure 4

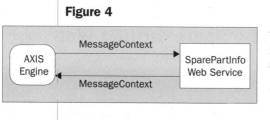

When we place the `AxisRequestLogger` in the Request stream, it will appear as shown below:

Figure 5

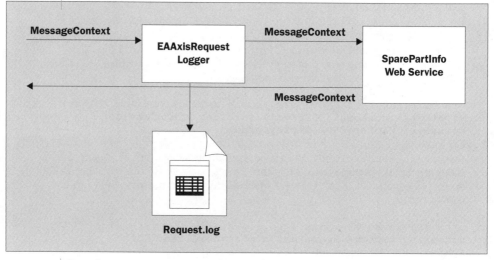

So, what our `AxisRequestLogger` does is intercepts the SOAP Request message, extracts the information that it is interested in logging, and log that information into the `Request.log` file as shown. Let us move on now to writing the code for this.

Writing the Handler – AxisRequestLogger

In the introduction to Handlers in this chapter, we discussed the support that AXIS provides for writing your own handlers via pre-built classes like `org.apache.axis.handlers.BasicHandler`. To recap that section, all we need to do to write our Handler is to extend the `org.apache.axis.handlers.BasicHandler` class and provide the implementation for the `invoke()` method that gets invoked by the Axis Engine.

The source code for the `AxisRequestLogger.java` file is shown below:

```
// AxisRequestLogger.java
package wroxaxis.chapter4.handlers;

import org.apache.axis.AxisFault;
import org.apache.axis.Handler;
import org.apache.axis.MessageContext;
import org.apache.axis.handlers.BasicHandler;
```

```
import org.apache.axis.SOAPPart;

import java.io.FileOutputStream;
import java.io.PrintWriter;
import java.util.Date;

public class AxisRequestLogger extends BasicHandler {

  public AxisRequestLogger() {
  }
```

The invoke() method is the method that we are interested it. The AXIS Engine passes the MessageContext as a parameter to the invoke() method. The MessageContext contains useful information like the Message object, the TargetService, etc. If any exceptions are caught, you are expected to throw an instance of org.apache.axis.AxisFault, which will wrap the SOAP <Fault> element.

```
public void invoke(MessageContext messageContext)
  throws AxisFault {
  try {
```

Then we collect the information from the MessageContext element that we are interested in logging. For illustration we will collect three data points of interest, the **TargetService** (SparePartInfo), the **TransportName** (HTTP) and the **PastPivot** property (The latter is a boolean value indicating if the Pivot was invoked or not. Since we are in the Request stream, the Pivot is not yet invoked and so it will be always false. A Pivot Handler, if you recollect, is a Handler that actually sends a request and gets back a response. Normally it is the point at which your actual back-end service functionality will be invoked).

```
//Collect data from the Request
String targetServiceName = messageContext.getTargetService();
String transportName = messageContext.getTransportName();
boolean getPastPivot = messageContext.getPastPivot();
```

The getOption() method shown below is used to retrieve information from the <parameter> elements that have configured for the <handler> element in the WSDD file. In the WSDD file that we will see later, we will see how to configure this <parameter> element having the **name: logfilename** and a **value: C:\\wrox-axis\\Request.log**, which will indicate the file that we want the above information to get logged into. The getOption() method takes a String identifying the parameter name and returns the parameter value for it.

```
String logfilename = (String) getOption("logfilename");
```

Finally, we use the java.io.FileOutputStream object to log the information along with a DateTime stamp.

```
if ((logfilename == null) || (logfilename.equals(""))) {
  throw new AxisFault("Server.NoLogFileConfigured",
              "The logfilename parameter option for" +
              " AxisRequestLogger was not set", null, null);
}

FileOutputStream os = new FileOutputStream(logfilename,
                                            true);
```

```
        PrintWriter writer = new PrintWriter(os);
        StringBuffer logStr = new StringBuffer();
        logStr.append(
            "##################################################" +
            "\r\n");
        logStr.append(
            "##########      Request Details     ##############" +
            "\r\n");
        logStr.append(
            "##################################################" +
            "\r\n");
        logStr.append("Request Intercepted at : " +
                    new Date().toString() + "\r\n");
        logStr.append("Target Service Name : " +
                    targetServiceName + "\r\n");
        logStr.append("Transport Name : " + transportName + "\r\n");
        logStr.append("getPivotPoint property : " + getPastPivot +
                    "\r\n");

        writer.println(logStr);
        writer.close();
    }
    catch (Exception e) {
```

As mentioned before, any exception that is caught needs to be wrapped into an `org.apache.axis.AxisFault` object. The `AxisFault` class has a utility static method called `makeFault` that takes as an argument a `java.lang.Exception` and returns an `org.apache.axis.AxisFault` instance that can be thrown.

```
        throw AxisFault.makeFault(e);
    }
  }
}
```

AxisRequestLogger – WSDD details

Since the `AxisRequestLogger` must intercept the Request Flow of the SparePartInfo Web Service, we need to add a `<requestFlow>` element to the `<service>` element of the `SparePartInfo` Web Service definition.

First we define our `<handler>` with name="AxisRequestLogger" and the type attribute indicating the Java class file that has its implementation. Note the `<parameter>` element with name="logfilename" and the value-"c:\\wrox-axis\\Request.log". As mentioned before, the `getOption()` method in the `invoke()` method of the source file for the Logger will retrieve the parameter and it will then know which file the information needs to be logged into.

```
<!-- SPI-deployWithHandler.wsdd -->
<deployment name="SparePartInfo"
            xmlns="http://xml.apache.org/axis/wsdd/"
            xmlns:java=
              "http://xml.apache.org/axis/wsdd/providers/java">
            xmlns:xsi=
              "http://www.w3.org/2000/10/XMLSchema-instance">
  <!-- Define the Handler i.e. AxisRequestLogger -->
  <handler name="AxisRequestLogger"
    type="java:wroxaxis.chapter4.handlers.AxisRequestLogger">
    <parameter name="logfilename"
```

```
                value="c:\\wrox-axis\\Request.log"/>
   </handler>
```

The next part should be familiar to you now. We define a <requestFlow> element that references the <handler> that we defined above.

```
<!-- Define the Service (SparePartInfo) -->
<service name="SparePartInfo" provider="java:RPC">
   <requestFlow>
      <handler type="AxisRequestLogger"/>
   </requestFlow>
   <parameter name="className"
              value="wroxaxis.chapter4.SparePartInfo"/>
   <parameter name="allowedMethods" value="getPartInfo"/>
</service>
</deployment>
```

Deploying and invoking the SparePartInfo Web Service

Let us run the same SparePartInfoServiceClient program and verify that our Handler is able to intercept the request and log the information into the file specified. Follow the steps given below:

1. Copy the AxisRequestLogger.java file into the
    %AXIS_DEVHOME%\wroxaxis\chapter4\handlers directory and compile
    it.

2. Copy the AxisRequestLogger.class file to the
    %AXIS_DEPLOYHOME%\WEB-INF\classes\wroxaxis\chapter4\handlers
    directory.

3. Copy the SPI-deployWithHandler.wsdd file into the
    %AXIS_DEVHOME%\wroxaxis\chapter4 directory. Go to the
    %AXIS_DEVHOME% directory. Deploy the SparePartInfo Web Service by using
    the AXIS AdminClient and the SPI-deployWithHandler.wsdd file as shown
    below:

    wrox-axis\chapter4> java org.apache.axis.client.AdminClient
    -l http://localhost:8080/axis/services/AdminService SPI-
    deployWithHandler.wsdd

    Go to %AXIS_DEVHOME% and run the SparePartInfoServiceClient Java
    program; the output should be as before.

4. We are more interested in determining if the information did get logged into `c:\\wrox-axis\\Request.log`. Navigate to that directory and check if `Request.log` is present. If so, view the file. You should see the SOAP Request information from a couple of sample runs as shown below.

```
####################################################
##########    Request Details   ###############
####################################################
Request Intercepted at : Wed Apr 10 15:12:10 BST 2002
Target Service Name : SparePartInfo
Transport Name : http
getPivotPoint property : false
####################################################
##########    Request Details   ###############
####################################################
Request Intercepted at : Wed Apr 10 15:14:32 BST 2002
Target Service Name : SparePartInfo
Transport Name : http
getPivotPoint property : false
```

Performance Monitoring Logger

In the previous section, we added a Request Handler. In this section, we will have not only the Request Handler but also a Response Handler for the SparePartInfo Web Service. The Request Handler (`SOAPRequestLogger`) will log the entire SOAP Request into a log file: `SOAP.log`. Then we will use both the handlers in conjunction with each other to determine the time that it took to execute the call to the Web Service. The Response Handler (`SOAPResponseLogger`) will then log that duration along with the SOAP Response into the `SOAP.log` file. So, in this way, we have written our own simple little performance monitoring system.

To recap, look at the diagram shown below:

Figure 6

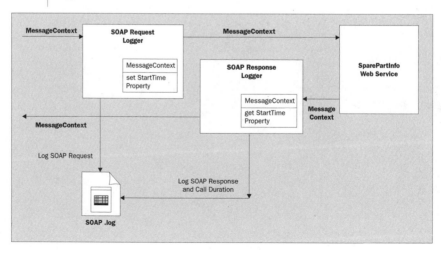

Let us trace how our Handlers will work in combination to achieve our goal of determining how much time it takes to make the call to `SparePartInfo` Web Service. As we cover the flow, we will also show the relevant code.

The `invoke()` method of the `SOAPRequestLogger` is called. We use the `getRequestMessage()` on the `MessageContext` object to retrieve the Request Message, which is of type `org.apache.axis.Message`. The `Message` object has utility methods that allow you to get the `org.apache.axis.message.SOAPEnvelope` object that encapsulates the SOAP Envelope element.

We then call the `getAsDOM()` method on the `org.apache.axis.message.SOAPEnvelope` instance to retrieve the SOAP Envelope as an `org.w3c.dom.Element` object. We use the utility class in AXIS, `org.apache.axis.utils.XMLUtils`, which gives us a convenient method to get a `String` representation of the SOAP Envelope, which we want to log into a file.

Finally, we use the `java.io.FileOutputStream` object to log the SOAP Envelope string into the `SOAP.log` file that was mentioned as a parameter to the `<handler>` configured in the WSDD. We shall see the `<handler>` definition in the WSDD, a little later in the text, but it follows the same pattern as our `AxisRequestLogger` that we built in the previous section.

```java
// SOAPRequestLogger.java
package wroxaxis.chapter4.handlers;

import org.apache.axis.AxisFault;
import org.apache.axis.MessageContext;
import org.apache.axis.Handler;
import org.apache.axis.Message;
import org.apache.axis.SOAPPart;
import org.apache.axis.message.SOAPEnvelope;
import org.apache.axis.handlers.BasicHandler;

import org.w3c.dom.Element;
import org.apache.axis.utils.XMLUtils;

import java.io.FileOutputStream;
import java.io.PrintWriter;
import java.util.Date;

public class SOAPRequestLogger extends BasicHandler {

  public SOAPRequestLogger() {}

  public void invoke(MessageContext messageContext)
            throws AxisFault {
    try {
      Message reqMessage = messageContext.getRequestMessage();
      SOAPEnvelope env = reqMessage.getSOAPEnvelope();
      Element envElement = env.getAsDOM();
      String strSOAPBody = XMLUtils.ElementToString(envElement);
      String logfilename = (String) getOption("logfilename");
      if ((logfilename == null) || (logfilename.equals(""))) {
        throw new AxisFault("Server.NoLogFileConfigured",
          "The logfilename parameter option for" +
          "SOAPRequestLogger was not set", null,null);
      }
```

```
FileOutputStream os = new FileOutputStream(
  logfilename, true);
PrintWriter writer  = new PrintWriter(os);
StringBuffer logStr = new StringBuffer();
logStr.append("====SOAP Request : " +
  new Date().toString() + " : =====\r\n");
logStr.append(strSOAPBody);
writer.println(logStr);
writer.close();
```

Now, we have to track the time that we started the call. For this we use the `System.currentTimeMillis()` that returns us the current time in milliseconds. Once we obtain the current time, we use the `setProperty()` method of the `MessageContext` object to set the a custom property called "**StartTime**" and its value (current time). The custom properties that we set in this manner are then present throughout the lifecycle of the entire chain through the `MessageContext` object. Thus as we move along the Request Chain and then into the Response Chain, we can use the `MessageContext` and retrieve the property value using the `getProperty()` method. This is exactly how we will retrieve the value in our Response Handler when we have to calculate the total duration of the method call.

```
    //Track the time the call was made
    Long startTime = new Long(System.currentTimeMillis());
    //Store the startTime in the messageContext
    messageContext.setProperty("StartTime",(Long) startTime);
  }
  catch (Exception e) {
    throw AxisFault.makeFault(e);
  }
 }
}
```

In the Response Chain, we will first determine the current time and then using the `getProperty()` method of the `MessageContext` object, we will retrieve the **StartTime** of the call. Then we will perform a simple subtraction and represent the duration of the call in seconds.

```
// SOAPResponseLogger.java

package wroxaxis.chapter4.handlers;

import org.apache.axis.AxisFault;
import org.apache.axis.MessageContext;
import org.apache.axis.Handler;
import org.apache.axis.Message;
import org.apache.axis.SOAPPart;
import org.apache.axis.message.SOAPEnvelope;
import org.apache.axis.handlers.BasicHandler;
import org.apache.axis.utils.XMLUtils;

import org.w3c.dom.Element;

import java.io.FileOutputStream;
import java.io.PrintWriter;
import java.util.Date;

public class SOAPResponseLogger extends BasicHandler {

  public void invoke(MessageContext messageContext)
```

```
  throws AxisFault {
  try {

    //Get the current Time
    long currentTimeMills = System.currentTimeMillis();

    //Retrieve the startTime from the messageContext "StartTime"
    //property that was set by the SOAPRequestLogger
    Long startTime =
      (Long) messageContext.getProperty("StartTime");
    long startTimeMills = startTime.longValue();

    //Determine the duration of the call in seconds
    float duration =
      ((float)(currentTimeMills - startTimeMills))/1000;
    String strDuration = "Time to make call : " +
      String.valueOf(duration) + "seconds";
```

Finally we will log this value along with the SOAP Response into the same log file, SOAP.log. Note that both SOAPRequestHandler and SOAPResponseHandler will be configured with identical child <parameter> elements that will point the parameter name i.e. **logfilename** to the same parameter value "**c:\\wrox-axis\\SOAP.log**".

```
//Reterive the SOAPResponse from the messageContext / Message
    Message resMessage = messageContext.getResponseMessage();
    SOAPEnvelope env = resMessage.getSOAPEnvelope();
    Element envElement = env.getAsDOM();
    String strSOAPResponse = XMLUtils.ElementToString(
      envElement);

    //Log the SOAPResponse in the same SOAP.log file
    String logfilename = (String) getOption("logfilename");
    if ((logfilename == null) || (logfilename.equals(""))) {
      throw new AxisFault("Server.NoLogFileConfigured",
      "The logfilename parameter option for AccessLogHandler " +
      "was not set", null,null);
    }
    FileOutputStream os = new FileOutputStream(
      logfilename, true);
    PrintWriter writer = new PrintWriter(os);

    StringBuffer logStr = new StringBuffer();
    logStr.append("==== SOAP Response   : " +
      new Date().toString() + " : =====\r\n");
    logStr.append(strSOAPResponse);
    logStr.append("--------------------------------------");
    logStr.append(strDuration);

    writer.println(logStr);
    writer.close();
  }
  catch (Exception e) {throw AxisFault.makeFault(e);
  }
 }
}
```

WSDD File Details for the Loggers

The WSDD for the above scenario should be simple to follow now. We will first define two handlers, SOAPRequestHandler and SOAPResponseHandler. Note that the <parameter> elements for both the handlers point to the same log file, c:\\wrox-axis\\SOAP.log file. The important part to note is that we are improvising on the same WSDD file that we saw before. In fact, we are not even removing our first Request Handler: AxisRequestLogger. It is perfectly fine to have one or more handlers in the same Request Flow and it also underscores the point that you can add and remove your handlers without affecting the function of the service.

```xml
<!-- SPI-deployWithSOAPLogger.wsdd -->
<deployment name="SparePartInfo"
    xmlns="http://xml.apache.org/axis/wsdd/"
    xmlns:java="http://xml.apache.org/axis/wsdd/providers/java"
    xmlns:xsi="http://www.w3.org/2000/10/XMLSchema-instance">

<!-- Define the Request Handler i.e. AxisRequestLogger -->
  <handler name="AxisRequestLogger"
    type="java:wroxaxis.chapter4.handlers.AxisRequestLogger">
    <parameter name="logfilename"
            value="c:\\wrox-axis\\Request.log"/>
  </handler>

  <!-- Define the Handler i.e. SOAPRequestLogger -->
  <handler name="SOAPRequestLogger"
        type="java:wroxaxis.chapter4.handlers.SOAPRequestLogger">
    <parameter name="logfilename"
            value="c:\\wrox-axis\\SOAP.log"/>
  </handler>

  <!-- Define the Handler i.e. SOAPResponseLogger -->
  <handler name="SOAPResponseLogger"
    type="java:wroxaxis.chapter4.handlers.SOAPResponseLogger">
    <parameter name="logfilename"
            value="c:\\wrox-axis\\SOAP.log"/>
  </handler>

  <!-- Define the Service (SparePartInfo) -->
  <service name="SparePartInfo" provider="java:RPC">
    <requestFlow>
      <handler type="AxisRequestLogger"/>
      <handler type="SOAPRequestLogger"/>
    </requestFlow>
    <responseFlow>
      <handler type="SOAPResponseLogger"/>
    </responseFlow>
    <parameter name="className"
            value="wroxaxis.chapter4.SparePartInfo"/>
    <parameter name="allowedMethods" value="getPartInfo"/>
  </service>
</deployment>
```

Deploying and Invoking the SparePartInfo Web Service

To invoke the SparePartInfo Web Service with our Performance Monitoring handlers, follow the steps given below:

1. Copy the SOAPRequestLogger.java and SOAPResponseLogger.java files into the %AXIS_DEVHOME%\wroxaxis\chapter4\handlers directory. Compile SOAPRequestLogger.java and SOAPResponseLogger.java.

2. Copy the SOAPRequestLogger.class and SOAPResponseLogger.class files to the %AXIS_DEPLOYHOME%\WEB-INF\classes\wroxaxis\chapter4\handlers directory.

3. Copy the SPI-deployWithSOAPLogger.wsdd file into the %AXIS_DEVHOME%\wroxaxis\chapter4 directory. Go to %AXIS_DEVHOME% and deploy the SparePartInfo Web Service by using the AXIS **AdminClient** and the SPI-deployWithHandler.wsdd file as shown below:

    ```
    java org.apache.axis.utils.AdminClient -l
    http://localhost:8080/wrox-axis/services/AdminService
    wroxaxis/chapter4/SPI-deployWithSOAPLogger.wsdd
    ```

4. Go to %AXIS_DEVHOME% and run the SparePartInfoServiceClient Java program. The output will be same as before since there is nothing that we have changed in the SparePartInfo Web Service.

5. Navigate to the c:\wrox-axis directory and check if SOAP.log file is present in this directory. View the SOAP.log file. A sample run is shown below. Note that our SOAPRequestLogger logs the entire SOAP Request, whereas the SOAPResponseLogger logs the entire SOAP Request and the call duration.

    ```
    ====SOAP Request : Wed Apr 10 15:28:18 BST 2002 : =====
    <SOAP-ENV:Envelope SOAP-
    ENV:encodingStyle="http://schemas.xmlsoap.org/soap/encoding/"
            xmlns:SOAP-ENC="http://schemas.xmlsoap.org/soap/encoding/"
            xmlns:SOAP-ENV="http://schemas.xmlsoap.org/soap/envelope/"
            xmlns:xsd="http://www.w3.org/2001/XMLSchema"
            xmlns:xsi="http://www.w3.org/2001/XMLSchema-instance">
     <SOAP-ENV:Body>
      <ns1:getPartInfo xmlns:ns1="SparePartInfo">
       <sku xsi:type="xsd:string">SKU-123</sku>
      </ns1:getPartInfo>
     </SOAP-ENV:Body>
    </SOAP-ENV:Envelope>
    ==== SOAP Response  : Wed Apr 10 15:28:18 BST 2002 : =====
    ```

```
<SOAP-ENV:Envelope xmlns:SOAP-
ENV="http://schemas.xmlsoap.org/soap/envelope/"
        xmlns:xsd="http://www.w3.org/2001/XMLSchema"
        xmlns:xsi="http://www.w3.org/2001/XMLSchema-instance">
 <SOAP-ENV:Body>
  <ns1:getPartInfoResponse SOAP-
ENV:encodingStyle="http://schemas.xmlsoap.org/soap/encoding/"
        xmlns:ns1="SparePartInfo">
   <getPartInfoResult xsi:type="xsd:string">SKU-123 - Part Info</getPartInfoResult>
  </ns1:getPartInfoResponse>
 </SOAP-ENV:Body>
</SOAP-ENV:Envelope>
─────────────────Time to make call : 0.08seconds
```

Now that we have seen how to write our own custom Handlers in AXIS, it is also appropriate to look at how to handle faults in custom Handlers. It is essential to handle faults correctly in order to make your own Handlers behave like good citizens in the AXIS Architecture.

Fault Handling

In this section, we will look at how to handle faults in your AXIS Handlers. We will cover how AXIS handles faults in its processing chain and what steps you as a programmer have to take to ensure that your Handlers intercept the Fault correctly.

Understanding Faults in AXIS

As an example, let us consider the Web Service-specific Chain shown below:

Figure 7

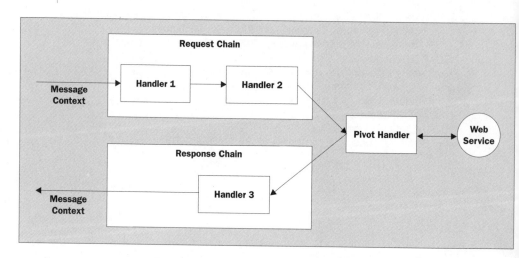

We are keeping the details to a minimum in the diagram. For our Web Service, we have the **Pivot Handler**, which is the `java:RPC` Provider that AXIS provides. Similarly, we have a Request Chain (Handler 1 and Handler 2) and a Response Chain (Handler 3) for the Web service as seen in the diagram.

So far so good, but what would happen if a particular Handler got an exception in its `invoke()` method? We have seen that the `invoke()` method throws an instance of the `org.apache.axis.AxisFault` class that wraps the SOAP Fault element. There could also be a possibility that the Web Service code itself throws an exception. For example, in the `SparePartInfo` Web Service that we covered previously, an invalid part SKU could throw an exception.

In this case, the AXIS Engine will invoke the `onFault()` method of each Handler in the reverse order to the way it called the `invoke()` methods of the Handlers. The `onFault()` method is similar to the `invoke()` method: it has the same parameter (an instance of the `MessageContext`) passed to it. The `onFault()` method provides the Handler a chance to undo any changes that it made in the `invoke()` method that should be reversed in the case of a fault. The Handler may also choose to release allocated resources, in the `onFault()` method.

The `onFault()` method has a default do-nothing implementation in the `org.apache.axis.handlers.BasicHandler` class that we extend. So, in order to handle faults in addition to the `invoke()` method, we must implement the `onFault()` method too:

```
import org.apache.axis.Handler;
import org.apache.axis.handlers.BasicHandler;
import org.apache.axis.MessageContext;
import org.apache.axis.AxisFault;

public class MyHandler extends BasicHandler {

  public void invoke(
    org.apache.axis.MessageContext messageContext)
    throws org.apache.axis.AxisFault
  {
    try {
      //Handler Code here
      }
      catch (Exception e) {
        throw AxisFault.makeFault(e);
      }
    }
   public void onFault(
    org.apache.axis.MessageContext messageContext)
   {
     //Fault Handling Code over here.
   }
}
```

Now that we are clear on how we can handle the faults in our own Handlers, it is still important to understand how the AXIS Engine propagates a fault condition throughout the Chain of Handlers. We mentioned before that if a particular Handler throws a fault, AXIS will call the `onFault()` methods of all the Handlers preceding it, in the reverse order of invocation.

Note that it will not call the onFault() method of the Handler that threw the AxisFault. It is the responsibility of that Handler to handle the exception.

To help understand this better, let us take a look at some examples. The examples are explained with reference to the diagram shown earlier in this section. It also assumes that all the handlers – **Handler 1**, **Handler 2**, and **Handler 3** – have onFault() methods implemented.

1. **Exception in Handler 3**

    In this scenario, let us assume that the invoke() method of Handler 3 had some exception and it threw a AxisFault. The sequence of onFault() methods called will be as follows:
    onFault() **of Handler 2**
    onFault() **of Handler 1**

2. **Exception in web service**

    In this scenario, the Pivot Handler will throw an AxisFault, which will result in the following onFault() methods being called:

    onFault() **of Handler 2**
    onFault() **of Handler 1**

3. **Exception in Handler 2**

    In this scenario, the AxisFault is thrown from the invoke() method of Handler 2. So, the following onFault() method will be called:

    onFault() **of Handler 1**

Now, that we are clear on how fault handling can be done in your own custom handlers and also how AXIS takes care of it, it is time to see that in action.

Faults in Action

In this section, we will look at the first scenario given in the previous section, where Handler 3 throws an exception. We do not want to write a new Web Service, so we will use the SparePartInfo Web Service. However, we will write a new deployment descriptor (WSDD) file for it, so that although we are referencing the same Web Service, we can define a new <service> element with its own custom flows. This is another nice AXIS feature to note.

The WSDD file for this is shown below. It defines three handlers: Handler1, Handler2 and Handler3. All the handlers have the same <parameter> element, a logfilename, that has a value of "c:\\wrox-axis\\fault.log".

The <service> element has a new name – "FaultService" – but it references the same class, SparePartInfo. It has a <requestFlow> that has Handler 1 and Handler 2 in that sequence. In addition, it has a <responseFlow> that has Handler 3.

```
<!-- faultdeploy.wsdd -->
<deployment name="FaultService"
      xmlns="http://xml.apache.org/axis/wsdd/"
      xmlns:java="http://xml.apache.org/axis/wsdd/providers/java"
      xmlns:xsi="http://www.w3.org/2000/10/XMLSchema-instance">

  <handler name="Handler1"
          type="java:wroxaxis.chapter4.handlers.Handler1">
    <parameter name="logfilename"
              value="c:\\wrox-axis\\fault.log"/>
  </handler>
  <handler name="Handler2"
          type="java:wroxaxis.chapter4.handlers.Handler2">
    <parameter name="logfilename"
              value="c:\\wrox-axis\\fault.log"/>
  </handler>
  <handler name="Handler3"
          type="java:wroxaxis.chapter4.handlers.Handler3">
    <parameter name="logfilename"
              value="c:\\wrox-axis\\fault.log"/>
  </handler>

  <!-- Define the Service (FaultService) -->
  <service name="FaultService" provider="java:RPC">
    <requestFlow>
      <handler type="Handler1"/>
      <handler type="Handler2"/>
    </requestFlow>
    <responseFlow>
      <handler type="Handler3"/>
    </responseFlow>
    <parameter name="className"
              value="wroxaxis.chapter4.SparePartInfo"/>
    <parameter name="allowedMethods" value="getPartInfo"/>
  </service>
</deployment>
```

Next are the request handlers: Handler1.java and Handler2.java. Each of the
Handlers implement the invoke() method and the onFault() method. The
methods currently make an entry in the log file if invoke() or onFault() are
called. We could easily include functionality in the onFault() method that could
for example, send an e-mail to a particular contact person reporting that some error
occurred, etc. The handler code should be straightforward at this stage to follow.
The important point to note is that we are simulating an exception on purpose in the
Request Handler. If you go through the code for Handler 3, you will find that we
throw an exception in the code. This section of code has been highlighted.

Request Handler – Handler1

```java
// Handler1.java
package wroxaxis.chapter4.handlers;

import org.apache.axis.AxisFault;
import org.apache.axis.Handler;
import org.apache.axis.MessageContext;
import org.apache.axis.handlers.BasicHandler;

import org.apache.axis.SOAPPart;

import java.io.FileOutputStream;
import java.io.PrintWriter;
import java.util.Date;

public class Handler1 extends BasicHandler {
```

```
public Handler1() {
}

public void invoke(
  org.apache.axis.MessageContext messageContext)
  throws org.apache.axis.AxisFault {
  try {
    String logfilename = (String) getOption("logfilename");
    if ((logfilename == null) || (logfilename.equals(""))) {
      throw new AxisFault("Server.NoLogFileConfigured",
      "The logfilename parameter option for Handler1 was" +
      " not set",null,null);
    }
    StringBuffer logStr = new StringBuffer();
    logStr.append("----Handler 1 called----" + "\r\n");
    logMessage(logfilename,logStr.toString());
  }
  catch (Exception e) {
    throw AxisFault.makeFault(e);
  }
}
public void onFault(MessageContext messageContext) {
  try {
    String logfilename = (String) getOption("logfilename");
    if ((logfilename == null) || (logfilename.equals(""))) {
      throw new AxisFault("Server.NoLogFileConfigured",
        "The logfilename parameter option for Handler1 was" +
        "not set",null,null);
    }

    StringBuffer logStr = new StringBuffer();
    logStr.append("Fault in Handler 1 called" + "\r\n");
    logMessage(logfilename,logStr.toString());
  }
  catch (Exception e) {}
}

private void logMessage(String logfileName,String logStr)
        throws Exception {
  try {
    FileOutputStream os =
      new FileOutputStream(logfileName, true);
    PrintWriter writer = new PrintWriter(os);
    writer.println(logStr);
    writer.close();
  }
  catch (Exception e) {
    throw new Exception(e.getMessage());
  }
}
}
```

Request Handler – Handler2

To avoid repeating the same code unnecessarily for Handler2 and Handler3 we'll
only show those parts which are different from Handler1, basically the `invoke()`
and `onFault()` methods.

```
// Handler2.java

//imports as for Handler1

  public Handler2() {
  }

  public void invoke(
    org.apache.axis.MessageContext messageContext)
    throws org.apache.axis.AxisFault
  {
    try {
      String logfilename = (String) getOption("logfilename");
      if ((logfilename == null) || (logfilename.equals(""))) {
        throw new AxisFault("Server.NoLogFileConfigured",
        "The logfilename parameter option for Handler2 was not" +
        "set", null,null);
      }
      StringBuffer logStr = new StringBuffer();
      logStr.append("----Handler 2 called----" + "\r\n");
      logMessage(logfilename,logStr.toString());
    }
    catch (Exception e) {
      throw AxisFault.makeFault(e);
    }
  }
  public void onFault(MessageContext msgContext) {
    try {
      String logfilename = (String) getOption("logfilename");
      if ((logfilename == null) || (logfilename.equals(""))) {
        throw new AxisFault("Server.NoLogFileConfigured",
        "The logfilename parameter option for Handler2 was not" +
        " set", null,null);
      }

      StringBuffer logStr = new StringBuffer();
      logStr.append("Fault in Handler 2 called" + "\r\n");
      logMessage(logfilename,logStr.toString());
    }
    catch (Exception e) {}
  }
...
```

Response Handler – Handler3

```
// Handler3.java

...

public class Handler3 extends BasicHandler {

  public Handler3() {
  }

  public void invoke(
    org.apache.axis.MessageContext messageContext)
    throws org.apache.axis.AxisFault {
    try {
      String logfilename = (String) getOption("logfilename");
      if ((logfilename == null) || (logfilename.equals(""))) {
        throw new AxisFault("Server.NoLogFileConfigured",
```

```
              "The logfilename parameter option for Handler3 was not" +
              " set", null,null);
        }
        StringBuffer logStr = new StringBuffer();
        logStr.append("----Handler 3 called----" + "\r\n");
        logMessage(logfilename,logStr.toString());
        throw AxisFault.makeFault(new Exception(
                                  "Exception here"));
      }
    catch (Exception e) {
       throw AxisFault.makeFault(e);
    }
  }

  public void onFault(MessageContext msgContext) {

    try {
      String logfilename = (String) getOption("logfilename");
      if ((logfilename == null) || (logfilename.equals(""))) {
        throw new AxisFault("Server.NoLogFileConfigured",
        "The logfilename parameter option for Handler3 was not" +
        " set",null,null);
      }
      StringBuffer logStr = new StringBuffer();
      logStr.append("Fault in Handler 3 called" + "\r\n");
      logMessage(logfilename, logStr.toString());
    }
    catch (Exception e) {}
  }
}
...
```

We also write a Java client to invoke the `FaultService`. It follows the same pattern that we have been explaining so far.

FaultService Client

`FaultServiceClient.java` is shown below. It is in many ways the same as `SparePartInfoServiceClient`. The only difference is the service name, `FaultService`. The statements that are different from `SparePartInfoServiceClient` are shown below:

```
package wroxaxis.chapter4;

import java.net.URL;
import org.apache.axis.client.Service;
import org.apache.axis.client.Call;
import org.apache.axis.encoding.XMLType;

import javax.xml.rpc.ParameterMode;
import javax.xml.rpc.namespace.QName;

public class FaultServiceClient {

  public FaultServiceClient() {}

  public static void main (String args[]) {
    try {

      // EndPoint URL for the FaultService  Web Service
      String endpointURL =
            "http://localhost:8080/axis/services/FaultService";
```

```
        // Method Name to invoke for the SparePartInfo Web Service
        String methodName  = "getPartInfo";

        // Create the Service call
        Service service = new Service();
        Call call = (Call) service.createCall();
        call.setTargetEndpointAddress(new
                              java.net.URL(endpointURL));
        call.setOperationName(new QName("FaultService",methodName));
        call.addParameter("sku",XMLType.XSD_STRING,
                        ParameterMode.PARAM_MODE_IN);
        call.setReturnType(XMLType.XSD_FLOAT);

        //Setup the Part SKU to be passed as input parameter to the
        //SparePartInfo Web Service
        Object[] params = new Object[] {"SKU-123"};

        //Invoke the SparePartInfo Web Service
        String info = (String) call.invoke(params);

        //Print out the result
        System.out.println("Spare Part Information : " + info);
      }
    catch (Exception e) {
        System.err.println(e.toString());
    }
  }
}
```

Deploying and Invoking the FaultService

1. Copy the Handler1.java, Handler2.java, and Handler3.java files into the %AXIS_DEVHOME%\wroxaxis\chapter4\handlers directory. Compile Handler1.java, Handler2.java and Handler3.java

2. Copy the Handler1.class, Handler2.class the and Handler3.class files to the %AXIS_DEPLOYHOME%\WEB-INF\classes\wroxaxis\chapter4\handlers directory.

3. Copy the faultdeploy.wsdd file into the %AXIS_DEVHOME%\wroxaxis\chapter4 directory. Go to %AXIS_DEVHOME% and deploy the FaultService Web Service by using the AXIS **AdminClient** and faultdeploy.wsdd file as shown below:

   java org.apache.axis.utils.AdminClient -l
   http://localhost:8080/axis/services/AdminService
   wroxaxis/chapter4/faultdeploy.wsdd

4. Copy FaultServiceClient.java to the %AXIS_DEVHOME%\wroxaxis\chapter4 directory. Go to the %AXIS_DEVHOME% directory and compile the file as shown below:
   javac wroxaxis/chapter4/FaultServiceClient.java

5. Finally, run the FaultServiceClient Java program as shown below. Verify the output with the output shown below. This is the exception that was thrown by Handler 3 and it has been propagated to the client correctly.

   java wroxaxis.chapter4.FaultServiceClient
   java.lang.Exception: Exception here

The next point we should check is to view the `fault.log` file in the `c:\\wroxaxis` directory. The file contents for the sample run above are shown below. You will note that the `invoke()` method were of the Handlers called first. So the process was **Handler 1 -> Handler 2 -> Handler 3**. Then there was an exception thrown in Handler 3. This did not result in a call to `onFault()` of Handler 3 since we had mentioned that the `AxisEngine` does not invoke the `onFault()` method of the handler that threw the fault. The `onFault()` methods of the preceding handlers are called in the reverse fashion – **Handler 2 -> Handler 1**.

```
—Handler 1 called—
—Handler 2 called—
—Handler 3 called—

Fault in Handler 2 called
Fault in Handler 1 called
```

Conclusion

In this chapter we covered how to extend the functionality of AXIS by providing our own custom Handlers. We covered the basics of writing Custom Handlers and looked at several different configurations of Handlers within the context of the AXIS Architecture.

Handlers can be written to handle the Request Flow, Response Flow, and Fault Flow for the Transport Chain, Global Chain, or Web Service Chain. Handlers are a powerful mechanism available within AXIS to help introduce incremental functionality into it in a non-intrusive manner.

axis

5

Advanced AXIS Features

In the previous chapters, we discussed basic features, the architecture, and writing handlers for request and response flows. In this chapter, we take you to the next level by focusing on some of the more advanced features AXIS provides.

We will be covering how to:

❑ Send and receive application-specific or custom data types (for example a JavaBean) from the client application to an AXIS web service

❑ Send and receive SOAP Attachments using Java Activation Framework (JAF)

❑ Develop a Java Message Service (JMS)-based Transport handler and plug it into the AXIS message processing system. We will be using WebLogic 6.1 as the messaging server

❑ Write a custom serializer and deserializer to plug into the AXIS Message processing system

❑ Use the security features available in AXIS to demonstrate HTTP Basic Authentication and SSL-based authentication

Custom Data Types

In previous examples, we have just used Java primitive types or `java.lang.String` for the input parameters and the return type but in many cases, you need to send and receive application-specific data types. For example, in Java-based applications, we might use a Java Bean to pass information (for instance employee details) between different parts of an application. In this section, we demonstrate how to use Java beans as the input parameter and return type passed between a client application and the web service. We will be discussing the following:

❑ Sending a `String` object as input parameter and receiving a Java bean as the return type

❑ Sending a Java bean as the input parameter and receiving a `String` object as the return type

We'll create a `SparePartService` that will accept a given SKU number and return the details of a spare part, wrapped in a bean called `SparePartBean`. The service will also accept a `SparePartBean` and add the spare part details contained in the bean to a list of available spare parts. To keep the code simple, the spare parts list is just contained in a flat file, although in real a application, a database would probably a more suitable solution.

First we'll create the Java Bean to wrap the spare part details. SparePartBean contains three attributes, namely sku, price, and description, and their respective accessor methods.

```java
// SparePartBean.java

package wroxaxis.chapter5;

public class SparePartBean {

  public String sku = null;
  public float price = 0.0f;
  public String description = null;

  // Default constructor to creates new SparePartBean
  public SparePartBean() {
  }
  // Get methods
  public String getSku() {
    return sku;
  }
  public float getPrice() {
    return price;
  }
  public String getDescription(){
        return description;
  }
  // Set methods
  public void setSku(String sku) {
    this.sku = sku;
  }
  public void setPrice(float price) {
        this.price = price;
  }
  public void setDescription(String description) {
    this.description = description;
  }
}
```

Now we'll develop the SparePartService web service class with methods to add a new spare part and to query the spare part list. The two methods we define are: getSparePart(), which given a SKU number returns the details of the matching spare part and addSparePart() to add a new spare part to the spare part list.

```java
// SparePartService.java

package wroxaxis.chapter5;
```

```
import java.io.*;
import java.util.*;
public class SparePartService {
```

The service uses a file called sparepartlist.txt for storing the spare part list. The file path shown here is applicable for the Windows system. If you are using some other operating system, you will need to change it to one suitable for that system.

```
  String fileName = "c:/wrox-
axis/wroxaxis/chapter5/sparepartlist.txt";
  String delimiter = "|";
```

The getSparePart() method accepts the sku as an input parameter and searches the file sparepartlist.txt to find an existing spare part for the sku. If there is a spare part in the file matching the given sku, a SparePartBean object is created and returned to the client. If there is no match for the sku, then an object with the default attribute values is returned.

```
public SparePartBean getSparePart(String PartSKU) {
  SparePartBean spBean = new SparePartBean();
  try {
    BufferedReader br = new BufferedReader(new
                                   FileReader(fileName));
    String line = null;
    while ( (line = br.readLine()) != null){
      StringTokenizer sToken = new StringTokenizer(line,
                                            delimiter);
      while(sToken.hasMoreTokens()){
        String sku = sToken.nextToken();
        if(sku.equalsIgnoreCase(PartSKU)) {
          spBean.setPrice(Float.parseFloat(sToken.nextToken()));
          spBean.setDescription(sToken.nextToken());
          break;
        }
      }
    }
  } catch(IOException e) {
    System.out.println(e);
  }
  return spBean;
}
```

The addSparePart() method is used to add a new spare part to the list of existing spare parts. The spare part details are passed to the service as a SparePartBean object. Once the file is updated with the new spare part, the method returns a string to indicate the successful update.

5

```
    public String addSparePart(SparePartBean spBean) {
      try {
        FileOutputStream fout = new FileOutputStream(fileName, true);
        PrintWriter out = new PrintWriter(fout);
        out.print("\n");
        out.print(spBean.getSku() + delimiter);
        out.print(spBean.getPrice() + delimiter);
        out.print(spBean.getDescription() + delimiter);
        out.close();
        fout.flush();
        fout.close();
      } catch (Exception e) {
        System.out.println(e);
        return e.toString();
      }
      return "SparePart with SKU: " + spBean.getSku()
            + " has been added successfully!";
    }
}
```

Now we need to compile and deploy the service. Compile the
SparePartBean.java and SparePartService.java files by giving the
following commands:

```
wrox-axis>javac wroxaxis/chapter5/SparePartBean.java
wrox-axis>javac wroxaxis/chapter5/SparePartService.java
```

Deployment Descriptor

The deployment descriptor for deploying the spare part service
(SparePartServiceDeploy.wsdd) is as shown below:

```
<deployment name="SparePartService"
  xmlns="http://xml.apache.org/axis/wsdd/"
  xmlns:java="http://xml.apache.org/axis/wsdd/providers/java">

  <service name="SparePartDetails" provider="java:RPC">
    <parameter name="className"
               value="wroxaxis.chapter5.SparePartService"/>
    <parameter name="allowedMethods"
               value="getSparePart addSparePart"/>
    <beanMapping qname="wroxaxisNS:SparePartBean"
                 xmlns:wroxaxisNS="SparePartDetails"
      languageSpecificType="java:wroxaxis.chapter5.SparePartBean"/>
  </service>
</deployment>
```

There is also a new element in the WSDD file, <beanMapping>, which is used to specify serializer and deserializer for marshaling and unmarshaling the SparePartBean. The <beanMapping> tag maps a Java bean to a QName and its format is as shown below:

```
<beanMapping qname="ns:local"
             xmlns:ns="someNameSpace"
             languageSpecificType="java:[the bean class]"/>
```

Hence in our example, the JavaBean: SparePartBean is mapped to the qname wroxaxisNS:SparePartBean. The attribute 'qname' defines a qualified name.

▶▶ QNames

It is quite likely that in real applications elements with the same name but a different meaning will exist. For instance, our spare part has a <description> element, but other JavaBeans might also define a <description> element. This could create a problem when processing an XML document that contains more than one type of <description> element. By defining a namespace that is (hopefully) unique and prefixing that to the element name, naming collisions can be avoided.

In our example all instances of the element in the SparePartBean will be prefixed with 'SparePartDetails:' when the bean is serialized.

Now you may be a little surprised that we have not specified any serializers and deserializers in the <beanMapping> element. Actually the <beanMapping> tag is a shorthand representation for a <typeMapping> tag with serializer= "org.apache.axis.encoding.ser.BeanSerializerFactory" and deserializer= "org.apache.axis.encoding.ser.BeanDeserializerFactory". The BeanSerializerFactory class returns an object of type org.apache.axis.encoding.ser.BeanSerializer and the BeanDeserializerFactory returns an object of type org.apache.axis.encoding.ser.BeanDeserializer.

Now deploy the service using the following command:

```
wrox-axis> java org.apache.axis.client.AdminClient -1
http://localhost:8080/axis/services/AdminService
wroxaxis/chapter5/SparePartServiceDeploy.wsdd
-Processing file wroxaxis/chapter5/SparePartServiceDeploy.wsdd
<Admin>Done processing</Admin>
```

and copying SparePartBean.class and SparePartService.class to the %AXIS_DEPLOYHOME%\WEB-INF\classes\chapter5 directory.

5

Client Applications

We'll create two client applications that invoke the SparePartService:

❑ Client 1 – which gets the details of an existing spare part

❑ Client 2 – which adds a new spare part to the spare part list

Although both the methods could be called from the same application, they have been separated for the sake of clarity.

Client 1

This client application invokes the getSparePart() method of SparePartService class to get spare part details for a given SKU number. The basic process of creating a Call object from the Service interface and setting method name and endpointURL remains same as in previous chapters.

```java
// SparePartServiceClient1.java

package wroxaxis.chapter5;

import java.net.URL;
import org.apache.axis.client.Service;
import org.apache.axis.client.Call;
import org.apache.axis.encoding.XMLType;

import javax.xml.rpc.ParameterMode;
import javax.xml.rpc.namespace.QName;
import org.apache.axis.encoding.ser.BeanSerializerFactory;
import org.apache.axis.encoding.ser.BeanDeserializerFactory;

public class SparePartServiceClient1 {

  public SparePartServiceClient1() {}

  public static void main(String args[]) {
    try {
      // Get the SKU number from the command prompt. If the SKU number is
      // not supplied display the usage.
      if (args.length == 0) {
        System.out.println(" Usage: java SparePartServiceClient"
                           + " <sku-number>");
        System.exit(1);
      }

      // EndPoint URL for the SparePartPrice  Web Service
      String endpointURL =
        "http://localhost:8080/axis/services/SparePartDetails";
```

```
    // Method Name to invoke for the SparePartDetails Web Service
    String methodName = "getSparePart";

    // Create the Call object and set properties like endPointURL
    //and method
    Service service = new Service();
    Call call = (Call) service.createCall();
    call.setTargetEndpointAddress(new java.net.URL(endpointURL));
    call.setOperationName(new QName("SparePartDetails",methodName));
    call.addParameter("sku", XMLType.XSD_STRING,
                    ParameterMode.PARAM_MODE_IN);
    QName qname = new QName("SparePartDetails", "SparePartBean");
    Class cls = wroxaxis.chapter5.SparePartBean.class;
```

Since the method returns an application-specific JavaBean, we need to register
the TypeMapping for the serializer and deserializer factory. The return type is set
as the qname; this is used to map the serializer and deserializer factory in the
TypeMapping.

```
    // register the SparePartBean class
    call.registerTypeMapping(cls, qname,
                            BeanSerializerFactory.class,
                            BeanDeserializerFactory.class);
    call.setReturnType(qname);
```

Set up the Parameters (the part SKU) to be passed as the input parameter to the
SparePartDetails web service

```
    Object[] params = new Object[] { args[0] };
```

Since the return type of the invoke() method in the Call class is of type
java.lang.Object, we need to type cast it to SparePartBean as shown
below. Then we display the results on the console output.

```
    // Invoke the SparePartPrice Web Service
    SparePartBean spBean = (SparePartBean) call.invoke(params);

    // Print out the result
    System.out.println("The price is $" + spBean.getPrice());
    System.out.println("The descrption is " +
                    spBean.getDescription());
    } catch (Exception e) {
    System.err.println(e.toString());
    }
  }
}
```

5

Client 2

This client application invokes the addSparePart() method of
SparePartService class to add a new spare part to the list of spare parts. The
method returns a string object to indicate a successful addition to the list. The
process of creating a Call object from the Service interface and setting
method name and endpointURL remains same as in Client 1.

```
// SparePartServiceClient2.java

package wroxaxis.chapter5;

import java.net.URL;
import org.apache.axis.client.Service;
import org.apache.axis.client.Call;
import org.apache.axis.encoding.XMLType;

import javax.xml.rpc.ParameterMode;
import javax.xml.rpc.namespace.QName;
import org.apache.axis.encoding.ser.BeanSerializerFactory;
import org.apache.axis.encoding.ser.BeanDeserializerFactory;


public class SparePartServiceClient2 {

  public SparePartServiceClient2() {}

  public static void main(String args[]) {
    try {

      // EndPoint URL for the SparePartPrice  Web Service
      String endpointURL =
        "http://localhost:8080/axis/services/SparePartDetails";

      // Method Name to invoke for the SparePartPrice Web Service
      String methodName = "addSparePart";

      // Create the Call object and set the properties
      Service service = new Service();
      Call call = (Call) service.createCall();
      call.setTargetEndpointAddress(new java.net.URL(endpointURL));
      call.setOperationName(new QName("SparePartDetails",
                                     methodName));
```

Here we create a new spare part by setting the values of a SparePartBean
instance.

```
SparePartBean spBean = new SparePartBean();
spBean.setSku("SKU-333");
spBean.setPrice(50.00f);
spBean.setDescription("Air Filter Model: 12345");
```

Then we create qualified name and register TypeMapping for the serializer and
deserializer as we did for Client 1.

```
      QName qname = new QName("SparePartDetails",
"SparePartBean");
      Class cls = wroxaxis.chapter5.SparePartBean.class;
```

```
        // register the SparePartBean class
        call.registerTypeMapping(cls, qname,
                            BeanSerializerFactory.class,
                            BeanDeserializerFactory.class);
```

Then we set the input parameter type by specifying the qname and parameter mode in the addParameter() method of the Call object.

```
        call.addParameter("SparePart", qname,
                        ParameterMode.PARAM_MODE_IN);
```

Since this method returns a String, we set the return type as XMLType.XSD_STRING.

```
        call.setReturnType(XMLType.XSD_STRING);
```

Finally, we invoke the service by passing the spare part bean as input parameter. Then we display the response on the console.

```
        // Setup the Parameters i.e. the Part SKU to be passed as
        // input parameter to the SparePartPrice Web Service
        Object[] params = new Object[] { spBean };

        // Invoke the SparePartPrice Web Service
        String result = (String) call.invoke(params);

        // Print out the result
        System.out.println("The response: " + result);
    } catch (Exception e) {
        System.err.println(e.toString());
    }
. }
}
```

Running the Clients

Before we can run the clients, we need to create a sparepartlist.txt file with a few example spare parts for Client 1 to query:

```
SKU-111|100.00f|Honda Spark Plug
SKU-112|20.00f|Toyota Spark Plug
SKU-113|40.00f|Nissan Spark Plug
```

Save this as c:/wrox-axis/wroxaxis/chapter5/sparepartlist.txt.

Compile both SparePartServiceClient1 and SparePartServiceClient1 and then run examples:

```
wrox-axis>javac wroxaxis\chapter5\SparePartServiceClient1.java
wrox-axis>javac wroxaxis\chapter5\SparePartServiceClient2.java
wrox-axis>java wroxaxis.chapter5.SparePartServiceClient1 SKU-
112
The price is $20.0
The descrption is Toyota Spark Plug

wrox-axis>java wroxaxis.chapter5.SparePartServiceClient2
The response: SparePart with SKU: SKU-333 has been added
successfully!
```

Now if you open the file `sparepartlist.txt`, you will find a new entry for a spare part with SKU-333 that was added by the Client 2 application.

Using Attachments

In a SOAP transaction apart from the actual request/response message, there is often a need to send some additional data, such as image files, spreadsheets or other binary data. It would be very inefficient to encode this sort of data so it could be sent as part of the actual SOAP message. These additional documents can be sent or received as attachments to the SOAP messages, in a similar fashion to e-mail attachments.

AXIS supports sending SOAP messages with attachments based on the W3C guidelines given at http://www.w3c.org/TR/SOAP-attachments. Multipurpose Internet Mail Extension (MIME) messages with content type of 'multipart/related' are used to send attachments with SOAP messages. The MIME multipart message may contain many parts where each part specifies the type of content it contains. AXIS uses JavaBeans Activation Framework (JAF) from Sun to provide MIME support. JAF provides features to determine the MIME data type and the commands available for manipulating that sort of data. A detailed description of the JAF can be found at http://java.sun.com/beans/glasgow/jaf.html.

In this section, we will create a web service called `SparePartAttachmentService` that accepts image attachments and saves them to a file. The service uses a `DataHandler` object to read and write the content of image.

The `javax.activation.DataHandler` class encapsulates a `Data` object, and provides methods that act on its data. The `Service` class contains an `addImage()` method to read the contents of image from the `DataHandler` and store it in a file at the specified location as shown below:

```java
// SparePartAttachmentService.java

package wroxaxis.chapter5;

import javax.activation.DataHandler;
import java.io.*;

public class SparePartAttachmentService {

  public SparePartAttachmentService() {}

  public String addImage(String sku, DataHandler dataHandler) {
    try {
      String filepath = "c:/wrox-axis/wroxaxis/chapter5/" + sku +
        "-image.jpg";
      FileOutputStream fout = new FileOutputStream(new File(filepath));

      BufferedInputStream in =
        new BufferedInputStream(dataHandler.getInputStream());
      while (in.available() != 0) {
        fout.write(in.read());
      }
    } catch (Exception e) {
```

```
        return e.toString();
    }
    return "Image: " + sku + " has been added successfully!!";
  }
}
```

Compile `SparePartAttachmentService.Java` located at `%AXIS-DEVHOME%\wroxaxis\chapter5` then place the `.class` file in the `AXIS_DEPLOYHOMR\WEB-INF\classes\wroxaxis\chapter5` directory.

Deployment Descriptor

The deployment descriptor (`AttachmentServiceDeploy.wsdd`) for deploying the attachment service is shown below. The `SparePartAttachmentService` is deployed with the name '`AttachmentService`'.

```
<deployment
            xmlns="http://xml.apache.org/axis/wsdd/"
            xmlns:java="http://xml.apache.org/axis/wsdd/providers/java">
  <service name="AttachmentService" provider="java:RPC">
    <parameter name="className"
                value="wroxaxis.chapter5.SparePartAttachmentService"/>
    <parameter name="allowedMethods"
                value="addImage"/>
  </service>

  <typeMapping qname="ns1:DataHandler" xmlns:ns1="AttachmentService"
      languageSpecificType="java:javax.activation.DataHandler"
      serializer="org.apache.axis.encoding.ser.
                  JAFDataHandlerSerializerFactory"
      deserializer="org.apache.axis.encoding.ser.
                    JAFDataHandlerDeserializerFactory"
      encodingStyle="http://schemas.xmlsoap.org/soap/encoding/"/>
</deployment>
```

Whereas the `<typeMapping>` tag in the WSDD file is used to explicitly specify the serializer and deserializer classes.

```
<typeMapping qname="ns:local" xmlns:ns="someNamespace"
            languageSpecificType="java:wroxaxis.chapter5.SparePartBean"
            serializer="wroxaxis.chapter5.SomeSerializer"
            deserializer="wroxaxis.chapter5.SomeDeserializerFactory"
            encodingStyle="http://schemas.xmlsoap.org/soap/encoding/"/>
```

The above code snippet looks similar to that of the `<beanMapping>` tag we saw earlier, with the exception of two extra attributes: `serializer` and `deserializer` to specify the Java class name of the serializer class and the deserializer factory class respectively. The serializer factory contains the method `getSerializerAs()` that returns a serializer based on the parsing mechanism. This service uses `JAFDataHandlerSerializerFactory` and `JAFDataHanderDeserializerFactory` classes that return `JAFDataHanderSerializer` and `JAFDataHanderDeserializer` objects for marshaling and unmarshaling the `DataHandler` object.

Deploy the service as shown below:

```
wrox-axis> javac wroxaxis\chapter5\SparePartAttachmentService.java
wrox-axis> java org.apache.axis.client.AdminClient -l
http://localhost:8080/axis/services/AdminService
wroxaxis/chapter5/AttachmentServiceDeploy.wsdd
- Processing file wroxaxis/chapter5/AttachmentServiceDeploy.wsdd
<Admin>Done processing</Admin>
```

then copy AttachmentService.class to the %AXIS_DEPLOYHOME%/WEB-INF/classes/wroxaxis/chapter5 directory.

The Client

Now we need to write a client application that sends an image file (.jpg) to the SparePartAttachmentService.

```java
// AttachmentServiceClient.java

package wroxaxis.chapter5;

import java.net.URL;
import org.apache.axis.client.Service;
import org.apache.axis.client.Call;
import org.apache.axis.encoding.XMLType;

import javax.xml.rpc.ParameterMode;
import javax.xml.rpc.namespace.QName;
import org.apache.axis.encoding.ser.JAFDataHandlerSerializerFactory;
import org.apache.axis.encoding.ser.JAFDataHandlerDeserializerFactory;
import javax.activation.FileDataSource;
import javax.activation.DataHandler;

public class AttachmentServiceClient {

  public AttachmentServiceClient() {}

  public static void main(String args[]) {
    try {
```

The client application reads an image called sparkplug.jpg into a DataHandler object (a suitable image file is provide in the book's code download).

```java
      String filename = "wroxaxis/chapter5/sparkplug.jpg";

      // Create the data for the attached file.
      DataHandler dhSource = new DataHandler(new
                                  FileDataSource(filename));

      // EndPoint URL for the SparePartPrice  Web Service
      String endpointURL =
        "http://localhost:8080/axis/services/AttachmentService";

      // Method Name to invoke for the Attachment Web Service
      String methodName = "addImage";
```

```
      // Create Call object and set parameters
      Service service = new Service();
      Call call = (Call) service.createCall();
      call.setTargetEndpointAddress(new java.net.URL(endpointURL));
      call.setOperationName(new QName("AttachmentService",
                                         methodName));
```

The addImage() method of Attachment Service takes two input parameters, the
SKU name of the spare part and the image of the spare part as a DataHandler
object. Since the first parameter (the SKU number) is of type
java.lang.String, the XMLType.XSD_STRING is used as the qualified name.

```
      call.addParameter("sku", XMLType.XSD_STRING,
                         ParameterMode.PARAM_MODE_IN);
```

For the DataHandler object, we define the QName as the service name specified
in the deployment descriptor.

```
      QName qname = new QName("AttachmentService", "DataHandler");
```

Then we add the DataHandler object as an input parameter to the
addImage() method:

```
      call.addParameter("image", qname, ParameterMode.PARAM_MODE_IN);
```

Then we register the TypeMapping for the DataHandler by using the class
name, the qualified name, and the JAFDataHandlerSerializer and
Deserializer as shown below:

```
      // register the SparePartBean class
      call.registerTypeMapping(dhSource.getClass(), qname,
                              JAFDataHandlerSerializerFactory.class,
                              JAFDataHandlerDeserializerFactory.class);

      call.setReturnType(XMLType.XSD_STRING);
```

Finally the service is invoked by passing the input parameters and the response
is then displayed on the console.

```
      // Setup the Parameters i.e. the Part SKU to be passed as
      // input parameter to the Attachment Web Service
      Object[] params = new Object[] { "SKU-111", dhSource };

      // Invoke the SparePartPrice Web Service
      String result = (String) call.invoke(params);

      // Print out the result
      System.out.println("The response: " + result);
    } catch (Exception e) {
      System.err.println(e.toString());
    }
  }
}
```

5

Compile `AttachmentServiceClient.java` and then run the client:

```
wrox-axis> javac wroxaxis\chapter5\SparePartAttachmentService.java
wrox-axis> java wroxaxis.chapter5.AttachmentServiceClient
The response: Image: SKU-111 has been added successfully!!
```

Now if you check in the `wrox-axis\wroxaxis\chapter5` directory, you will find a new `.jpg` file named `SKU-111-image.jpg`.

JMS Transport Handler

By default, the beta version of AXIS only comes with an HTTP-based Transport Handler. However, SOAP does not mandate the use of HTTP for transporting messages and applications may use other protocols like SMTP, FTP, and even asynchronous messaging protocols like the Java Message Service for sending and receiving SOAP messages. To demonstrate the steps needed to create a new AXIS Transport Handler we will develop a JMS Transport.

JMS defines a standard way for Java applications to create and exchange messages via a Message-Oriented Middleware (MOM) application, in our case WebLogic. The use of MOM allows you to create self-contained and independent applications that are loosely coupled. Messages can be exchanged asynchronously, which is particularly useful in situations where a permanent network connection cannot be guaranteed

JMS defines two types of messaging styles known as Point-to-Point (P2P) and Publish/Subscribe (Pub/Sub).

Point to Point (P2P)

In the P2P model, messages are exchanged between the producer and consumer through a channel called a queue. A queue is a destination to which producers send messages and from which receivers consume those messages. In the P2P model, the producer of message is called a sender and the consumer is called a receiver with the queue as the mode of communication channel between them. Multiple receivers may connect to a queue, but each message may only be consumed by one receiver. A message is removed from a queue after a receiver consumes it.

Publish/Subscribe (Pub/Sub)

This model is a one-to-many model since a message published by a message producer may be consumed by more than one subscriber. In Pub/Sub a message producer is called as a publisher and the receiver is called a subscriber with a topic as the mode of communication channel between them. In this model, messages are exchanged through a topic, which is an administered object of type destination. A publisher publishes a message to a particular topic and all registered subscribers receive their own copy of each message.

The Pub/Sub model is very useful in broadcast type applications; where a particular message is delivered to more than one client in an asynchronous way. For instance, this model could be used in a Web-based auction, where bid information needs to be sent to more than one client. For more information on JMS refer to http://java.sun.com/products/jms/index.html or *Professional JMS* (Wrox Press) ISBN 1-861004-93-1.

In our application, we will be using the P2P messaging method as shown in Figure 1. The `JMSClient` is a client application that creates a `Call` object, sets target point URL, method name, input parameters, and also the `Transport` object to be used. The `JMSSender` is the Java class that acts as message sender. The JMS Server contains two queues namely 'WroxAxisQueue' for SOAP requests and 'WroxAxisReplyQueue' for SOAP Responses. The `JMSListener` is a queue receiver application.

So that we can concentrate developing the JMS transport we'll reuse the `SparePartPrice` web service that was developed in Chapter 2.

Figure 1

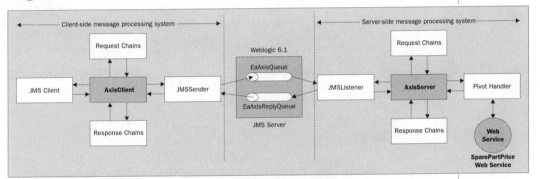

Defining JMS Administered Objects in WebLogic 6.1

An evaluation edition of BEA WebLogic 6.1 can be downloaded from http://commerce.bea.com/downloads/weblogic_server.jsp. BEA WebLogic Server includes an automated installation program for both Windows and UNIX systems; just run the installer and accept the default options. If needed, full installation instructions are provided at http://e-docs.bea.com/wls/docs61/install/index.html.

Administered objects are pre-configured JMS objects created by an administrator for the use of clients. JMS defines the following two types of administered objects:

❑ Connection Factory

❑ Destination

• Topic

• Queue

Since we are using the BEA's Weblogic 6.1 for JMS implementation, we can define the queues either by using the Weblogic's default console (http://localhost:7001/console) or by making entries in the `config.xml` file located in the **%BEA_HOME%\wlserver6.1\config\mydomain** directory.

We need a connection factory to talk to the JMS server. We define a connection factory with the JNDI name `AxisConnectionFactory` in `config.xml` (only the relevant portion of the `config.xml` file is shown.):

```
<Domain Name ="mydomain">
  ...
  <JMSConnectionFactory JNDIName="AxisConnectionFactory"
       Name="Axis Connection Factory" Targets="myserver"/>
```

We also need to define the actual sending and receiving queues for the Point-to-Point (P2P)-based JMS Connection. We define two queues with JNDI names: 'WroxAxisQueue' for SOAP requests and 'WroxAxisReplyQueue' for SOAP responses.

```
<JMSServer Name="myserver" Targets="myserver">
  <JMSQueue JNDIName="WroxAxisQueue" Name="JMSQueue"/>
  <JMSQueue JNDIName="WroxAxisReplyQueue" Name="JMSReplyQueue"/>
</JMSServer>#
</Domain>
```

Now once we start the WebLogic server, we can access the administered objects with an `InitialContext` object by looking up the JNDI names. Now we'll write the Java classes needed for the JMS based transport.

Utility Class

`JMSUtil` is a utility class that contains attributes and methods used by the other classes. It describes the WebLogic Administered objects: JNDI Factory, JMS Factory, and the Queues and has a method to get the Initial Context.

```java
// JMSUtil.java

package wroxaxis.chapter5;

import javax.naming.InitialContext;
import javax.naming.NamingException;

import java.util.Properties;

public class JMSUtil {
  public static final String providerURL = "t3://localhost:7001";

  // Defines the JNDI context factory.
  public static final String JNDI_FACTORY =
    "weblogic.jndi.WLInitialContextFactory";

  // Defines the JMS context factory.
  public static final String JMS_FACTORY = "AxisConnectionFactory";

  // Defines the queues
  public static final String QUEUE = "WroxAxisQueue";
  public static final String QUEUE1 = "WroxAxisReplyQueue";
```

```
public static final InitialContext getInitialContext()
        throws javax.naming.NamingException {

   Properties props = new Properties();
   props.put(javax.naming.Context.PROVIDER_URL, providerURL);
   props.put(javax.naming.Context.INITIAL_CONTEXT_FACTORY,
           JNDI_FACTORY);
   InitialContext ictx = new javax.naming.InitialContext(props);
   return ictx;
 }
}
```

The Message Sender

The message sender class, JMSSender, extends BasicHandler class to enable
it to be pluged into the Axis message processing system.

```
// JMSSender.java

package wroxaxis.chapter5;

import org.apache.axis.AxisFault;
import org.apache.axis.Message;
import org.apache.axis.MessageContext;
import org.apache.axis.encoding.Base64;
import org.apache.axis.handlers.BasicHandler;
import org.apache.axis.message.MessageElement;
import org.apache.axis.utils.JavaUtils;
import org.apache.commons.logging.Log;
import org.apache.commons.logging.LogFactory;
import org.apache.axis.message.SOAPEnvelope;
import org.w3c.dom.Element;
import org.apache.axis.utils.XMLUtils;

import javax.jms.*;
import javax.naming.InitialContext;

public class JMSSender extends BasicHandler {

   static Log log = LogFactory.getLog(JMSSender.class.getName());

   //Define JMS Queue family classes
   private QueueConnectionFactory queueConnFactory;
   private QueueConnection queueConn;
   private QueueSession session;
   private QueueSender sender;
   private QueueReceiver receiver;
   private Queue queue;

   //Define TextMessage for wrapping the SOAP (request) Envelope
   private TextMessage jmsMsg;
```

In the init() method we initialize the QueueConnectionFactory,
QueueConnection, QueueSesssion, Queue etc. We also create message
sender and the receiver to receive the reply message.

```
public JMSSender() {
   try {
     System.out.println("---In constructor JMSSender()---\n");

      // Get the initial context to lookup the AdministeredObjects
```

```
      InitialContext ictx = JMSUtil.getInitialContext();

      // Initialize Queue related objects.
      queueConnFactory =
        (QueueConnectionFactory) ictx.lookup(JMSUtil.JMS_FACTORY);
      queueConn = queueConnFactory.createQueueConnection();
      session = queueConn.createQueueSession(false,
                                      Session.AUTO_ACKNOWLEDGE);
      queue = (Queue) ictx.lookup(JMSUtil.QUEUE);
      sender = session.createSender(queue);

      // Create an object of TextMessage
      jmsMsg = session.createTextMessage();

      // Create a queue for receiving the SOAP (response) Envelope
      Queue queue1 = (Queue) ictx.lookup(JMSUtil.QUEUE1);
      jmsMsg.setJMSReplyTo(queue1);
      receiver = session.createReceiver(queue1);
      queueConn.start();
      }catch(Exception e){
      System.out.println(e);
      System.exit(0);
}
  }
```

AxisClient invokes the Transport Handler by calling the invoke() method.

```
// Axis Engine calls this method
public void invoke(MessageContext msgContext) throws AxisFault {
   try {
      if (log.isDebugEnabled()) {
         log.debug(JavaUtils.getMessage("enter00", "JMSSender::invoke"));
      }
```

The SOAP request is passed to the Transport Handler as a Message object placed in a MessageContext. Hence we need to get the SOAP request using the getSOAPEnvelope() method and then convert it to a String object. The message is echoed to the console and placed in a TextMessage object (jmsMsg).

```
      // Get the request Message from MessageContext
      org.apache.axis.Message axisMsg = msgContext.getRequestMessage();

      // Get a string representation of SOAP Envelope
      SOAPEnvelope soapEnvelope = axisMsg.getSOAPEnvelope();
      Element envElement = soapEnvelope.getAsDOM();
      String strSOAPBody = XMLUtils.ElementToString(envElement);

      System.out.println("---SOAP Request:\n");
      System.out.println(strSOAPBody + "\n");

      // Set SOAP Envelope as the text message
      jmsMsg.setText(strSOAPBody);
```

Then the message is sent to the JMS Server by placing it in the WroxAxisQueue.

```
      System.out.println("---Sending SOAP Request---");
      sender.send(jmsMsg);
      System.out.println("---Sent SOAP Request---\n");
```

The receiver then waits for the SOAP response; when the response is received, it's placed in a `TextMessage` object and then echoed to the console.

```
        System.out.println("---Receiving SOAP Response---");
        TextMessage replyMsg = (TextMessage) receiver.receive();
        System.out.println("---Received SOAP Response---\n");
        System.out.println("---SOAP Response:");
        System.out.println("\n");
        System.out.println("" + replyMsg.getText());
        System.out.println("\n");
```

From the response `TextMessage`, we get the text and wrap it as a message object to put into `MessageContext` as response message. Then the control is returned back to `JMSClient`.

```
    org.apache.axis.Message responseMsg =
        new org.apache.axis.Message(replyMsg.getText());
    msgContext.setResponseMessage(responseMsg);
    System.out.println("---Returning control back to JMSClient---\n");
    }
    catch (Exception e) {
    throw AxisFault.makeFault(e);
  }
}
```

The `cleanUp()` method releases the resources used by closing the `QueueConnection` and `QueueSession`:

```
  public void cleanUp() {
    try {
      sender.close();
      receiver.close();
      session.close();
      queueConn.close();
    } catch (Exception e) {
    System.out.println(e);
    System.exit(0);
    }
  }
}
```

The Message Listener

The Message Listener (`JMSListener.java`) is a JMS Queue receiver application that implements the `MessageListener` interface.

```
// JMSListener.java

package wroxaxis.chapter5;

import java.io.*;
import org.apache.axis.AxisEngine;
import org.apache.axis.AxisFault;
import org.apache.axis.Message;
import org.apache.axis.MessageContext;
import org.apache.axis.configuration.FileProvider;
import org.apache.axis.server.AxisServer;
import org.apache.axis.message.SOAPEnvelope;
```

```
import org.apache.axis.message.SOAPFaultElement;
import org.apache.log4j.Category;
import javax.xml.rpc.namespace.QName;
import org.apache.axis.Constants;
import java.util.Properties;
import javax.jms.*;
import javax.naming.InitialContext;
import javax.naming.NamingException;
import org.apache.axis.message.SOAPEnvelope;

import org.w3c.dom.Element;
import org.apache.axis.utils.XMLUtils;

public class JMSListener implements MessageListener {

  //Define JMS Queue family classes
  private QueueConnectionFactory queueConnFactory;
  private QueueConnection queueConn;
  private QueueSession session;
  private QueueSender sender;
  private QueueReceiver receiver;
  private Queue queue;
  private boolean quit = false;

  // Define TextMessage for wrapping the SOAP (request) Envelope
  private TextMessage jmsMsg;

  private AxisEngine engine = null;
  private String factoryName;

  private String transportName;

  javax.jms.Message msg;
  static Category category =
    Category.getInstance(JMSListener.class.getName());

  public JMSListener() {}
```

In JMSListener, we get an instance of AxisServer by loading the
configuration details specified in the server-config.wsdd deployment
descriptor. As discussed earlier in Chapter 3, the Axis message processing system
uses FileProvider to load the configuration information. The configuration
information consists of deployed services, Handlers, Chains and, Transports.

```
public AxisEngine getAxisEngine() throws Exception {

  if (engine != null) {
    return engine;

  }
  String prefix = "c:/jakarta-tomcat/webapps/axis/WEB-INF/;
  String config = prefix + "server-config.wsdd";
  System.out.println("filename :" + config);
  FileProvider provider = new FileProvider(config);
  return new AxisServer(provider);
}
```

In the `init()` method, we initialize the `QueueConnection`, `QueueSession` etc.

```
private void init() throws AxisFault {

   try {
      InitialContext ictx = JMSUtil.getInitialContext();
      queueConnFactory =
         (QueueConnectionFactory) ictx.lookup(JMSUtil.JMS_FACTORY);

      // Look up the Queue
      queue = (Queue) ictx.lookup(JMSUtil.QUEUE);
      queueConn = queueConnFactory.createQueueConnection();

      // Create a session (non-transactional) that automatically
      // acknowledges message receipt.
      session = queueConn.createQueueSession(false,
                                 Session.AUTO_ACKNOWLEDGE);

      receiver = session.createReceiver(queue);
      queueConn.start();

      System.out.println("Ready to receive messages!!\n");

      // Let this JMSListener be notified everytime a message is
      // received by its associated queue.
      receiver.setMessageListener(this);

   } catch (Exception e) {
      // System.out.println(e);
      throw AxisFault.makeFault(e);
   }
}
```

Whenever a message arrives in the `WroxAxisQueue`, the JMS Message notifies the `JMSListener` by invoking the `onMessage()` method.

```
public void onMessage(javax.jms.Message msg) {

   System.out.println("---In onMessage()---");
   quit = true;
   MessageContext msgContext = null;
   org.apache.axis.Message responseMsg = null;

   try {
      String msgTxt = null;
      TextMessage jmsMsg = (TextMessage) msg;
      System.out.println(jmsMsg.getText());
      Queue replyQueue = (Queue) msg.getJMSReplyTo();
      sender = session.createSender(replyQueue);

      // Create an instance of AxisServer
      AxisEngine engine = getAxisEngine();

      // Creae a MessageContext and associate with the engine
      msgContext = new MessageContext(engine);
```

We get the SOAP request from the JMS `TextMessage` and create
an object of type Message to wrap the SOAP request and put into
`MessageContext`. Then we pass the message context to the
`AxisServer` by calling the `invoke()` method. The
`AxisServer` invokes all the request chains and the pivot
handler and the response chains. Since the service invocation is
done using RPC mechanism, the pivot handler is the class Java
Provider, `org.apache.axis.providers.java.RPCProvider`.

```java
// Wrap the incoming TextMessage into Axis Message
org.apache.axis.Message soapMessage =
  new org.apache.axis.Message(jmsMsg.getText());

System.out.println("SOAP Request:");
System.out.println(jmsMsg.getText() + "\n");

// Set the request message in MessageContext
msgContext.setRequestMessage(soapMessage);

System.out.println("---Invoking AxisServer.invoke()---");

// Invoke AxisEngine (AxisServer)
engine.invoke(msgContext);

System.out.println("---AxisServer.invoke() is completed---");
System.out.println(
  "---Getting response message from MessageContext---");
```

Once the `AxisServer` message processing is completed, The SOAP response is
put into JMS `TextMessage`. The `TextMessage` is then sent to the
`WroxAxisReplyQueue`.

```java
// Get the response message from the MessageContext
responseMsg = msgContext.getResponseMessage();

// Get a String representation of response
SOAPEnvelope envelope = responseMsg.getSOAPEnvelope();
Element envElement = envelope.getAsDOM();
String strSOAPBody = XMLUtils.ElementToString(envElement);

System.out.println("SOAP Response:");
System.out.println(strSOAPBody);

// Create an instance of TextMessage to wrap the SOAP (response)
TextMessage jmsResponseMsg = session.createTextMessage();
jmsResponseMsg.setText(strSOAPBody);

// Put the response into the queue: 'replyQueue'
System.out.println("\n---Sending SOAP Response using the Queue:"
                  + " WroxAxisReplyQueue ---");
sender.send(jmsResponseMsg);
System.out.println("---Sent SOAP Response---\n");
System.out.println("---Waiting for new SOAP Requests---");

} catch (Exception e) {
e.printStackTrace();
if (!(e instanceof AxisFault)) {
  e = AxisFault.makeFault(e);
}
responseMsg = msgContext.getResponseMessage();
if (responseMsg == null) {
  responseMsg = new org.apache.axis.Message((AxisFault) e);
```

5

```
          msgContext.setResponseMessage(responseMsg);
      } else {
        try {
          SOAPEnvelope env = responseMsg.getSOAPEnvelope();
          env.clearBody();
          env.addBodyElement(new SOAPFaultElement((AxisFault) e));
        } catch (AxisFault af) {
          af.printStackTrace();
        }
      }
    }
  }
}
```

This is the main method required to run the listener application. The listener keeps listening to `WroxAxisReplyQueue` for JMS Messages.

```
public static void main(String args[]) throws Exception {
  JMSListener listener = new JMSListener();
  listener.init();

  // Wait until a "quit" message has been received.
  synchronized (listener) {
    while (!listener.quit) {
      try {
        listener.wait();
      } catch (InterruptedException ie) {}
    }
  }
}
```

The `weblogic.jar`, which is located at `%BEA-HOME%\wlserver6.1\lib` must be added to the classpath. Compile `JMSListener.java` file and run the class as shown below:

```
wrox-axis> javac -classpath %WL_HOME%\lib\weblogic.jar
wroxaxis/chapter5/JMSListener.java
wrox-axis> java -classpath
%CLASSPATH%;%WL_HOME%\lib\weblogic.jar
wroxaxis.chapter5.JMSListener
Ready to receive messages!
```

Note, it may take quite a while for the listener application to be initialized.

The Transport

In the client application, we will be setting the transport handler to an instance of the `JMSTranport` class. The `JMSTranport` class extends to `org.apache.axis.client.Transport` and overrides the value of the `transportName` attribute.

```
// JMSTransport.java

package wroxaxis.chapter5;

import org.apache.axis.client.Transport;

public class JMSTransport extends Transport {
```

```
public JMSTransport() {
    transportName = "JMSTransport";
}
}
```

The Deployment Descriptor

Previously we have only need to configure the deployed services to the AXIS
server-side message processing system but now we need to add functionality to
the client side as well. AxisEngine (AxisClient) at the client side message
processing system loads the configuration information by reading from the
deployment descriptor: client-config.wsdd. Hence, we need to specify the
details of JMSTransport in client-config.wsdd. The following deployment
descriptor (JMSClientDeploy.wsdd) specifies the Pivot and Transport
Handlers. As shown below, we set JMSSender as the pivot handler and
JMSTransport as the transport handler. The AxisClient reads the WSDD file
to create an instance of the pivot handler to send the SOAP request.

```xml
<?xml version="1.0" encoding="UTF-8"?>
<deployment xmlns="http://xml.apache.org/axis/wsdd/"
        xmlns:java="http://xml.apache.org/axis/wsdd/providers/java">
    <handler name="JMSDispatcher"
            type="java:wroxaxis.chapter5.JMSSender"/>
    <transport name="JMSTransport" pivot="JMSDispatcher"/>
</deployment>
```

We can deploy this WSDD file using the Admin utility class provided by AXIS as
shown below:

wrox-axis\wroxaxis\chapter5\> **java org.apache.axis.utils.Admin
client wroxaxis\chapter5\JMSClientDeploy.wsdd**

When you execute the above, the Admin class creates the client-config.wsdd
and appends the deployment details provided in JMSClientDeploy.wsdd. The
option 'client' given at the command prompt indicates that the deployment
information is for the client-side message processing system.

The Client

Now we will write a client to invoke the SparePartPrice web service that we
developed in Chapter 2 via our JMS Transport. Given the SKU number, the web
service returns the price of the spare part. The client program is similar to the
client program (SparePartPriceServiceClient.java) except for the
addition of setting up the Transport Handler to the Call object. The complete
code for the JMS client (JMSClient.java) is listed below:

```java
// JMSClient.java

package wroxaxis.chapter5;

import java.net.URL;
import org.apache.axis.client.Service;
import org.apache.axis.client.Call;
import org.apache.axis.encoding.XMLType;

import javax.xml.rpc.ParameterMode;
import javax.xml.rpc.namespace.QName;
```

```
public class JMSClient {

  public JMSClient() {}

  public static void main(String args[]) {
    try {

      // EndPoint URL for the SparePartPrice  Web Service
      String endpointURL =
        "http://localhost:8080/axis/services/SparePartPrice";

      // Method Name to invoke for the SparePartPrice Web Service
      String methodName = "getPrice";

      // Create the Service call
      Service service = new Service();
      Call call = (Call) service.createCall();
      call.setTargetEndpointAddress(new java.net.URL(endpointURL));
      call.setOperationName(new QName("SparePartPrice",
                                      methodName));
      call.addParameter("sku", XMLType.XSD_STRING,
                        ParameterMode.PARAM_MODE_IN);
```

As shown below, using the setTransport() method, we can plug in any new or application-specific Transport Handler.

```
      call.setTransport(new JMSTransport());
```

The rest of the example is the same as before – invoking the service by passing the SKU number and displaying the result on the console.

```
      call.setReturnType(XMLType.XSD_FLOAT);

      // Setup the Parameters i.e. the Part SKU to be passed as
      // input parameter to the SparePartPrice Web Service
      Object[] params = new Object[] {
        "SKU-123"
      };

      System.out.println("---Start call.invoke()---\n");

      // Invoke the SparePartPrice Web Service
      Float price = (Float) call.invoke(params);
      System.out.println("---End call.invoke()---");

      // Print out the result
      System.out.println("---Displaying the result---");
      System.out.println("The price is $" + price.floatValue());
    } catch (Exception e) {
      System.err.println(e.toString());
    }
  }
}
```

Compile the `JMSTransport`, `JMSClient`, and `JMSSender` Java files and run the `JMSClient` class as shown below:

```
C:\wrox-axis>java -classpath %CLASSPATH%;%WL_HOME%\lib\weblogic.jar wroxaxis.cha
pter5.JMSClient
---Start call.invoke()---

---In constructor JMSSender()---

---SOAP Request:

<SOAP-ENV:Envelope SOAP-ENV:encodingStyle="http://schemas.xmlsoap.org/soap/encod
ing/" xmlns:SOAP-ENC="http://schemas.xmlsoap.org/soap/encoding/" xmlns:SOAP-ENV=
"http://schemas.xmlsoap.org/soap/envelope/" xmlns:xsd="http://www.w3.org/2001/XM
LSchema" xmlns:xsi="http://www.w3.org/2001/XMLSchema-instance">
 <SOAP-ENV:Body>
  <ns1:getPrice xmlns:ns1="SparePartPrice">
   <sku xsi:type="xsd:string">SKU-123</sku>
  </ns1:getPrice>
 </SOAP-ENV:Body>
</SOAP-ENV:Envelope>

---Sending SOAP Request---
---Sent SOAP Request---

---Receiving SOAP Response---
---Received SOAP Response---

---SOAP Response:

<SOAP-ENV:Envelope xmlns:SOAP-ENV="http://schemas.xmlsoap.org/soap/envelope/" xm
lns:xsd="http://www.w3.org/2001/XMLSchema" xmlns:xsi="http://www.w3.org/2001/XML
Schema-instance">
 <SOAP-ENV:Body>
  <ns1:getPriceResponse SOAP-ENV:encodingStyle="http://schemas.xmlsoap.org/soap/
encoding/" xmlns:ns1="SparePartPrice">
   <getPriceResult xsi:type="xsd:float">10.99</getPriceResult>
  </ns1:getPriceResponse>
 </SOAP-ENV:Body>
</SOAP-ENV:Envelope>

---Returning control back to JMSClient---

---End call.invoke()---
---Displaying the result---
The price is $10.99

C:\wrox-axis>
```

You can see the flow clearly. The JMSClient constructs the call object and invokes the `AxisClient`. `AxisClient` checks the Transport object in the deployment descriptor (`client-config.wsdd`) and loads the Transport Handler defined for the 'JMS' transport type. Then the SOAP request is passed to the `AxisServer` in a `MessageContext` through `WroxAxisQueue`.

`AxisServer` sends a SOAP response to the `WroxAxisReplyQueue` wrapped in a message object. Then the control is given back to JMSClient by returning from the `invoke()` method. Then the return value is displayed on the console.

The output at the JMS receiver (JMSListener) is shown opposite. You can see it receiving the SOAP request, invoking `AxisServer`, wrapping up the return value in a SOAP response, and placing it in the `WroxAxisReplyQueue`.

```
Command Prompt - java -classpath .;C:\wrox-axis;C:\xml-axis-beta1\lib\axis.jar;C:\xml-axis-beta1\li...  _ □ X
Ready to receive messages!!

---In onMessage()---
<SOAP-ENV:Envelope SOAP-ENV:encodingStyle="http://schemas.xmlsoap.org/soap/encod
ing/" xmlns:SOAP-ENC="http://schemas.xmlsoap.org/soap/encoding/" xmlns:SOAP-ENV=
"http://schemas.xmlsoap.org/soap/envelope/" xmlns:xsd="http://www.w3.org/2001/XM
LSchema" xmlns:xsi="http://www.w3.org/2001/XMLSchema-instance">
 <SOAP-ENV:Body>
  <ns1:getPrice xmlns:ns1="SparePartPrice">
   <sku xsi:type="xsd:string">SKU-123</sku>
  </ns1:getPrice>
 </SOAP-ENV:Body>
</SOAP-ENV:Envelope>
filename :c:\jakarta-tomcat\webapps\axis\WEB-INF\server-config.wsdd
SOAP Request:
<SOAP-ENV:Envelope SOAP-ENV:encodingStyle="http://schemas.xmlsoap.org/soap/encod
ing/" xmlns:SOAP-ENC="http://schemas.xmlsoap.org/soap/encoding/" xmlns:SOAP-ENV=
"http://schemas.xmlsoap.org/soap/envelope/" xmlns:xsd="http://www.w3.org/2001/XM
LSchema" xmlns:xsi="http://www.w3.org/2001/XMLSchema-instance">
 <SOAP-ENV:Body>
  <ns1:getPrice xmlns:ns1="SparePartPrice">
   <sku xsi:type="xsd:string">SKU-123</sku>
  </ns1:getPrice>
 </SOAP-ENV:Body>
</SOAP-ENV:Envelope>

---Invoking AxisServer.invoke()---
---AxisServer.invoke() is completed---
---Getting response message from MessageContext---
SOAP Response:
<SOAP-ENV:Envelope xmlns:SOAP-ENV="http://schemas.xmlsoap.org/soap/envelope/" xm
lns:xsd="http://www.w3.org/2001/XMLSchema" xmlns:xsi="http://www.w3.org/2001/XML
Schema-instance">
 <SOAP-ENV:Body>
  <ns1:getPriceResponse SOAP-ENV:encodingStyle="http://schemas.xmlsoap.org/soap/
encoding/" xmlns:ns1="SparePartPrice">
   <getPriceResult xsi:type="xsd:float">10.99</getPriceResult>
  </ns1:getPriceResponse>
 </SOAP-ENV:Body>
</SOAP-ENV:Envelope>

---Sending SOAP Response using the Queue: WroxAxisReplyQueue ---
---Sent SOAP Response---

---Waiting for new SOAP Requests---
```

5

Custom Serialization

Earlier in the chapter, we used a built-in AXIS serializer (BeanSerializer) and
deserializer (BeanDeserializer) to send and receive a SparePartBean
between the SparePartServiceClient and the SparePartService. This is
fine for standard JavaBeans but sometimes you'll have to write custom serializers
and deserializers for application-specific data types. To keep things simple we'll
write a custom serializer/deserializer for the JavaBean we developed earlier, even
though this is can be handled fine by the built-in bean serilaizer

In this section, we will show you how to write a custom serializer and
deserializer and plug them into the Axis Message Processing system. To create a
new serializer and deserializer, we need to develop the following four classes:

❑   Serializer Factory – A factory class that returns a Serializer based on the
    parsing mechanism

❑   Deserializer Factory – A factory class that returns a Deserializer based on the
    parsing mechanism

❑   Serializer – This class is responsible for converting the JavaBean to a
    corresponding XML structure

❑   Deserializer – This class is responsible for converting the XML structure to its
    corresponding JavaBean

We will then deploy the service with the above serializer and deserializer to the AXIS message processing system using a deployment descriptor. Finally, we'll write a client application to access the service.

Serializer Factory

The WroxAxisSerializerFactory is a factory class for obtaining a serializer based on a particular parsing mechanism type.

```java
// WroxAxisSerializerFactory.java

package wroxaxis.chapter5;

import org.xml.sax.Attributes;
import org.xml.sax.SAXException;

import javax.xml.rpc.namespace.QName;

import org.apache.axis.encoding.Serializer;
import org.apache.axis.encoding.SerializerFactory;
import org.apache.axis.encoding.SerializationContext;
import org.apache.axis.Constants;

import java.util.Iterator;
import java.util.Vector;

public class WroxAxisSerializerFactory implements SerializerFactory {

    private Vector mechanisms;

    public WroxAxisSerializerFactory() {
    }
```

The factory class has a getSerializersAs() method to return an instance of a serializer based on the specified parsing mechanism. The method returns an instance of WroxAxisSerializer, which is the serializer class that we are going to develop.

```java
    public javax.xml.rpc.encoding.Serializer getSerializerAs(String
                                                             mechanismType)
    {
        return new WroxAxisSerializer();
    }
```

As shown below, the factory class has a method called getSupportedMechanismTypes() that returns all the parsing mechanisms being supported. The factory class maintains a vector of all supported mechanism types; to keep things simple the current version of WroxAxisSerializerFactory supports only SAX-based parsing mechanism.

```java
    public Iterator getSupportedMechanismTypes() {
        if (mechanisms == null) {
            mechanisms = new Vector();
            mechanisms.add(Constants.AXIS_SAX);
        }
        return mechanisms.iterator();
    }
}
```

5

Deserializer Factory

Similarly, the deserializer factory has methods to get an instance of a deserializer based on parsing mechanism type and to get a list of all the supported parsing mechanisms.

The WroxAxisDeserializerFacotry supports only SAX-based deserializers and returns instances of WroxAxisDeserialzer.

```java
// WroxAxisDeserializerFactory.java

package wroxaxis.chapter5;

import org.xml.sax.Attributes;
import org.xml.sax.SAXException;

import javax.xml.rpc.namespace.QName;
import java.io.IOException;

import org.apache.axis.encoding.Deserializer;
import org.apache.axis.encoding.DeserializerFactory;
import org.apache.axis.encoding.DeserializationContext;
import org.apache.axis.encoding.DeserializerImpl;
import org.apache.axis.Constants;

import java.util.Iterator;
import java.util.Vector;

public class WroxAxisDeserializerFactory implements
DeserializerFactory {
  private Vector mechanisms;

  public WroxAxisDeserializerFactory() {}

  public javax.xml.rpc.encoding.Deserializer
    getDeserializerAs(String mechanismType) {
      return new WroxAxisDeserializer();
  }
  public Iterator getSupportedMechanismTypes() {
    if (mechanisms == null) {
      mechanisms = new Vector();
      mechanisms.add(Constants.AXIS_SAX);
    }
    return mechanisms.iterator();
  }
}
```

Serializer

The WroxAxisSerializer class is responsible for transforming objects of type SparePartBean into a corresponding XML structure. The WroxAxisSerializer class defines a QName for mapping all the attributes of SparePartBean like SKU, price, and description.

```java
// WroxAxisSerializer.java

package wroxaxis.chapter5;

import org.apache.axis.encoding.SerializationContext;
```

```
import org.apache.axis.encoding.Serializer;
import org.apache.axis.message.SOAPHandler;
import org.apache.axis.Constants;
import org.xml.sax.Attributes;
import org.xml.sax.SAXException;
import org.apache.axis.Constants;
import org.apache.axis.wsdl.fromJava.Types;

import javax.xml.rpc.namespace.QName;
import java.io.IOException;
import java.util.Hashtable;

public class WroxAxisSerializer implements Serializer
{
  public static final String SKU = "sku";
  public static final String PRICE = "price";
  public static final String DESCRIPTION = "description";
```

The AXIS message processing system invokes the serialize() method by passing the SerializationContext. The serialize() method transforms each attribute of SparePartBean in to XML structure based on the mapping defined between the QName of the attribute and the attribute itself.

```
public void serialize(QName name,  Attributes attributes,
                      Object value, SerializationContext context)
      throws IOException {
```

If you try to pass anything else but a SparePartBean to the serializer, it throws an exception.

```
System.out.println("Inside WroxAxisSerializer");
if (!(value instanceof SparePartBean)) {
  throw new IOException("Can't serialize a "
                       + value.getClass().getName()
                       + " with a WroxAxisSerializer.");
}
```

Now we read the values from the SparePartBean using its get methods and write them to XML using the SerializationContext.serialize() method.

```
SparePartBean spBean = (SparePartBean) value;

context.startElement(name, attributes);
context.serialize(new QName("", SKU), null, spBean.getSku(),
                  String.class);
context.serialize(new QName("", PRICE), null, ""
                  + spBean.getPrice(), float.class);
context.serialize(new QName("", DESCRIPTION), null,
                  spBean.getDescription(), String.class);
context.endElement();
}
public String getMechanismType() {
  return Constants.AXIS_SAX;
}

public boolean writeSchema(Types types) throws Exception {
  return false;
}
}
```

Deserializer

The WroxAxisDeserializer class is responsible for transforming the XML structure to SparePartBean.

```java
// WroxAxisDeserializer.java

package wroxaxis.chapter5;

import org.apache.axis.encoding.DeserializationContext;
import org.apache.axis.encoding.Deserializer;
import org.apache.axis.encoding.DeserializerImpl;
import org.apache.axis.encoding.FieldTarget;
import org.apache.axis.Constants;
import org.apache.axis.message.SOAPHandler;
import org.xml.sax.Attributes;
import org.xml.sax.SAXException;

import javax.xml.rpc.namespace.QName;
import java.io.IOException;
import java.util.Hashtable;

public class WroxAxisDeserializer extends DeserializerImpl {
  public static final String SKU = "sku";
  public static final String PRICE = "price";
  public static final String DESCRIPTION = "description";

  private Hashtable typesByMemberName = new Hashtable();
```

In the constructor, we map each attribute of SparePartBean to the corresponding XSD type.

```java
  public WroxAxisDeserializer() {
    System.out.println("inside wroxaxis deserializer");
    typesByMemberName.put(SKU, Constants.XSD_STRING);
    typesByMemberName.put(PRICE, Constants.XSD_FLOAT);
    typesByMemberName.put(DESCRIPTION, Constants.XSD_STRING);
    value = new SparePartBean();
  }
```

The onStartChild() method will be invoked by the parser by passing the DeserializationContext.

```java
  public SOAPHandler onStartChild
   (String namespace,
   String localName,
   String prefix,
   Attributes attributes,
   DeserializationContext context)
        throws SAXException {

   QName typeQName = (QName) typesByMemberName.get(localName);
   if (typeQName == null) {
     throw new SAXException("Invalid element in SparePartBean"
                          + " struct - " + localName);

     // These can come in either order.
   }
   Deserializer dSer = context.getDeserializerForType(typeQName);
   try {
     dSer.registerValueTarget(new FieldTarget(value, localName));
   } catch (NoSuchFieldException e) {
     throw new SAXException(e);
```

```
        }

    if (dSer == null) {
      throw new SAXException("No deserializer for a " + typeQName +
                          "???");
    }
    return (SOAPHandler) dSer;
  }
}
```

Deployment Descriptor

Now we need to deploy the serializer and deserializer for the SparePartBean
by creating a WSDD file, SerializerServiceDeploy.wsdd. We will use the
same SpartPartService that we deployed earlier. For the sake of clarity, we
deploy the SpartPartService with a different name, SpartPartServiceSer.

```
<deployment xmlns="http://xml.apache.org/axis/wsdd/"
            xmlns:java="http://xml.apache.org/axis/wsdd/providers/java">
  <service name="SparePartDetailsSer" provider="java:RPC">
    <parameter name="allowedMethods" value="addSparePart"/>
<parameter name="className" value="wroxaxis.chapter5.SparePartService"/>
```

We use the <typeMapping> tag as shown below; this is similar to the
<beanMapping> element we used earlier with the addition of serializer and
deserializer attributes that refer to the WroxAxsiSerializerFactory and
WroxAxisDeserializerFactory classes.

```
    <typeMapping qname="WroxAxisNS:SparePartBean"
        xmlns:WroxAxisNS="SparePartDetailsSer"
        languageSpecificType="java:wroxaxis.chapter5.SparePartBean"
        serializer="wroxaxis.chapter5.WroxAxisSerializerFactory"
        deserializer="wroxaxis.chapter5.WroxAxisDeserializerFactory"
        encodingStyle="http://schemas.xmlsoap.org/soap/encoding/"/>
  </service>
</deployment>
```

Compile all the Java files and deploy the WSDD file as shown below:

```
wrox-axis> javac wroxaxis/chapter5/WroxAxisSerializer.java
wrox-axis> javac wroxaxis/chapter5/WroxAxisDeserializer.java
wrox-axis> javac wroxaxis/chapter5/WroxAxisSerializerFactory.java
wrox-axis> javac wroxaxis/chapter5/WroxAxisDeserializerFactory.java
wrox-axis> java org.apache.axis.client.AdminClient -1
http://localhost:8080/axis/services/AdminService
wroxaxis/chapter5/SerializerServiceDeploy.wsdd
- Processing file wroxaxis/chapter5/SerializerServiceDeploy.wsdd
<Admin>Done processing</Admin>
```

Then copy the .class files to the %AXIS_DEPLOY%\WEB-
INF\classses\wroxaxis\chapter5 directory

5

Client

The Client application is almost the same as `SerializerServiceClient` used earlier with a few changes as highlighted below. The endpoint URL is points to the service `SparePartDetailsSer`.

```java
// SerializerServiceClient.java+

package wroxaxis.chapter5;

import java.net.URL;
import org.apache.axis.client.Service;
import org.apache.axis.client.Call;
import org.apache.axis.encoding.XMLType;

import javax.xml.rpc.ParameterMode;
import javax.xml.rpc.namespace.QName;

public class SerializerServiceClient {

  public SerializerServiceClient() {}

  public static void main(String args[]) {
    try {

      // EndPoint URL for the SparePartPrice  Web Service
      String endpointURL =
        "http://localhost:8080/axis/services/SparePartDetailsSer";

      // Method Name to invoke for the SparePartPrice Web Service
      String methodName = "addSparePart";

      // Create the Service call
      Service service = new Service();
      Call call = (Call) service.createCall();
      call.setTargetEndpointAddress(new java.net.URL(endpointURL));
      call.setOperationName(new QName("SparePartDetailsSer",
                                      methodName));

      SparePartBean spBean = new SparePartBean();
      spBean.setSku("SKU-114");
      spBean.setPrice(50.00f);
      spBean.setDescription("Air Filter Model: 12345");

      QName qname = new QName("SparePartDetailsSer",
                              "SparePartBean");
      Class cls = wroxaxis.chapter5.SparePartBean.class;
```

We will register the `TypeMapping` for the `WroxAxisSerializer` and `WroxAxisDeserializer` classes. For more information on Type Mapping please refer the Chapter 3.

```java
      // register the SparePartBean class
      call.registerTypeMapping(cls, qname,
                               WroxAxisSerializerFactory.class,
                               WroxAxisDeserializerFactory.class);

      call.addParameter("SparePart", qname,
                        ParameterMode.PARAM_MODE_IN);
      call.setReturnType(XMLType.XSD_STRING);

      // Setup the Parameters i.e. the Part SKU to be passed as
```

```
        // input parameter to the SparePartPrice Web Service
        Object[] params = new Object[] { spBean };

        // Invoke the SparePartPrice Web Service
        String result = (String) call.invoke(params);

        // Print out the result
        System.out.println("The response: " + result);
    } catch (Exception e) {
        System.err.println(e.toString());
    }
  }
}
```

Compile and run the client program as shown below:

```
wrox-axis> javac wroxaxis\chapter5\SerializerServiceClient.java
wrox-axis> java wroxaxis.chapter5.SerializerServiceClient
inside WroxAxisSerializer
The response: Sparepart with SKU: SKU-114 has been added sucessfully!!
```

The SOAP Request for the service is also given below to show the XML structure for SparePartBean. The highlighted portion shows the serialized XML structure of SparePartBean. You can see the attributes of SparePartBean with values in the following XML structure.

```
POST /axis/services/SparePartDetailsSer HTTP/1.0
Content-Length: 780
Host: localhost
Content-Type: text/xml; charset=utf-8
SOAPAction: ""

<?xml version="1.0" encoding="UTF-8"?>
<SOAP-ENV:Envelope
  SOAP-ENV:encodingStyle="http://schemas.xmlsoap.org/soap/encoding/"
  xmlns:SOAP-ENV="http://schemas.xmlsoap.org/soap/envelope/"
  xmlns:xsd="http://www.w3.org/2001/XMLSchema"
  xmlns:xsi="http://www.w3.org/2001/XMLSchema-instance"
  xmlns:SOAP-ENC="http://schemas.xmlsoap.org/soap/encoding/">
  <SOAP-ENV:Body>
    <ns1:addSparePart xmlns:ns1="SparePartDetailsSer">
      <SparePart href="#id0"/>
    </ns1:addSparePart>
    <multiRef id="id0" SOAP-ENC:root="0"
      xsi:type="ns2:SparePartBean" xmlns:ns2="SparePartDetailsSer">
      <sku xsi:type="xsd:string">SKU-114</sku>
      <price xsi:type="xsd:float">50.0</price>
      <description xsi:type="xsd:string">
        Air Filter Model: 12345
      </description>
    </multiRef>
  </SOAP-ENV:Body>
</SOAP-ENV:Envelope>
```

Security

Security is vital in any Business-to-Business (B2B) transaction. While several initiatives are underway to enable secure SOAP transactions currently AXIS only supports HTTP basic authentication and the SSL protocol. In this section, we will concentrate on using the basic security features supported by AXIS by writing examples to demonstrate BASIC-AUTH and SSL over HTTP to access the `SparePartPrice` web service developed in Chapter 2.

HTTP Basic Authentication

The most common security mechanism implemented by services accessible via HTTP is "Basic Authentication" because of its simplicity and easy implementation. HTTP Basic authentication (also known as BASIC-AUTH) requests a username and password for authentication. When a client application (a Java client or a web browser) sends an HTTP request to access a resource, the web server authenticates the supplied username and password. If the authentication is successful, the user can then access the resources. If the authentication fails, then the web server returns the HTTP response '401 Unauthorized'.

BASIC-AUTH is based on two elements: **Realm** and an **Access Control List** (ACL). Realm refers to a set of web resources. ACL contains a list of the available services and the entities (users) permitted to use each service. In AXIS, these details are maintained in the files perms.1st and users.1st located at `%TOMCAT_HOME%\webapps\axis\WEB-INF`.

The file perms.1st contains a list of mappings between users (entities) and the names of the deployed service as shown below:

```
wroxuser1 AuthSparePartService
wroxuser2 AttachmentService
```

The file users.1st contains a list of username and passwords as shown below:

```
wroxuser1 password1
wroxuser2 password2
```

We are going to reuse the `SparePartPrice` service that we created in Chapter 2 to enable access control. We need to add a couple of elements to the WSDD file:

```
<deployment
    xmlns="http://xml.apache.org/axis/wsdd/"
    xmlns:java="http://xml.apache.org/axis/wsdd/providers/java">
    xmlns:xsi="http://www.w3.org/2000/10/XMLSchema-instance">
  <service name="AuthSparePartPrice" provider="java:RPC">
    <parameter name="className"
              value="wroxaxis.chapter2.SparePartPrice"/>
    <parameter name="allowedMethods" value="getPrice"/>
    <parameter name="allowedRoles" value="wroxuser1"/>
    <requestFlow name="auth">
      <handler
type="java:org.apache.axis.handlers.SimpleAuthenticationHandler"/>
      <handler
type="java:org.apache.axis.handlers.SimpleAuthorizationHandler"/>
```

5

```
      </requestFlow>
    </service>
</deployment>
```

Basic authentication can be enabled for a service by adding SimpleAuthenticationHandler and SimpleAuthorizationHandler to the service's request flow. To distinguish it from the service developed in Chapter 2 give it a new name, AuthSparePartPrice, save this file as AuthSparePartPriceDepoly.wsdd.

Now we need to deploy the service:

```
wrox-axis> java org.apache.axis.client.AdminClient
wroxaxis/chapter5/AuthSparePartPriceServiceDeploy.wsdd -1
http://localhost:8080/axis/services/AdminService
```

Now we write a client application, BasicAuthClient, to access the SparePartPrice service using BASIC-AUTH.

In BASIC-AUTH-based authentication, the server (Tomcat engine) expects username and password in the HTTP request coming from the client application. Hence, the client application must include the user credentials in the HTTP request. AXIS provides methods in the org.apache.axis.client.Call class to set the username and password values.

```java
// BasicAuthClient.java

package wroxaxis.chapter5;

import java.net.URL;
import org.apache.axis.client.Service;
import org.apache.axis.client.Call;
import org.apache.axis.encoding.XMLType;

import javax.xml.rpc.ParameterMode;
import javax.xml.rpc.namespace.QName;

public class BasicAuthClient {

  public static void main(String args[]) {
    try {
      if (args == null) {
        System.out
          .println("Usage: java wroxaxis.chapter5.BasicAuthClient "
                 + "<username> <password>");
        System.exit(0);
      }
```

The user's credentials are passed at the command prompt and arguments are then assigned to username and password respectively. As before, we set other values like endpoint URL, method name, input parameters, and return type to the Call object.

```java
      // For HTTP Basic Authentication
      String username = args[0];
      String password = args[1];

      // For HTTP Basic Authentication
      // EndPoint URL for the SparePartPrice  Web Service
```

5

```
        String endpointURL =
          "http://localhost:8080/axis/services/AuthSparePartPrice";

        // Method Name to invoke for the SparePartPrice Web Service
        String methodName = "getPrice";

        // Create the Service call
        Service service = new Service();
        Call call = (Call) service.createCall();
        call.setTargetEndpointAddress(new java.net.URL(endpointURL));
        call.setOperationName(new QName("SparePartPrice", methodName));
        call.addParameter("sku", XMLType.XSD_STRING,
                        ParameterMode.PARAM_MODE_IN);
        call.setReturnType(XMLType.XSD_FLOAT);
```

Then we set the username and password by calling the setter method of the Call object.

```
        call.setUsername(username);
        call.setPassword(password);
```

Finally, we invoke the SparePartPrice service and print the return value (price) on the console window.

```
        // Setup the Parameters (the Part SKU) to be passed the
        // SparePartPrice Web Service
        Object[] params = new Object[] { "SKU-123" };

        // Invoke the SparePartPrice Web Service
        Float price = (Float) call.invoke(params);

        // Print out the result
        System.out.println("The price is $" + price.floatValue());
      } catch (Exception e) {
        System.err.println(e.toString());
      }
    }
}
```

Now compile the client and run the application:

wrox-axis> **javac wroxaxis\chapter5\BasicAuthClient.java**

wrox-axis> **java wroxaxis.chapter5.BasicAuthClient wroxuser1 password1**
The price is $10.99

wrox-axis> **java wroxaxis.chapter5.BasicAuthClient abcd abcd**
user 'abcd' not authenticated

wrox-axis> **java wroxaxis.chapter5.BasicAuthClient wroxuser2 wroxuser2**
unauthorized

From these responses we can see that "wroxuser1" can access the service, "abcd" not in the password file (users.lst) so is not authenticated, and "wroxuser2" is authenticated but not authorized to access the AuthSparePartPrice service.

The following output is the HTTP Request from the client to the Server. The HTTP header contains the field 'Authorization' with it's type as 'Basic' and username and password encoded in BASE-64 format (dG9tY2F00nRvbWNhdA==).

```
POST /axis/services/protected/SparePartPrice HTTP/1.0
Content-Length: 504
Host: localhost
Content-Type: text/xml; charset=utf-8
Authorization: Basic dG9tY2F0OnRvbWNhdA==
SOAPAction: ""

<?xml version="1.0" encoding="UTF-8"?>
<SOAP-ENV:Envelope SOAP-
ENV:encodingStyle="http://schemas.xmlsoap.org/soap/encoding/" xmlns:SOAP-
ENV="http://schemas.xmlsoap.org/soap/envelope/"
xmlns:xsd="http://www.w3.org/2001/XMLSchema"
xmlns:xsi="http://www.w3.org/2001/XMLSchema-instance" xmlns:SOAP-
ENC="http://schemas.xmlsoap.org/soap/encoding/">
 <SOAP-ENV:Body>
  <ns1:getPrice xmlns:ns1="SparePartPrice">
   <sku xsi:type="xsd:string">SKU-123</sku>
  </ns1:getPrice>
 </SOAP-ENV:Body>
</SOAP-ENV:Envelope>
```

For valid user name and password, the HTTP response will contain HTTP header and SOAP response. But if authentication is not successful, the HTTP response is a '401 Unauthorized' message.

SSL Communication

Secure Sockets Layer (SSL) is a protocol for transmitting data in a secure way by encrypting it. SSL was originally developed by Netscape has been widely used for authenticated and encrypted communication between clients and servers. The SSL protocol runs above TCP/IP and below higher-level protocols like HTTP. During the process of communication, an SSL-enabled server authenticates it to an SSL-enabled client, and allows the client to authenticate itself to the server to establish a secure connection. These authentication processes are known as server authentication (one-way) and client authentication (two-way) respectively. Cryptography is a complex subject; if you are intending to use encryption to protect sensitive data it is vital that you have a good understanding of the many issues such as key management and security architectures that are beyond the scope of this book. An excellent reference on these aspects of security is *Professional Java Security* (Wrox Press) ISBN: 1-861004-25-7

In this section, we will briefly discuss the authentication types and then write code that uses SSL with AXIS.

One-way authentication

In one-way authentication, the client application validates the server using the server certificate. The client application could be an internet browser such Internet Explorer and Netscape or a Java application. Here we use a Java program as the client application.

5

The following diagram shows the steps needed for one-way SSL transport.

Figure 2

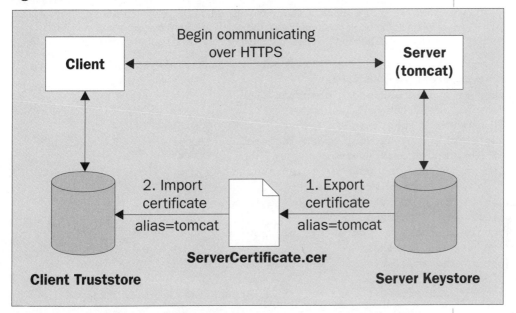

The server in this case is Tomcat and the client is the Java application that we are going to write. The server key store contains the key pairs and certificates for server authentication. Hence, we need to export the certificate and import it into a trust store at the client side. A trust store contains all the certificates that the client application can trust and allow communication.

First, we need to create server key store and client trust store following these steps:

1.   Generate key store for the Tomcat server

2.   Export server certificate

3.   Import server certificate into client trust store

We use the keytool utility that comes with the Java SDK for creating and managing keys and certificates. It generates self-signed certificate with public-private key pairs, puts them in a key store file, and protects private keys with a password. For more information on keytool refer to http://java.sun.com/j2se/1.4/docs/tooldocs/win32/keytool.html.

5

Generate Server Key Store

Go to the `%AXIS_DEVHOME%\wroxaxis\chapter5` directory and give the command shown below. You will be asked for different information pertaining to the certificate like Name, Organization, State, etc. To use the keys generated with the Tomcat setup used in the book you must name the certificate 'localhost', set the password to 'changeit'. The alias 'tomcat' is the default one used by the Tomcat server.

```
wrox-axis\wroxaxis\chapter5> keytool -v -genkey -keyalg RSA -keystore
serverkeystore -alias tomcat
Enter keystore password:  changeit
What is your first and last name?
  [Unknown]:  localhost
What is the name of your organizational unit?
  [Unknown]:  tomcat-server
What is the name of your organization?
  [Unknown]:  Wrox Press Inc.
What is the name of your City or Locality?
  [Unknown]:  Chicago
What is the name of your State or Province?
  [Unknown]:  Illinois
What is the two-letter country code for this unit?
  [Unknown]:  US
Is CN=localhost, OU=tomcat-server, O=Wrox Press Inc., L=Chicago,
ST=Illinois, C=US correct?
  [no]:  yes

Generating 1,024 bit RSA key pair and self-signed certificate
(MD5WithRSA)
        for: CN=localhost, OU=tomcat-server, O=Wrox Press Inc.,
L=Chicago, ST=Illinois, C=US
Enter key password for <tomcat>
        (RETURN if same as keystore password):
[Saving serverkeystore]
```

Export Certificate

Export the server certificate into a file named `ServerCertificate.cer`:

```
wrox-axis\wroxaxis\chapter5> keytool -v -export -rfc -file
ServerCertificate.cer  -keystore serverkeystore -alias tomcat
Enter keystore password:  Password
Certificate stored in file <ServerCertificate.cer>
```

Import Certificate

Import the above Server certificate into a client trust store called `clienttruststore` as shown below:

```
wrox-axis\wroxaxis\chapter5> keytool -v -import -file
ServerCertificate.cer
-keystore clienttruststore -storetype JCEKS -alias tomcat
```

```
Enter keystore password: changeit
Owner: CN=localhost, OU=tomcat-server, O=Wrox Press Inc., L=Chicago,
ST=Illinois, C=US
Issuer: CN=localhost, OU=tomcat-server, O=Wrox Press Inc.,
L=Chicago, ST=Illinois, C=US
Serial number: 3cb71e17
Valid from: Fri Apr 12 18:49:11 BST 2002 until: Thu Jul 11 18:49:11
BST 2002
Certificate fingerprints:
        MD5:  7C:1D:08:B0:5A:EB:AC:64:E8:67:C6:F5:21:DA:E7:9E
        SHA1:
76:70:8C:56:7C:7E:F4:53:64:AA:8E:7F:FD:ED:90:59:54:99:E5:A3
Trust this certificate? [no]: yes
Certificate was added to keystore
[Saving clienttruststore]
```

To enable SSL on Tomcat, we need to enable the SSL configuration present in
the server.xml file which can be found in the %CATALINA_HOME%\conf
directory. The entry shown below is present by default in the server.xml file
but it is commented out, so just uncomment it. This is done by removing the
comment directives '<!–' and '-->' present at the beginning and at the end of
the XML Connector element shown below.

```
...
<!-- Define an SSL HTTP/1.1 Connector on port 8443 -->

  <Connector
className="org.apache.catalina.connector.http.HttpConnector"
            port="8443" minProcessors="5" maxProcessors="75"
            enableLookups="true"
            acceptCount="10" debug="0" scheme="https"
secure="true">
    <Factory
className="org.apache.catalina.net.SSLServerSocketFactory"
            clientAuth="false" protocol="TLS"
            keystoreFile="c:/wrox-
axis/wroxaxis/chapter5/serverkeystore"
            keypass="changeit"/>
  </Connector>
...
```

In the above code listing, the attribute clientAuth contains values false for
one way authentication and true for two way authentication. You also need to
add the attribute keystoreFile, which specifies the location of the server
keystore and the attribute keypass, used to specify the keystore password.

If you restart Tomcat and navigate a suitable Internet browser to
https://localhost:8443 a secure connection to the Tomcat server should be
established.

SSL Client

Now, let us write the client application to access the same SparePartPrice
service by making a SOAP call over HTTPS.

```
package wroxaxis.chapter5;
```

```
import java.net.URL;
import org.apache.axis.client.Service;
import org.apache.axis.client.Call;
import org.apache.axis.encoding.XMLType;

import javax.xml.rpc.ParameterMode;
import javax.xml.rpc.namespace.QName;

public class SSLClient {

  public static void main(String args[]) {

    try
    {
```

The following lines set the SSL protocol handler and the SSL provider implementation class for handling SSL-based connections.

```
// Set the protocol for handling SSL based connecting
System.setProperty("java.protocol.handler.pkgs",
                   "com.sun.net.ssl.internal.www.protocol");

// Add the provider implementation class for handling SSL
//connections
java.security.Security.addProvider(new
com.sun.net.ssl.internal.ssl.Provider());
```

Then we set the property to specify the trustStore for the client application to get the server certificates to authenticate the server. The password for the key store is also specified.

```
// Set the truststore for authentication
System.setProperty("javax.net.ssl.trustStore",
                   "wroxaxis/chapter5/clienttruststore");
System.setProperty("javax.net.ssl.trustStorePassword", "changeit");
```

By default, Tomcat uses port 8443 for the HTTPS transport. Hence we will make a SOAP call over HTTPS at port 8443.

```
// EndPoint URL for the SparePartPrice  Web Service
String endpointURL =
    "https://localhost:8443/axis/services/SparePartPrice";
```

The rest of the code is defining the method name and setting the attributes for the Call class in the same way as in Chapter 2 to invoke the SparePartPrice service.

```
// Method Name to invoke for the SparePartPrice Web Service
String methodName  = "getPrice";
// Create the Service call
Service service = new Service();
Call call = (Call) service.createCall();
call.setTargetEndpointAddress(new java.net.URL(endpointURL));
call.setOperationName(new QName("SparePartPrice",methodName));

call.addParameter("sku",XMLType.XSD_STRING,ParameterMode.PARAM_MODE_IN);
call.setReturnType(XMLType.XSD_FLOAT);

//The Part SKU to be passed as parameter to the SparePartPrice
Service
Object[] params = new Object[] {"SKU-123"};

//Invoke the SparePartPrice Web Service
```

```
      Float price = (Float) call.invoke(params);

      //Print out the result
      System.out.println("The price is $" + price.floatValue());
    }
    catch (Exception e) {
      System.err.println(e.toString());
    }
  }
}
```

Compile the SSLClient.java file and run the class as shown below:

```
wrox-axis> javac wroxaxis\chapter5\SSLClient.java
wrox-axis> java wroxaxis.chapter5.SSLClient
The price is $10.99
```

Two-way authentication

In a two-way authentication, the client that is making a call to the server needs to be authenticated. Hence, the server needs to validate the client certificate. The following diagram depicts the steps involved in two-way authentication. Please note that since we are using self-signed certificates generated by the keytool utility, it is required for the server trust store to have the client certificates. If the client certificate is signed by a Certification Authority (CA) like Verisign or Thawte, then it is only required to have the CA's root certificate in the server trust store.

Figure 3

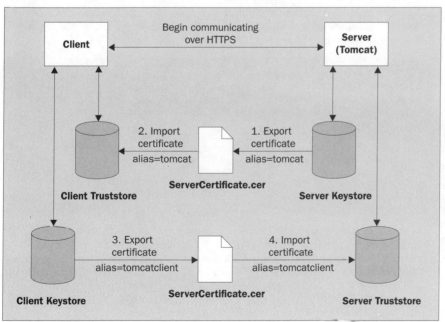

Since Steps 1 and 2 are the same as for one-way authentication we just need to complete Steps 3 and 4 to create the client certificate.

Generate Client Key Store

Follow the same procedure that we use before but this time give the key a different alias "tomcat_client" and save it to a different file:

```
wrox-axis\wroxaxis\chapter5>keytool -v -genkey -keyalg RSA -keystore
clientkeystore -alias tomcatclient
```

Export Certificate

Export the client certificate into a file named ClientCertificate.cer. The command to export the certificate from the client key store is as shown below:

```
wrox-axis\wroxaxis\chapter5> keytool -v -export -file
ClientCertificate.cer -alias tomcatclient
```

Import Certificate

Import the above server certificate into the server trustStore called servertruststore as shown below:

```
wrox-axis\wroxaxis\chapter5> keytool -v -import -file
ClientCertificate.cer -alias tomcatclient -keystore servertruststore
```

Enable SSL Two-way Authentication in Tomcat

We have discussed that the attribute clientAuth is used to specify one-way or two-way authentication with false or true values respectively. Hence, just change the value of clientAuth from false to true.

```
<!-- Define an SSL HTTP/1.1 Connector on port 8443 -->

  <Connector className="org.apache.catalina.connector.http.HttpConnector"
          port="8443" minProcessors="5" maxProcessors="75"
          enableLookups="true"
          acceptCount="10" debug="0" scheme="https" secure="true">
    <Factory className="org.apache.catalina.net.SSLServerSocketFactory"
          clientAuth="true" protocol="TLS"
          keystoreFile="c:\wrox-axis\wroxaxis\chapter5\serverkeystore"
          keypass="changeit" trustpass="changeit"/>
  </Connector>
...
```

In addition, we need to specify the location of the servertruststore. Unfortunately, there isn't a truststoreFile attribute for the <factory> element. You can get round this limitation by setting some system properties to the JVM that Tomcat runs in. The easiest way to do this is create an environment variable called CATALINA_OPTS and set it to

```
CATALINA_OPTS="-Djavax.net.ssl.trustStore= c:\wrox-
axis\wroxaxis\chapter5\
          servertruststore -
Djavax.net.ssl.trustStorePassword=changeit"
```

If you restart Tomcat and visit https://localhost:8443/ Tomcat's default page is no longer displayed, as there won't be an appropriate certificate installed in your browser for the server to authenticate.

The Client

The only addition to the client application is specifying the location of `clientkeystore`. Hence, you need to add the following lines to `SSLClient.java` file.

```
// Set the keystore for authentication
System.setProperty("javax.net.ssl.keyStore",
  "wroxaxis/chapter5/clientkeystore");
System.setProperty("javax.net.ssl.keyStorePassword",
                    "changeit");
```

Recompile `SSLClient.java` and run the class as we did for one-way authentication. You should see the same result.

Summary

In this chapter, we have covered the following AXIS features:

❑ Sending and receiving custom data types between the client application and an AXIS service

❑ Sending SOAP attachments by using the `DataHandler` class defined in the Java Activation Framework for sending MIME Messages of type `multipart/related`.

❑ Developing custom Transport Handlers and plugging them into the Axis Message Processing system

❑ Writing custom serializers and deserializers for marshaling and unmarshaling application-specific data types

❑ Finally, how to configure HTTP Basic Authentication and SSL over HTTP using AXIS

AXiS

6

Interoperability

Since their inception, web services have evolved based on open standards like SOAP, WSDL, and UDDI. One of the key advantages of this approach should be **interoperability**. Web services promise the seamless exchange of data between various implementations of the SOAP protocol for different platforms, and there has been enormous effort by both standards organizations and the developer community to achieve this. In this chapter, we'll discuss the issues involved with interoperability and the efforts made to meet these challenges. Then we will write applications to access a .NET service from an AXIS client and vice versa.

Let us start with looking into some of the interoperability issues that have come up when exchanging SOAP messages between various implementations:

❑　　　**Parameter Types** – The SOAP specification makes it optional to send type information for encoded parameters, such as the input parameters in a SOAP request or the return type of a SOAP response. Hence, if an implementation assumes that the SOAP message contains type information, it may not work with another implementation that chooses not to send that information.

❑　　　**SOAPAction** – When SOAP messages are exchanged over HTTP, the intent of the message is represented using a SOAPAction HTTP header. However, since the usage of SOAPAction is not clearly defined in the SOAP specification, some implementations use SOAPAction and some just ignore it. For example, in AXIS, it is not mandatory to have a value assigned to a SOAPAction header, but it is a mandatory requirement in Cape Clear's SOAP implementation. AXIS uses the namespace concept to dispatch the request to the correct service whereas Cape Clear uses the SOAPAction header attribute to find and invoke the service. The ambiguities in the SOAP specification and the amount of trouble they cause show just how vital it is to have strong standards.

❑　　　**Sparse Arrays** – Section 5 of the SOAP specification describes two possibilities for representing a null value in a SOAP message: either omitting the XML element representing the value, or using an XML element with the xsi:nil attribute set to true. Here lies a problem: some SOAP implementations don't use the names of method arguments, instead they use the ordinal positioning to match the elements with the real arguments. However, other implementations ignore all the arguments with null values. Hence, it is far from clear how to represent and send a so called sparse array across the wire. Sparse arrays are discussed further in Chapter 7.

❑　　　**Void Returns** – The SOAP specification is unclear how the void return type in a Remote Procedure Call (RPC) based SOAP response should be represented. A void return type can be represented using an empty SOAP envelope or an empty SOAP method response element. Unfortunately, some implementations support only one of these approaches.

- ❑ **Multiple Bodies** – The SOAP specification does not clearly state which body entry in an RPC-encoded message to take as the main one (starting point). This means that SOAP implementations may not parse a method call correctly when a SOAP message contains more than one body entry, for instance in the case of multi-ref serialization.

- ❑ **XML Schemas** – When the SOAP specification was released, there was no standard XML schema to use for describing the metadata. Hence, the SOAP specification does not mandate the use of a specific XSD schema. If the partners involved in the exchange of a SOAP message use different toolkits that use different versions of the XML schema (for example 1999 vs. 2001), then they will encounter issues while deserializing the RPC encoded parameters,

Though the above list does not address all the issues involved, it will give us a good idea of the potential interoperability problems.

Achieving Interoperability

Much of the effort in achieving interoperability came from the developer community testing various implementations and reporting the failure scenarios. One of the most active communities involved in addressing interoperability issues is the **SOAPBuilders** Yahoo! group. Some of the areas discussed by the SOAPBuilders group are the following:

- ❑ The purpose of the SOAPAction HTTP Header

- ❑ Issues related to encoding styles used to represent input parameters and return types

- ❑ The various ways of representing arrays in WSDL and SOAP messages

Apart from resolving many interoperability issues, the SOAPBuilders group also developed an interoperability test suite called Interop Lab (http://www.xmethods.net/ilab). The Interop Lab tests include a collection of simple "echo" SOAP RPC invocations, in which the client application sends a parameter of a certain data type (int, float, string, etc.) and the server simply returns a parameter of the same type and value. The client application then examines the returned value to ensure that it exactly matches with the value that it sent. This test suite addresses SOAP connectivity, serialization and deserialization.

You can look at the interoperability results of AXIS with various SOAP implementation toolkits at http://www.apache.org/~rubys/ApacheClientInterop.html. These tests are based on the test suite specified by Interop Lab.

The Web Services Interoperability Organization

Another major push towards achieving interoperability is the formation of the Web Services Interoperability Organization (WS-I) in February 2002. The home page of WS-I (http://www.ws-i.org) states that – "WS-I is an open, industry organization chartered to promote web services interoperability across platforms, operating systems, and programming languages. The organization works across the industry and standards organizations to respond to customer needs by providing guidance, best practices, and resources for developing web services solutions."

This organization is supported by over 100 companies including every major commercial player in web services, with the notable exception of Sun Microsystems. It is involved in preparing **profiles** for the interoperability tests. A profile is a named group of web service specifications at specific version levels, along with conventions about how they work together. Profiles address web services interoperability at a granular level to help users, developers, and executives making investment decisions about web services and web services products. In the first phase, WS-I is targeted to address issues related to XML Schema 1.0, SOAP 1.1, WSDL 1.1, and UDDI 2.0.

Now we've looked at some of the issues let's write some applications to demonstrate interoperability using AXIS.

Using a Microsoft .NET Service from an AXIS Client

In this section, we will write an AXIS client application to access a .NET service. If you go to http://www.xmethods.com/, you will see a list of published services. These web services are deployed using various implementations such as Apache SOAP, GLUE from The Mind Electric, .NET from Microsoft, SOAP:Lite, etc. All the services published at XMETHODS provide the WSDL interface for client applications to generate stubs (Proxy classes) that actually call the services.

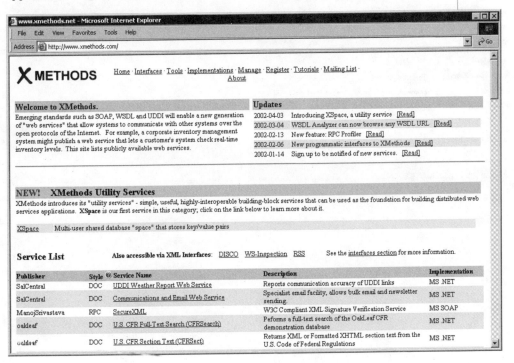

In this section, we will write a client application to access a .NET service. We will use a service called 'Daily Dilbert' published at the site http://www.esynaps.com. The steps involved are as shown below:

- ❑ Get the WSDL file for the .NET service
- ❑ Generate stub classes for an AXIS client
- ❑ Write a client application to access the service

Getting the WSDL File

Go to xmethods.com and select the service named as Daily Dilbert in the list of published services then click the link to the WSDL file as shown below:

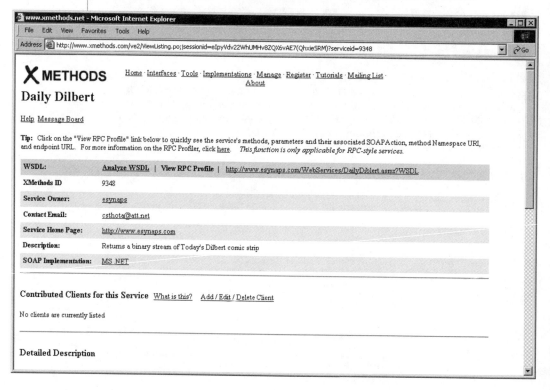

Interoperability

6

A snapshot of the WSDL file for the Daily Dilbert service is shown below:

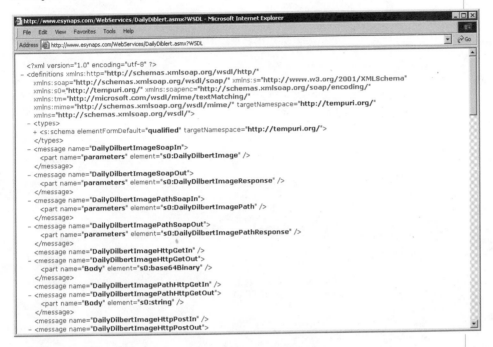

If you examine the WSDL you'll see that the Daily Dilbert service defines two operations: the first (`DailyDilbertImage`) retrieves an image (the comic strip) as a `Byte[]` data type and the second (`DailyDilbertImagePath`) returns the location of the image. We will save the byte array returned from the first method into a file. The comic strip returned to you is a GIF image, so once we save it, we should be able to view it in a web browser.

Generating Stub Classes

Now the next step is to generate stub or proxy classes. AXIS provides a utility class known as `WSDL2Java` for generating all the proxy classes from the details specified in the WSDL file.

As shown below, run the `WSDL2Java` class, passing the WSDL file. The `WSDL2Java` class generates a list of stub classes in the directory. `%AXIS_DEVHOME%/wroxaxis/chanpter6/dilbert`. Since we have already discussed the stub classes in detail in Chapter 2, we will not go into detail again. You can generate the stub classes by giving the URL for the location of the WSDL file. This can be obtained from the Dilbert Service page at the Xmethods site. The command to generate stub classes using the URL for WSDL file is shown below:

```
Wrox-axis> java org.apache.axis.wsdl.WSDL2Java -o . -p
"wroxaxis.chapter6.dilbert"
http://www.esynaps.com/WebServices/DailyDiblert.asmx?wsdl
```

Note it really is http://www.esynaps.com/WebServices/DailyDiblert.asmx?wsdl – they actually have the web service misspelled.

The above command generates the following files:

```
DailyDilbertImage.java
DailyDilbertImageResponse.java
DailyDilbertImagePath.java
DailyDilbertImagePathResponse.java
DailyDilbertSoap.java
DailyDilbertSoapStub.java
DailyDilbert.java
DialyDilbertLocator.java
```

Then compile all the above stub classes generated by the utility class WSDL2Java.

```
wrox-axis> javac wroxaxis/chapter6/dilbert/*.java
```

Writing a Client Application to Access the Service

Now, we will write an AXIS client (DilbertAXISClient.java) that uses the above stub classes to access the .NET DailyDilbert Web service.

The Java file is located at %AXIS_DEVHOME%/wroxaxis/chapter6/dilbert. Let us go through the client code:

```
package wroxaxis.chapter6.dilbert;

import java.io.*;

public class DilbertAXISClient {

  public DilbertAXISClient() {}
```

The client application uses the DailyDilbertLocator class to obtain an instance of the stub class. The DailyDilbertLocator initializes the stub class (DailyDilbertSoapStub) with the URL to the service (http://www.esynaps.com/WebServices/DailyDiblert.asmx).

```
public static void main(String args[]) throws Exception {
  DailyDilbertLocator locator = new DailyDilbertLocator();
  DailyDilbertSoapStub stub =
    (DailyDilbertSoapStub) locator.getDailyDilbertSoap();
```

By using the stub class, we invoke the service to get the location of the GIF file and print it on the console.

```
String ImagePath = (String) stub.dailyDilbertImagePath();
System.out.println(ImagePath);
```

Then we invoke the method `dailyDilbertImage()` to get the image as a byte array. We save the image to a file by opening an IO stream. If the application saves the image without any error, it returns a message indicating that the message is saved successfully.

```
Byte[] image = (Byte[]) stub.dailyDilbertImage();
File file = new File("./wroxaxis/chapter6/dilbert/dilbert.gif");
FileOutputStream os = new FileOutputStream(file);

for (int i = 0; i < image.length; i++) {
  os.write(image[i].intValue());
}
os.close();
System.out.println("Daily Dilbert Comic strip has been saved"
                 + "successfully");
  }
}
```

Compile and run the class file (`DilbertAXISClient`) as shown below:

```
wrox-axis> javac wroxaxis/chapter6/dilbert/DilbertAXISClient.java
wrox-axis> java wroxaxis.chapter6.dilbert.DilbertAXISClient
```

```
http://www.dilbert.com/comics/dilbert/archive/images/dilbert2012188820
20319.gif
 Daily Dilbert Comic strip has been saved successfully
```

Now navigate to `%AXIS_DEVHOME%/wroxaxis/chapter6/dilbert` and view `dilbert.gif` in your internet browser.

Using a GLUE Service from an AXIS Client

GLUE is a comprehensive web services platform developed in Java by The Mind Electric. It implements standards such as HTTP, SOAP, WSDL, and UDDI; it is interoperable with Microsoft .NET, IBM's Web Services Toolkit, and the Apache SOAP toolkit. For more details on GLUE, please visit http://www.themindelectric.com/glue/index.html.

In this section, we access a stock quote service deployed using the GLUE implementation. The sequence of steps remains same as in the previous case. So, go to xmethods.com and find the service named 'Delayed Quotes'. Click on the link to go to the detail section. Copy the URL to the WSDL file and generate stub classes as shown below:

```
wrox-axis> java org.apache.axis.wsdl.WSDL2Java -o . -p
"wroxaxis.chapter9.
stockquote" http://services.xmethods.net/soap/urn:xmethods-delayed-
quotes.wsdl
```

You will see a list of stub classes generated by the WSDL2Java class in the directory %AXIS_DEVHOME%/wroxaxis/chapter6/stockquote. Now let us write the AXIS client (StockQuoteAXISClient.java) to access the service. If you look at the generated stub class, it contains a getQuote() method to get the quote value of a given ticker symbol. Only the relevant portion of the stub (NetXmethodsServicesStockquoteStockQuoteBindingStub.java) is shown below. The getQuote() method takes the symbol as an object of type String and returns the stock price as a float value. The URL for the service (urn:xmethods-delayed-quotes#getQuote) is set using setSOAPActionURI() on the Call object.

```java
package wroxaxis.chapter6.stockquote;

public class NetXmethodsServicesStockquoteStockQuoteBindingStub
   extends org.apache.axis.client.Stub
     implements wroxaxis.chapter9.stockquote
       .NetXmethodsServicesStockquoteStockQuotePortType {

  public float getQuote(java.lang.String symbol)
        throws java.rmi.RemoteException {
    if (super.cachedEndpoint == null) {
      throw new org.apache.axis.NoEndPointException();
    }
    org.apache.axis.client.Call call = getCall();
    javax.xml.rpc.namespace.QName p0QName =
      new javax.xml.rpc.namespace.QName("", "symbol");
    call.addParameter(p0QName, new javax.xml.rpc.namespace.QName(
      "http://www.w3.org/2001/XMLSchema", "string"),
        javax.xml.rpc.ParameterMode.PARAM_MODE_IN);
    call.setReturnType(new javax.xml.rpc.namespace.QName(
      "http://www.w3.org/2001/XMLSchema", "float"));
    call.setUseSOAPAction(true);
    call.setSOAPActionURI("urn:xmethods-delayed-quotes#getQuote");
    call.setOperationStyle("rpc");
    call.setOperationName(new javax.xml.rpc.namespace.QName(
      "urn:xmethods-delayed-quotes", "getQuote"));

    Object resp = call.invoke(new Object[] { symbol });

    if (resp instanceof java.rmi.RemoteException) {
      throw (java.rmi.RemoteException) resp;
    } else {
      return ((Float) resp).floatValue();
    }
  }
}
```

Interoperability

6

194

Let's write an AXIS client (StockQuoteAXISClient.java) to invoke the stock quote service. The Java file is located at %AXIS_DEVHOME%/wroxaxis/chapter6/stockquote. The client application uses the service locator to bind the stub object to the service URI. Then using the stub class, we invoke the getQuote() method on the service. The return value is printed to the console.

```
package wroxaxis.chapter6.stockquote;

public class StockQuoteAXISClient {

  public static void main(String args[]) throws Exception {

    if (args.length == 0) {
      System.out.println("Usage java wroxaxis.chapter9.stockquote."
                         + "StockQuoteAXISClient <Ticker Symbol>");
      System.exit(0);
    }
    NetXmethodsServicesStockquoteStockQuoteServiceLocator locator =
      new NetXmethodsServicesStockquoteStockQuoteServiceLocator();
    NetXmethodsServicesStockquoteStockQuoteBindingStub stub =
      (NetXmethodsServicesStockquoteStockQuoteBindingStub) locator
       .getNetXmethodsServicesStockquoteStockQuotePort();
    float price = stub.getQuote(args[0]);
    System.out.println("The Trade value is: $" + price);
  }
}
```

Compile and run the client application as shown below:

> **javac wroxaxis\chapter9\stockquote\ *.java**

If you invoke the service with the ticker values IBM and SUNW, you can see the stock values of IBM and Sun Microsystems respectively:

> **java wroxaxis.chapter6.stockquote.StockQuoteAXISClient IBM**
The Trade value is: $97.25

> **java wroxaxis.chapter6.stockquote.StockQuoteAXISClient SUNW**
The Trade value is: $8.71

Using AXIS Services from .NET Clients

In this section, we'll write a .NET client application using C#. To compile and run .NET applications you will need the .NET Framework SDK, which is available from the Microsoft Developer Network downloads. Go to, http://msdn.microsoft.com/downloads then navigate to Software Development Kits | Microsoft .NET framework SDK using the left hand navigation bar.

Figure 1 shows an overview of the application that we are going to develop. The left portion under the title .NET Environment shows the classes involved at the client side. The right side under the title AXIS Environment shows the AXIS server-side message processing system. The client applications access the AXIS service to:

❑ **Get the details of a spare part for a given SKU number** – this is done by invoking the getSparePart() method, passing a String as the input parameter. The SparePartDetails service returns the spare part details in the form of a SparePartBean.

❑ **Add a new spare part to the list of existing spare parts** – the client application invokes the addSparePart() method, sending the spare part details wrapped in a SparePartBean. The service returns a String indicating the successful update to the spare part list.

Put simply, we are going to demonstrate passing information in a bean between the .NET and AXIS environments.

Luckily, we need to develop only the .NET client applications. We have already written the implementation class (SparePartService.java) for this service in Chapter 5 and deployed it with the name 'SparePartDetails'. We also wrote the SparePartBean that is required by the service.

Figure 1

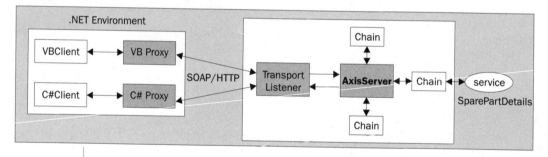

As the diagram shows, the first thing we need to do is generate the proxy classes required by the C# application to access the service. The .NET Framework comes with a utility tool called wsdl.exe, which generates the proxy classes for a given WSDL file. Hence, we just need the WSDL file for the SparePartDetails service. This can be obtained by typing the URL in the Internet browser as shown opposite. Make sure that Tomcat is running on your machine and you have the SparePartDetails service deployed on your system.

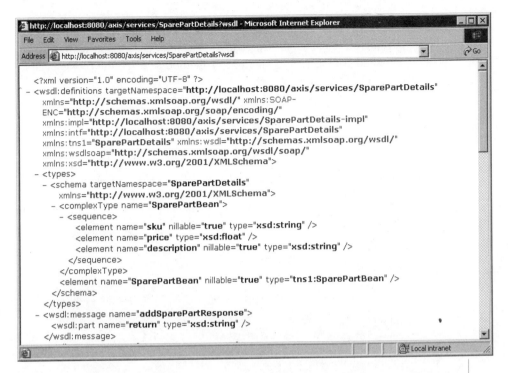

If you're using Internet Explorer select View | Source then save the file as
SparePartDetails.wsdl in the
%AXIS_DEVHOME%/wroxaxis/chapter6/dotnet directory. Let's run the
wsdl.exe to generate VB and C# proxy classes.

As shown below, by default the utility tool generates C# proxy classes. You could
generate VB proxy classes by explicitly setting the language attribute to 'VB'.

```
C:\wrox-axis\wroxaxis\Chapter6\dotnet>wsdl
SparePartDetails.wsdl
Microsoft (R) Web Services Description Language Utility
[Microsoft (R) .NET Framework, Version 1.0.3705.0]
Copyright (C) Microsoft Corporation 1998-2001. All rights
reserved.

Writing file 'C:\wrox-
axis\wroxaxis\Chapter6\dotnet\SparePartServiceService.cs'.
```

You can see that the utility-tool-generated SparePartServiceService.cs, note
that wsdl.exe appends the word Service to all the proxy classes.

Accessing an AXIS Service from a C# Client

Following is the C# proxy code. The only modification we need to make to the default generated code is to add the Main() method to make the proxy a client application.

```
using System.Diagnostics;
using System.Xml.Serialization;
using System;
using System.Web.Services.Protocols;
using System.Web.Services;
```

The [System.Web.Services.WebServiceBindingAttribute] attribute specifies the namespace and the web service. When this assembly is compiled, the .NET runtime will automatically supply the infrastructure required to make a SOAP request call.

```
[System.Web.Services.WebServiceBindingAttribute(Name=
  "SparePartDetailsSoapBinding", Namespace=
  "http://localhost:8080/
  axis/services/SparePartDetails")]
[System.Xml.Serialization.SoapIncludeAttribute(typeof(SparePartBean))]
```

The base class, System.Web.Services.Protocols.SoapHttpClientProtocol specifies that the implementation for communicating with the web services is over the HTTP protocol.

```
public class SparePartServiceService :
          System.Web.Services.Protocols.SoapHttpClientProtocol {
```

The constructor of the proxy class maintains the URL of the remote web service and stores it in the inherited Url property.

```
  [System.Diagnostics.DebuggerStepThroughAttribute()]
  public SparePartServiceService() {
    this.Url =
    "http://localhost:8080/axis/services/SparePartDetails";
  }

  [System.Diagnostics.DebuggerStepThroughAttribute()]
  [System.Web.Services.Protocols.SoapRpcMethodAttribute("",
    RequestNamespace= "http://localhost:8080/axis/services
    /SparePartDetails", ResponseNamespace=
    "http://localhost:8080/
    axis/services/SparePartDetails")]
  [return: System.Xml.Serialization.SoapElementAttribute("return")]
```

The signature of getSparePart() is the same as defined in the web service. The return type is cast to an instance of SparePartBean.

```
public SparePartBean getSparePart(string in0) {
  object[] results = this.Invoke("getSparePart", new object[] {in0});
  return ((SparePartBean)(results[0]));
}
```

By default, the wsdl.exe also generates methods to invoke the service asynchronously. The BeginInvoke() method starts an asynchronous invocation of a method on the web service and the EndInvoke() method ends the asynchronous invocation.

```
[System.Diagnostics.DebuggerStepThroughAttribute()]
public System.IAsyncResult BegingetSparePart(string in0,
  System.AsyncCallback callback, object asyncState) {
  return this.BeginInvoke("getSparePart", new object[] {
                  in0}, callback, asyncState);
}

[System.Diagnostics.DebuggerStepThroughAttribute()]
public SparePartBean EndgetSparePart(System. _
  IAsyncResult asyncResult) {
  object[] results = this.EndInvoke(asyncResult);
  return ((SparePartBean)(results[0]));
}

[System.Diagnostics.DebuggerStepThroughAttribute()]
[System.Web.Services.Protocols.SoapRpcMethodAttribute("",
  RequestNamespace= "http://localhost:8080/axis/services
  /SparePartDetails", ResponseNamespace=
  "http://localhost:8080/
  axis/services/SparePartDetails")]
[return: System.Xml.Serialization.SoapElementAttribute("return")]
```

The signature of the addSparePart() method is the same as the one defined by the web service. The invoke() method synchronously invokes a method of the web service.

```
public string addSparePart(SparePartBean in0) {
  object[] results = this.Invoke("addSparePart", new
                                  object[]{in0});

  return ((string)(results[0]));
}


[System.Diagnostics.DebuggerStepThroughAttribute()]
```

```
public System.IAsyncResult BeginaddSparePart(SparePartBean
  in0,
  System.AsyncCallback callback, object asyncState) {
  return this.BeginInvoke("addSparePart", new object[] {in0},
                          callback, asyncState);
}

[System.Diagnostics.DebuggerStepThroughAttribute()]
public string EndaddSparePart(System.IAsyncResult
                              asyncResult) {
  object[] results = this.EndInvoke(asyncResult);
  return ((string)(results[0]));
}
}
```

We need to add the main entry point for the C# proxy class. In the main method, we create a new instance of SparePartSericeService. Then we call the getSparePart() method by passing the SKU information. Then we print the details of the spare part on the console.

```
public static void Main() {
  SparePartServiceService service = new SparePartServiceService ();
  SparePartBean sparePart = service.getSparePart("SKU-112");
  Console.WriteLine("\n");
  Console.WriteLine("Printing Spare Part Details");
  Console.WriteLine("***************************");
  Console.WriteLine("SKU :"+sparePart.sku);
  Console.WriteLine("Description :"+sparePart.description);
  Console.WriteLine("Price : $"+sparePart.price);
  Console.WriteLine("\n");
```

Now we will call the method, addSparePart() to add a new spare part to the spare parts list. The SparePartBean is a bean class to capture the spare part information.

```
  Console.WriteLine("Adding new Spare Part Details");
  Console.WriteLine("****************************");
  SparePartBean newSparePart = new SparePartBean();
  newSparePart.sku = "SKU-114";
  newSparePart.description = "Air Filter";
  newSparePart.price = 22.16f;
  string response = service.addSparePart(newSparePart);
  Console.WriteLine("response :"+response);
}
}
```

Finally we have the bean class to wrap the spare-part information, which is essentially the same as a JavaBean class.

```
[System.Xml.Serialization.SoapTypeAttribute("SparePartBean",
                                "SparePartDetails")]
public class SparePartBean {

  public string sku;
  public System.Single price;
  public string description;
}
```

Now let us compile the `.cs` file and execute it. The .NET SDK provides a C# compiler called `csc.exe` that compiles a C# file in to an executable code (`.exe` file). Compile and run the proxy class as show below:

```
C:\wrox-axis\wroxaxis\chapter6\dotnet> csc SparePartServiceService.cs
Microsoft (R) Visual C# .NET Compiler version 7.00.9466
for Microsoft (R) .NET Framework version 1.0.3705
Copyright (C) Microsoft Corporation 2001. All rights reserved.
C:\wrox-axis\wroxaxis\chapter6\dotnet> SparePartServiceService

Printing Spare Part Details
***************************
SKU :sku-112
Description :Toyota Spark Plug
Price :$20

Adding Spare Part Details
*************************

response :SparePart with SKU-114 has been added successfully!!
```

You can see that the C# proxy got the spare part details from the AXIS service and displayed them on the console. Then it added a new spare-part to the spare part list. If you open the spare part list file (`sparepartlist.txt`) located in `%AXIS_DEVHOME%/wroxaxis/chapter5` you should see the entry of a new spare part with SKU-114.

Summary

In this chapter, we discussed interoperability issues, and the efforts various organizations are making to address them. We have shown examples of AXIS client applications accessing services implemented using .NET and GLUE and a .NET client application in C# that accesses a service deployed in the AXIS system.

In the next chapter we will look at some possible future directions for AXIS, including features that should be added now and other developments that might influence its future.

Axis

7

Future Directions for AXIS

The AXIS team are committed to tracking future developments in SOAP and its related protocols; one of the main reasons for creating a totally new SOAP implementation was to make this easier. After looking at what AXIS can do now, it is time to consider its future directions. While it is impossible to predict the developments in a collaborative project like AXIS, there is a published list of aims in the `requirements.html` document that can be found in the `docs` folder of the AXIS distribution, though it is not always completely up-to-date.

AXIS is still in development so it hasn't addressed all the issues yet, nor as web-services-related specifications are still in considerable flux, would this even be possible. This chapter covers some of AXIS's limitations, new topics relevant in the context of web services, and how AXIS may develop to take these into account.

XML Protocol (XMLP)

W3C is working on releasing a standardized version of the SOAP protocol known as XML protocol (XMLP). Since the W3C is using SOAP as the basis for its work, there should not be massive changes between SOAP 1.2 and XML Protocol. In addition to the SOAP specifications, XMLP will address other features like message correlation (correlating SOAP requests with the SOAP responses), encrypted message payloads, SOAP intermediaries, caching, routing, and quality of service.

W3C released a working draft of the XML Protocol Abstract Model (http://www.w3.org/TR/xmlp-am) on 9 July 2001 and a working draft for XML Protocol Usage Scenarios (http://www.w3.org/TR/xmlp-scenarios) on 17 December 2001.

Some of the message patterns addressed by XMLP are:

❑ Fire and Forget – a sender sends a message to one or more receivers. No acknowledgement or response is expected from the receiver.

❑ Request/Response – a sender sends a request message to a SOAP receiver. The receiver processes the message by invoking some business application. The response is sent back to the Sender.

❑ Remote Procedure Call – the communication between sender and receiver takes place by sending and receiving messages using the RPC mechanism.

❑ Request with Acknowledgement – a sender wishes to reliably exchange data with a receiver. But in this case, the sender wishes to be notified of the status of data delivery to the receiver. Hence the sender will be notified of the successful delivery of the message or the failure of delivery if some fault occurs.

- ❏ Request with Encrypted Payload – the sending and receiving applications agree on some encryption methodology and the payload is exchanged in encrypted form.

- ❏ Communication via Multiple Intermediaries – in this pattern, there can be one or more intermediaries between the sending and receiving applications.

- ❏ Asynchronous Messaging – a sender sends a message asynchronously to a receiver expecting some response at a later time.

XMLP addresses message identification and correlation using SOAP Headers. For example, an AXIS handler could be created that generates a unique message identifier and inserts it into a SOAP Header. The following code snippet shows a SOAP request message containing a message identifier.

```
<env:Envelope xmlns:env="http://www.w3.org/2001/12/soap-envelope">
  <env:Header>
    <n:MsgHeader xmlns:n="http://wrox.com/sparepartservice">
      <n:MessageId>
        uuid:09233523-345b-4351-b623-5dsf35sgs5d6
      </n:MessageId>
    </n:MsgHeader>
  </env:Header>
  <env:Body>
    ...
  </env:Body>
</env:Envelope>
```

The client application can then use the `<messageId>` to correlate the SOAP response message with the SOAP request.

```
<env:Envelope xmlns:env="http://www.w3.org/2001/12/soap-envelope">
  <env:Header>
    <n:MsgHeader xmlns:n="http:// wrox.com/sparepartservice ">
      <n:MessageId>
        uuid:09233523-567b-2891-b623-9dke28yod7m9</n:MessageId>
      <n:ResponseTo>
        uuid:09233523-345b-4351-b623-5dsf35sgs5d6
      </n:ResponseTo>
    </n:MsgHeader>
  </env:Header>
  <env:Body>
    ...
  </env:Body>
</env:Envelope>
```

XMLP also specifies usage scenarios for caching, routing, and tracking using Intermediaries. Caching is used to store data frequently requested by the sender (client) applications. When a client requests this data, the cache intermediary can provide data from its local cache instead of making an expensive network call to the final recipient.

XMLP is still in early stages and it will take some time for it to come out as a release candidate. But, since it is the follow up to the SOAP specification, future versions of AXIS will certainly provide support for it.

Transport Protocols

By default the current AXIS version, beta 1, only supports synchronous communication via the HTTP protocol. Later versions may support asynchronous communication by using the Java messaging service (JMS) using e-mail transfer protocols like SMTP.

For example, when using a JMS-based transport handler, the client application and the server will be interacting with the JMS server rather than talking with each other directly. At the server side, there will be a message listener that will be waiting for a message on a Queue/Topic. The client application sends the message to the Queue/Topic. Once a message arrives in a Queue/Topic, the message server notifies the listener and passes the message. The listener then passes the message to the AXIS server. The SOAP request received from the AXIS server is put back in a Queue or published to a Topic. The great advantage with these methods is that if the client or server is unavailable when a message is sent it will wait in the Queue or Topic. Chapter 5 shows an example of a JMS-based transport handler.

Security

AXIS Beta 1 has support for authentication using HTTP BASIC-AUTH and encryption with the secure socket layer protocol. Support for transport- and SOAP-based security is one of the few requirements listed as having a high priority. There are many XML standards being developed in the area of security, of which XML Signatures and the XML Key Management Specification (XKMS) are going to be most valuable from the web services point of view. Let us briefly look into these new standards.

XML Signatures

XML signatures, similar to digital signatures, are used in XML transactions to address authentication, data integrity, and non-repudiation of the data they sign. Using XML Signature, we can sign the complete XML document or a part of it. Hence, instead of signing a complete SOAP request, only the required portion would be signed with XML signature. Another valuable feature of XML Signature is that a single XML signature can sign more than one type of resource. For example, we can include character-encoded data (HTML), binary-encoded data (GIF or JPG), and obviously XML data, all in a single XML Signature. The following diagram shows the key elements of an XML Signature.

Figure 1

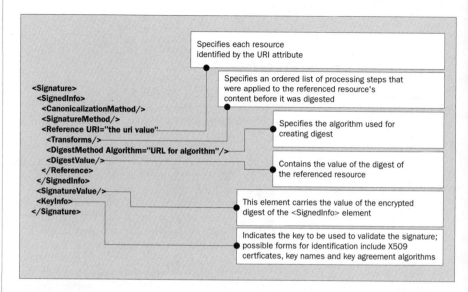

Let us briefly look at the steps involved in creating an XML Signature.

1. Identify the resources that need to be signed – this includes identifying all the resources through a Uniform Resource Identifier (URI).

2. Calculate the digest of each resource – a digest value is created for each referenced resource specified by the <Reference> element and is placed in the <DigestValue> element. The algorithm used to create the digest (for example: SHA1) is specified in <DigestMethod>.

3. Collect all the <Reference> elements – all resources and their digest values are placed within a <SignedInfo> element.

4. Sign the relevant portions of the XML document – calculate the digest of the <SignedInfo> element, sign it, and place the signature in a <SignatureValue> element.

5. Add the key information – including any X509 certificate for the sender. The certificate contains the public key needed to verify the signature. This information is enclosed in the <KeyInfo> element.

6. Finally enclose in a <Signature element> – Place the <SignedInfo>, <SignatureValue>, and <KeyInfo> elements into a <Signature> element.

A sample XML Signature is given below:

```
<Signature xmlns=http://www.w3.org/2000/09/xmldsig#">
  <SignedInfo Id="wroxAxis">
    <CanonicalizationMethod
      Algorithm="http://www.w3.org/TR/2001/REC-xml-c14n-20010315"/>
    <SignatureMethod
      Algorithm="http://www.w3.org/2000/09/xmldsig#dsa-sha1"/>
    <Reference URI="http://www.w3.org/TR/2000/REC-xhtml1-20000126/">
      <Transforms>
```

```
      <Transform
        Algorithm=
        "http://www.w3.org/TR/2001/REC-xml-c14n-20010315"/>
    </Transforms>
    <DigestMethod
        Algorithm="http://www.w3.org/2000/09/xmldsig#sha1"/>
    <DigestValue>j6lwx3rvEPO0vKtMup4NbeVu8nk=</DigestValue>
  </Reference>
 </SignedInfo>
 <SignatureValue>MC0CFFrVLtRlk=...</SignatureValue>
 <KeyInfo>
   <X509Data>
     <X509SubjectName>CN=WroxAuthor,o=Wrox Inc</X509SubjectName>
     <X509Certificate>content of the certificate</X509Certificate>
   </X509Data>
 </KeyInfo>
</Signature>
```

XML Key Management Specification (XKMS)

The XML Key Management Specification (XKMS) provides a service as an interface between an XML application and a Public Key Infrastructure (PKI). XKMS was published as a W3C Note in March 2001 by Verisign, Microsoft, and Web Methods. XKMS greatly simplifies the deployment of enterprise-strength Public Key Infrastructure (PKI) by transferring complex tasks from the client application to a third-party **Trust Service**.

XKMS has two major components: XML Key Information Service Specification (X-KISS), and XML Key Registration Service Specification (X-KRSS). X-KISS defines a protocol for a trust service to resolve public key information contained in the XML signature. X-KRSS defines a protocol for a trust service to accept registration of public key information. Once registered, the public key may be used in conjunction with other web services including X-KISS. X-KRSS supports all the functions associated with a public key lifecycle.

Since the above two standards play vital roles in web services security, AXIS should provide support for them in the future.

Java API for XML Messaging (JAXM)

In an effort support web services, Sun has released a series of Java APIs for XML

1. Java API for XML Processing (JAXP) – an API for processing XML documents

2. Java API for XML Messaging (JAXM) – Defines an API for sending SOAP messages over the internet in a standard way

3. Java API for XML Registry (JAXR) – Provides interfaces to access business registries of XML web services (UDDI registry or ebXML registry)

4. Java API for XML-based RPC (JAX-RPC) – this API is for sending SOAP method calls to remote services over the Internet and receiving the results

These APIs are collectively known as Java XML Pack (JAX Pack). AXIS already provides support for JAX-RPC and this is discussed in Appendix C. The most important of these standards in relation to AXIS is JAXM.

JAXM

In brief, the Java API for XML Messaging (JAXM) provides a standard way for Java applications to send and receive SOAP messages over the Internet from a Java platform. JAXM provides an API for developing and deploying SOAP-based applications that can be truly interoperable with applications developed on other platforms. JAXM is based on the SOAP1.1 and the SOAP with Attachments specifications.

The main difference between JAX-RPC and JAXM is that the JAX-RPC supports Remote Procedure Call (RPC)-based web services invocation whereas JAXM supports XML message-based web services invocation. JAXM supports both synchronous and asynchronous messaging.

JAXM Message Model

JAXM supports two message models: SOAP message without Attachments and SOAP message with Attachments. The JAXM API defines Java classes called SOAPMessage, SOAPPart, and SOAPEnvenlope to represent a SOAP Message, SOAP Part and SOAP Envelope. SOAPMessage is the root class for all SOAP Messages. If the SOAP message includes AttachmentPart objects, then the message is encoded as a MIME message.

Though the current version of JAXM is based on the SOAP 1.1 Message format, support for other message types is available. It is possible to plug in a new MessageFactory object for creating a SOAP Messages with additional application-specific features (for example, ebXML SOAP Message object instead of a basic SOAPMessage object). The steps listed below show the code to create an application specific SOAP Message.

```
//Get the Initial Context
InitialContext ictx = getInitialContext();

//Get the Provider Factory and a Connection
ProviderConnectionFactory connFactory =
  (ProviderConnectionFactory)ictx.lookup("WroxXML");
ProviderConnection conn = connFactory.createConnection();

// Create a MessageFactory
MessageFactory  ebxmlMsgFactory =
  connect.createMessageFactory("WroxXMLProvider");

//Create an ebXML SOAP Message
SOAPMessage message = ebxmlMsgFactory.createMessage();The
current version of JAXM also defines API for creating ebXML
SOAP Message.
```

Why AXIS should Support JAXM

Though AXIS already provides some of the same features as JAXM, it may support it because:

1. JAXM is Sun's Java-based standard API for invoking message-based web services; sooner or later all vendors that are providing SOAP implementations will start supporting it to make their implementations interoperable with other providers. Also one of the targets in the AXIS requirements document is to use standard APIs where ever possible.

2. JAXM defines a simple yet flexible API to define a SOAP Messages that can easily be extended. Hence, if in the future AXIS has to provide to support for sending XML documents to web services built on ebXML standards it would make sense to use JAXM. Similarly, if a future release of JAXM provides an API to define a SOAP Message based on the W3C XML protocol, then AXIS could use the API as the interface to talk to other Java implementations of the XML protocol.

SOAP Intermediaries

An intermediary is a SOAP processing node that sits between the service client and the service provider. It receives a SOAP message, processes it, and then forwards it to the next SOAP processing node; an intermediary may not be the final destination of the message. For instance, if the SOAP message contained information that was in a language unsuitable for the recipient you could send it via a translation service. There could even be more than one intermediary between the client and the service provider as shown below:

Figure 2

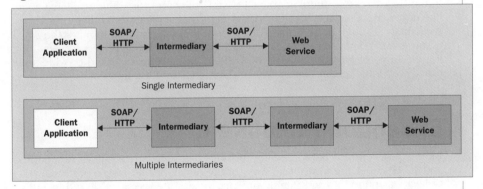

An intermediary can be placed either in the SOAP request path or in the SOAP response path as shown overleaf:

Figure 3

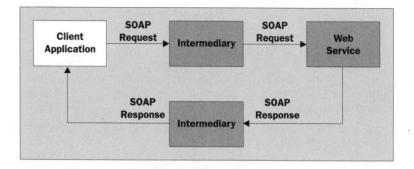

An Intermediary is required to remove the message headers that are not relevant to other nodes before forwarding the message to the next SOAP intermediary or end point. An intermediary may add new headers before forwarding the message to the next end point. If the incoming SOAP request messages are marked with the 'mustUnderstand=1' attribute, then the intermediary must be able to handle it otherwise a fault must be thrown.

In the current Beta 1 release of AXIS, there is no way of declaring intermediaries in the web service deployment descriptor (WSDD). Also AXIS does not support a mechanism for specifying which headers should be removed at the intermediary before the message is sent to the next message-processing node. Hopefully support for this will be added in future versions.

Administration and Monitoring

In the Beta 1 release, there is no GUI-based utility tool for administration activities like deploying a service, viewing all the deployed services, providing user credentials. Though there is the TCP Monitor tool (tcpmon) to monitor the SOAP requests and response messages on the wire, there is no GUI utility to view all the log messages of a particular service. AXIS, in future releases, could provide a JSP-based web interface for deploying, un-deploying, and listing services.

Exception Handling

Although the current Beta 1 version includes mapping between Java exceptions and SOAP faults, there is still no way for the developers to map a particular type of Java exception to a SOAP fault and vice versa. Later versions should include support for extensible Java exception mapping.

Versioning

Versioning of web services becomes a problem when you have to maintain different versions of a service. In a real-world scenario, an organization may create many different versions of its software services over time. Assume that we have already deployed the `SparePartPrice` as a web service, and there are three customers A, B, and C using the `SparePartPrice` who all have similar requirements. Then however a new customer, D, requires some customisation of the `SparePartPrice` so a new version is released.

However, if the service is deployed with the same name there will be a conflict between that and the existing version. One obvious solution is to use a different service name, which is not an ideal option; though if the service name includes a version number, it may be acceptable. The other workaround is to assign a different value for the SOAP Action URI. But this may fail with some implementations because some SOAP implementations use SOAP Action to locate and invoke a service. Hence there is a need to have a mechanism for maintaining different versions of the same service. Right now there is no particular standard to specifically address versioning of web services.

Providers

We discussed in the previous chapters that a Provider object is responsible for invoking the service, executing the method requested, and then placing the return value in the `MessageContext` by wrapping it with the `Message` object. We have also discussed the various providers supported by AXIS. In this section we will look at some of the providers and the support that may be provided in later versions of AXIS.

1. **BSF Provider** – the responsibility of the BSF provider is to invoke a service that is implemented using scripting languages. AXIS has still to provide a full implementation of a BSF Provider but it is a stated requirement.

2. **EJB Provider** – AXIS provides basic functionality in the EJB Provider to invoke services that are implemented as Enterprise Java Beans. The Beta version supports invoking a Stateless Session Bean but there is no support for invoking Stateful Session or Entity Beans.

3. **COM Provider** – this is for invoking services that are implemented as Microsoft COM components. There is no support for this in the current beta version but support may be provided in future versions.

4. **CORBA Provider** – the CORBA provider is responsible for invoking a service implemented as a CORBA component. This requires stubs and skeletons for the object request broker on which the CORBA component is deployed. There is no sign of a CORBA Provider and it is not listed on the current requirements list.

Support for Multidimensional and Sparse Arrays

SOAP supports using arrays in the SOAP request and response to transmit data. Currently AXIS just supports the use of simple arrays but it would be useful if it offered support for more complex structures such as multidimensional and sparse arrays.

Multidimensional Array

A multidimensional array contains more than one row and column. In this case, more than one size will appear within the size part of the `arrayType` attribute as shown below:

```
<list xsi:type="SOAP-ENC:Array" SOAP-ENC:arrayType="xsd:string[2,3]">
    <item xsi:type="xsd:String">r1c1</item>
    <item xsi:type="xsd:String">r1c2</item>
    <item xsi:type="xsd:String">r1c3</item>
    <item xsi:type="xsd:String">r2c1</item>
    <item xsi:type="xsd:String">r2c2</item>
    <item xsi:type="xsd:String">r2c3</item>
</list>
```

Sparse Array

SOAP provides support to transmit only part of an array in the SOAP message. An array is partly transmitted by specifying the required elements using SOAP-ENC:position attribute to indicate the position of the element in the array. Such an array is known as a sparse array.

A sparse array represents the array values with specified dimensions, which may or may not contain data. In sparse array format, the transmitted array contains any number of values that need not be adjacent in the array. The sparse array representation is useful for arrays where few elements are present, or where the elements present are widely separated. In the serialized form, a SOAP sparse array does not explicitly list every entry in the array and may contain any number of elements from an array, in any order. For example if we have an array containing five String elements, but only the first and third elements contain data, then the SOAP serialization for the sparse array shown below specifies only those elements using the attribute SOAP-ENC:position.

```
<list xsi:type="SOAP-ENC:Array" SOAP-ENC:arrayType="xsd:string[5]">
    <book SOAP-ENC:position="[1]">Pro. Java EAI</book>
    <book SOAP-ENC:position="[3]">Pro. Java Web Services</book>
</list>
```

The attribute 'arrayType' is composed of two distinct values: the first one, atype, is to specify the type of the elements contained in the array and the second value, asize, to specify the size of the array. An asize string contains one integer for each dimension of the array each separated with commas and enclosed in brackets. For example, an arrayType of "xsd:String[5]" contains an atype of "xsd:String" and an asize of "[5]".

A sparse array can be multidimensional as shown below. The following XML structure contains a two-dimensional array to represent a seating arrangement. Only two elements specified by their position are included in the SOAP request.

```
<seating-plan xsi:type="SOAP-ENC:Array"
              SOAP-ENC:arrayType="xsd:string[20,8]" >
  <seat SOAP-ENC:position="[12][1]">press reporter</seat>
  <seat SOAP-ENC:position="[15][2]">photographer</seat>
</seating-plan>
```

Let us look into some of the issues involved in AXIS supporting serialization of sparse arrays.

1. There is no mechanism to indicate that an array may always be sparse, never sparse, may be sparse, etc.

2. There in no mechanism to specify the semantics of omitted values. The absence of a value indicates that it is either null or some other default value. One way of indicating whether an accessor contains a null value would be to use the xsi:nil="true" attribute defined in the XML schema.

The AXIS beta version does not provide support to sparse or multidimensional arrays, but these are listed in the requirements.

Summary

In this chapter, we looked into some new topics and why they are relevant for providing support in AXIS. Since AXIS's architecture allows plugging in new Handlers, some of the features like providers for COM, BSF, etc. can be easily incorporated.

7

axis

8

Case Study

So far, we have covered short examples that demonstrate the features available in AXIS. It is time now to combine all that we have learned so far into a full-blown web services application. We shall make use of web applications and interacting web services to achieve business collaboration in a fictitious car manufacturer called UMW (**U**ltimate **M**achine from **W**rox).

We will assume that the reader is quite familiar with developing JSP-based applications and at the same time is now comfortable with the AXIS web services environment. A good reference for JSP is Wrox Press' *Professional JSP, 2nd Edition* (ISBN: 1861004958). Keeping that in mind, we will cover in detail only a particular scenario in the Case Study and the reader is free to run the entire application and delve into the source code for information about other functionality. Be assured that if you know simple RPC-based services, using custom parameter types along with WSDD details, you will understand the code with minimal effort. So, let's move on now to understanding what the application is all about.

UMW Case Study Description

Shown below, is a high-level diagram of the various organizations (**roles**) present in the Case Study.

Figure 1

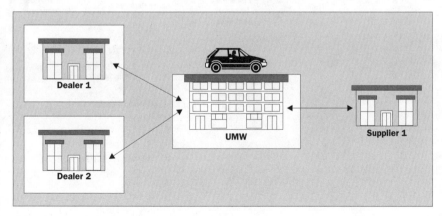

The main organization that we have is shown in the center. **UMW** is a Car Manufacturer that creates automobiles for a new age and is taking the world by storm! UMW has several Car Dealers or showrooms, where consumers go to look at its models, buy them, get the car servicing done, and so on. Two Dealers (Dealer 1 and Dealer 2) are shown in the figure. At the same time, UMW has several Suppliers that deliver spare which are used to manufacture the UMW Models. Therefore, this is a simplistic Car Manufacturer–Dealer–Supplier supply chain, which could scale to far more suppliers and complex interactions.

For the purposes of this case study, we will be concentrating on the Dealer and Manufacturer – UMW.

Current Implementation

In this section, we will describe the current systems that are present for the Dealer and the Manufacturer (henceforth referred to as UMW). For the sake of simplicity, we will assume that both the dealers in this case study, Dealer 1 and Dealer 2, have identical systems. In addition, we will focus on a few activities of the supply chain including inventory management, spare part ordering, etc.

Dealer

The current systems at the Dealer are shown below.

Figure 2

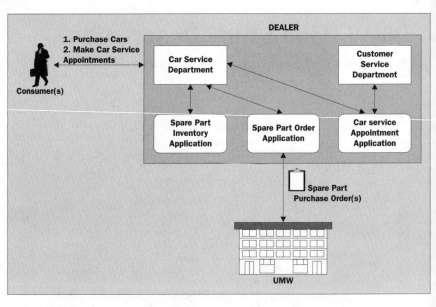

Basically they have three applications:

1. **Spare Part Inventory Application**: This application tracks the car spare part inventory available at the dealer. It can also be used to flag up when inventory levels have dipped below the minimum hold quantity. The car service department personnel use this application to track the inventory. When it is time to replenish the inventory, they **switch** to another application and the Spare Part Order application use.

2. **Spare Part Order Application**: This application as the name suggests is used to order additional quantities of the spare parts. All the spare part inventory items are ordered directly from the UMW central warehouse. The Spare Part Order Application will need to send a purchase order to the UMW site. Currently, this is sent off as an e-mail to the UMW Ordering department, which then needs to enter that information into its Ordering application.

3. **Car Service Appointment Application**: This application is used by the Customer Service Department to reserve appointments for car service. Consumers call the dealer and talk to a customer service representative over the phone to select an appointment of their choice. The customer service representative then uses this application to reserve the appointment for the consumer.

UMW

The current system at the car manufacturer, UMW is shown below.

Figure 3

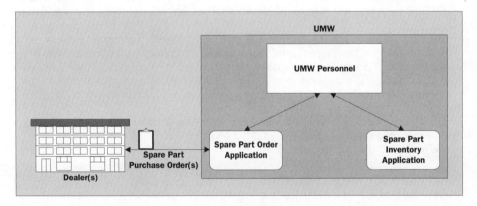

UMW has a supply chain application that encompasses the Spare Part Order and the Spare Part Inventory applications. The UMW sales personnel use the Spare Part Ordering application to record the purchase orders that they have received from the dealers in the form of an e-mail. The Spare Part Inventory Application is used to maintain a minimum inventory for the spare parts. If the spare part quantity needs to be replenished, then this application flags up a warning and the Supply Chain application then uses an ordering application that places the order to the spare part suppliers. To keep this case study simple, we are not showing this aspect of the application. But at the same time, you should be able to see that a spare part purchase order from the dealer could in turn trigger off a chain of orders, which finally culminates into a purchase order at the end of the supply chain – the manufacturer of the spare part.

Moving Forward

Now that we have described the existing systems at the dealer and UMW, it will be easy for you to notice that there are several inefficiencies in the whole process of Spare Part Ordering. The team that is allocated the task of investigating these issues might identify the following points:

1. The current mechanism of using e-mail to send purchase orders from the Dealer to UMW definitely needed an overhaul. The process not only introduced errors in the sales order entries but also consumed time of the personnel to process the e-mail requests. We could go a step further, by writing business logic to automatically generate a purchase order if the inventory of a part fell below a certain minimum level. This would help the organization to maintain optimum levels of inventory at any given time, thereby translating into tremendous cost savings.

2. The Spare Part Inventory application needed to be available to different applications internally. This would make it easy for the dealers Spare Part Ordering Application to integrate a current snapshot of the inventory into its view. This would make the process of ordering spare parts easier since you would not have to switch between the ordering and inventory applications.

3. Car Service Reservation needed to be done centrally. Currently the consumer must look up the dealer locations from the UMW web site before calling the individual dealers to make a reservation. This consumes a lot of time and there is a definite need to centrally automate the reservation process so that all the consumer needs to do is look at available appointments at different dealers and make the reservation electronically. The reservation would then be electronically sent to the dealer's car service appointment application.

The IT team were able to explore any new technologies that would help in demonstrating a prototype to the management. Simplicity and open-standards were one of the key decision making factors. It wasn't very difficult for them to decide that using web services would probably give them an opportunity to demonstrate a quick prototype and guarantee openstandards, low cost, etc.

The IT team came up with the following high-level architecture that shows the different web services interfaces that they will be building to reduce the inefficiencies that we just described.

8

Figure 4

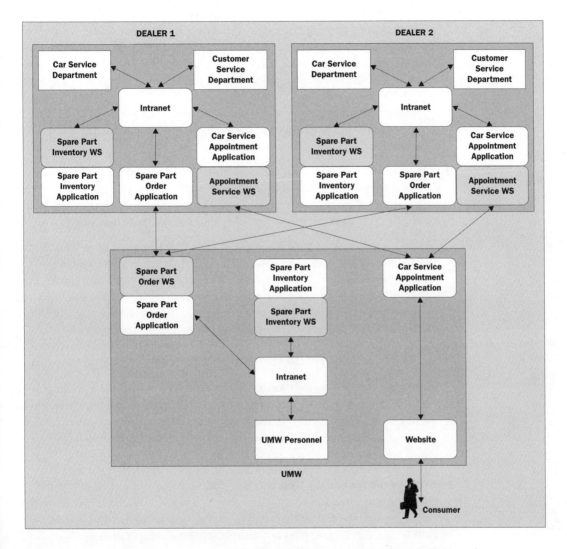

Let us concentrate first on the Dealer Application. All departments at the dealer location will use an intranet application to get access to the different applications. The Intranet will be responsible for communicating to the applications and presenting aggregated views from different applications as necessary. The applications that are shown are the same as we saw previously. You will find two web services:

- **Spare Part Inventory Web Service**: This web service will expose the Spare Part Inventory application. It is an internal web service. By providing a web service interface, it will be easier for the inventory information to be integrated into any application provided over the intranet. In the future, to provide increased supply chain visibility, it would be perfectly valid to make this an external web service too, so that UMW or other spare part providers can look at the current inventory status at the dealer.

  The Web Service interface is very simple. Given a unique part number, it will return the Inventory information for that part: the current quantity on hand, the reorder Level, minimum quantity to reorder, etc.

- **Appointment Web Service**: This web service will expose the Car Service Appointment application. It is an external web service. The UMW Car Service Appointment Application will invoke the appointment web service across the Internet. This web service basically exposes two kinds of functions :

- Provide current list of available appointments: When a consumer logs on to the UMW web site, they are presented with a list of dealer locations that are accepting online reservation requests. Once they select a particular dealer, the UMW Car Service Appointment Application will make a call to that dealer's appointment web service to retrieve the current list of available appointments. This list of available appointments will be shown to the consumer.

On the UMW side, we have the following Web Services:

- Provide a mechanism to reserve a particular appointment: The consumer will choose the particular appointment they are interested in and click a button to reserve the appointment. This will make the UMW Car Service Appointment application to make another web service call to the dealer's Appointment Web Service to reserve the appointment.

- **Spare Part Inventory Web Service**: This is similar in functionality to the dealer's Spare Part Inventory. Of course, it is very likely that in a real scenario, there would be different back-end inventory systems at the dealer(s) and UMW, but for the purposes of this case study, we will assume that the implementations are identical.

- **Spare Part Order Web Service**: This web service is used to interface with the Ordering Application at the dealer end. We discussed previously that whenever a dealer had to send a spare part order over to UMW, they did that by e-mail. The UMW Spare Part Order web service now eliminates this. You will notice in the diagram that the Spare Part Ordering Application on the dealer end makes the web service call to the UMW Spare Ordering web service. This web service is then responsible for entering the purchase order information into the UMW Ordering Application system.

UMW Application Functionality

To help understand the later parts of the chapter, where we will be covering the code in brief, it is important to list the applications developed in this chapter.

Dealer Application

The Dealer application comprises the following components:

1. **Dealer Applications (Spare Part Inventory, Spare Part Ordering, Car Service Appointment):** Since we want to keep the case study simple, we will basically design a simple database schema that will capture the essence of these applications. We will develop Java Data Access and Business classes, which will encompass the functionality of the respective applications.

2. **Dealer Intranet Web Site**: The personnel use this web site to interact with the above applications. The web site will have the following functionality:

- Order spare parts by communicating with the UMW Spare Part Ordering Web Service.

- View the purchase orders that were sent to UMW.

- View the Spare Part catalog and the current inventory levels. The internal Spare Part Inventory web service provides the current inventory levels.

- View the current car service reservations.

3. **Spare Part Inventory Web Service**: This internal web service will expose the Spare Part Inventory functionality.

4. **Appointment Web Service**: This external web service will provide an interface to the Car Service Appointment Application.

We will also assume that both the dealers in our case study have identical systems.

UMW Application

The UMW application comprises the following components:

1. **UMW Applications (Spare Part Inventory, Car Service Appointment):** Since we want to keep the case study simple, we will basically design a simple database schema that will capture the essence of these applications. We will develop data access and business classes in Java which will encompass the functionality of the respective applications.

2. **UMW Intranet Web Site**: The personnel use the intranet to interact with the above applications. We understand that there should be two web sites: an intranet and an external web site that will be used by the consumers to make car service appointments. However to keep things simple, we will push that external web site functionality into the intranet itself. It should not be much of an effort to move that functionality to another site if needed. The intranet will have the following functionality:

- View the Purchase Orders that were sent by the Dealers.

- View the Spare Part catalog and the current inventory levels. The internal Spare Part Inventory web service provides the current inventory levels.

- Allow the consumer to make their car service appointments.

1. **Spare Part Inventory Web Service**: This internal web service will expose the Spare Part Inventory functionality.

2. **Spare Part Order Web Service**: This web service will provide an interface to the UMW Spare Part Order Application. It will receive the purchase orders from the dealers and pass them on to the Spare Part Ordering Application. The Ordering Application will then log them into the database as sales orders.

Case Study Development

Both Dealer 1 and Dealer 2 applications and the UMW application are downloadable from the book web site. They are fully functional as described above. Detailed instructions for setting up the applications are provided later in this chapter. Since we cannot get into the details of all of the above functionality, we will do our best to describe as much is possible with the current context. We will assume a fair knowledge of AXIS and JSP-based web sites from the reader and will present the required source code to help understand the whole case study application.

Design

In this section, we will go through the database design for both the dealer application and the UMW application. The database design will provide enough information to help understand how the data access and business classes can be structured to provide the required functionality.

Once we have covered the database design, we will cover how the Java classes are structured to achieve the desired functionality. Finally, we will trace through the source code in detail for the Spare Part Inventory web service and the supporting Java classes. Since we follow the same code pattern for developing the other Web Services, you should have enough information on how the other web services are structured.

Database Design

Let us first go through the DEALER database schema shown below:

Figure 5

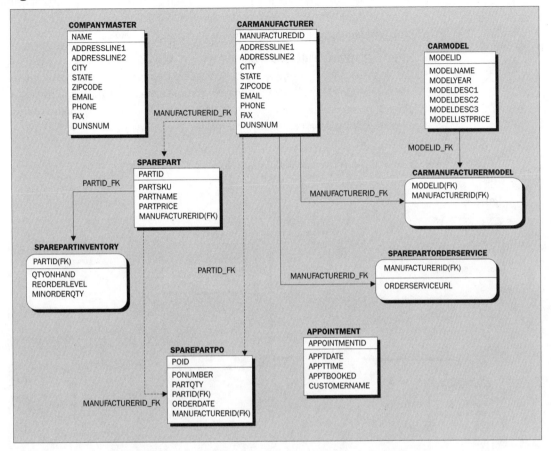

❑ COMPANYMASTER: **This table contains the DEALER information like name,** contact details and the dealer's DUNS number that will identify it to the Manufacturer (UMW), when it places the order.

❑ **CARMANUFACTURER**: This table contains details about the car manufacturer (in our case study here, there is only one manufacturer, UMW).

❑ **CARMODEL** and **CARMANUFACTURERMODEL**: The CARMODEL table contains a list of the current models offered by this dealer. The CARMANUFACTURERMODEL is a join that links the CARMODEL to the CARMANUFACTURER.

❑ **SPAREPART**: This table contains a master list of the spare parts in the dealers system. It references the MANUFACTURERID.

❑ **SPAREPARTINVENTORY**: This table contains information on the current inventory levels for the particular spare part.

❑ **SPAREPARTPO**: This table contains a list of the purchase orders that are sent out by the Spare Part Ordering Application.

❑ **SPAREPARTORDERSERVICE**: The Spare Part Ordering application invokes the UMW Spare Part Order web service to send the purchase order. This table contains the UMW Spare Part Order Service URL for example, http://www.umw.com:7001/axis/SparePartOrderWebService.

❑ **APPOINTMENT**: This table contains a list of the car service appointments. If the APPTBOOKED column is 'N', it means that the appointment is available and can be reserved. If APPTBOOKED is 'Y', then it makes that the appointment is already reserved and the CUSTOMERNAME field will contain the name of the customer, who reserved the appointment.

Let us now look at the UMW database schema shown below:

Figure 6

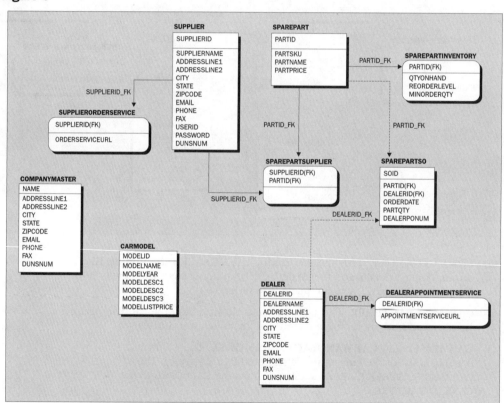

The following tables are similar to the Dealer database: CARMODEL, COMPANYMASTER, SPAREPART, SPAREPARTINVENTORY. The remaining tables are explained below:

- **SUPPLIER, SPAREPARTSUPPLIER,** and **SUPPLIERORDERSERVICE**: The SUPPLIER table contains a list of all the suppliers that UMW deals with. The SPAREPARTSUPPLIER links the SPAREPART to the SUPPLIER, so that we can track things like which supplier provides spare parts. The SUPPLIERORDERSERVICE contains the URL to the Order web service of the Supplier. Since we are not demonstrating or coding for this aspect of the functionality, it will not have any data. But since we have captured the database schema, it should be easy to build upon this.

- **DEALER** and **DEALERAPPOINTMENTSERVICE**: The DEALER table contains a list of all the dealers that UMW deals with and their information. The DEALERAPPOINTMENTSERVICE contains the Dealer Appointment web service URL.

- **SPAREPARTSO**: This table contains the sales order information that references the purchase orders that were sent to the UMW Spare Part Ordering Web Service by the dealer.

Dealer Java classes

The Dealer Application Java classes are shown below. The same pattern is followed in developing the classes for UMW also.

The **entity** classes are basically simple Java Beans that wrap a particular table in the database. There is an entity class for every database table.

The **dao** classes encapsulate the JDBC calls that are responsible for interacting with the database, finding unique records, getting a list of them, etc.

The Business Classes (**bo**) provide a façade to the data access classes. It is the façade class that we will expose as a web service.

Figure 7

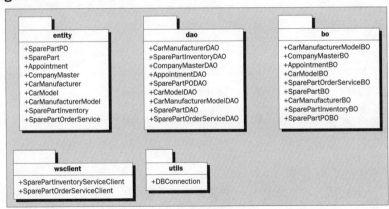

The **wsclient** package contains two AXIS web service clients: the SparePartInventoryServiceClient, which is responsible for invoking the internal Spare Part Inventory Web Service, and the SparePartOrderServiceClient, which invokes the UMW Spare Part Order web service.

Finally, the **utils** package encapsulates the details of getting the java.sql.Connection object.

Spare Part Inventory Application and Web Service

Let us look at the UML Sequence Diagram of getting Spare Part Inventory Information. From the above class structure, you will know that we are essentially dealing with 3 types of classes, the Business class, the DAO class, and the Entity class. So, for the Spare Part Inventory functionality, we are interested in the following three classes: SparePartInventoryBO, SparePartInventoryDAO, and SparePartInventory. Show, below is a sequence diagram that traces the getInventoryDetails() method of the SparePartInventoryBO class. This method takes a unique partId and returns the SparePartInventory entity object.

Figure 8

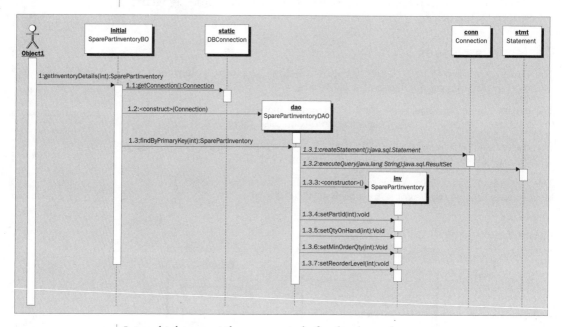

Let us look now at the source code for the three classes:

The entity class contains get and set methods for the Spare Part Inventory Information.

SparePartInventory.java

```
package com.dealer1.entity;
public class SparePartInventory implements java.io.Serializable {

    int partId;
    int qtyOnHand;
    int reorderLevel;
    int minOrderQty;


    public SparePartInventory() {}
```

```java
public int getMinOrderQty() {
  return minOrderQty;
}

public void setMinOrderQty(int minOrderQty) {
  this.minOrderQty = minOrderQty;
}

public int getPartId() {
  return partId;
}

public void setPartId(int partId) {
  this.partId = partId;
}

public int getQtyOnHand() {
  return qtyOnHand;
}

public void setQtyOnHand(int qtyOnHand) {
  this.qtyOnHand = qtyOnHand;
}

public int getReorderLevel() {
  return reorderLevel;
}

public void setReorderLevel(int reorderLevel) {
  this.reorderLevel = reorderLevel;
}

}
```

A DAO class, `SparePartInventoryDAO.java`, is shown below. The DAO class is responsible for communicating with the database, executing the SQL query, and returning the results.

SparePartInventoryDAO.java

```java
package com.dealer1.dao;

import java.util.*;
import java.sql.*;
import com.dealer1.entity.*;
import com.dealer1.utils.*;
```

```
public class SparePartInventoryDAO {
  private Connection conn;
```

The constructor is passed a `java.sql.Connection` object that will hold a connection to the **dealer1** database.

```
public SparePartInventoryDAO(Connection conn) {
  this.conn = conn;
}
```

The `findAll()` method is used to retrieve the inventory information for all the spare parts in the database. It returns an `ArrayList`, which contains a list of `SparePartInventory` (entity) objects.

```
public ArrayList findAll() throws Exception {
  ArrayList invList = new ArrayList();
  Statement stmt = null;
  ResultSet rs = null;
  String SQL = "SELECT * FROM SPAREPARTINVENTORY";
  try {
```

The next couple of statements use the `java.sql.Connection` object that was passed as a parameter to the constructor to create the `java.sql.Statement` object and retrieve the `java.sql.ResultSet` object that was simply a SELECT of all the records present in the SPAREPARTINVENTORY table.

```
    stmt = conn.createStatement();
    rs = stmt.executeQuery(SQL);
    while (rs.next()) {
```

For each record found, we create an instance of the entity object, in this case the `SparePartInventory` class. We use the setter methods for the `SparePartInventory` class and add this instance to `invList`, which is a `java.util.ArrayList` object.

```
      SparePartInventory inv = new SparePartInventory();
      inv.setPartId(rs.getInt("PARTID"));
      inv.setQtyOnHand(rs.getInt("QTYONHAND"));
      inv.setReorderLevel(rs.getInt("REORDERLEVEL"));
      inv.setMinOrderQty(rs.getInt("MINORDERQTY"));
      invList.add(inv);
    }
```

Finally, we return the `invList` object.

```
  return invList;
  }
  catch (Exception e) {
      throw e;
```

```
    }
    finally {
      try {
        if (rs != null) rs.close();
        if (stmt != null) stmt.close();
      }
      catch (Exception e) {
          throw e;
      }
    }
  }
}
```

The findByPrimaryKey() method is used to retrieve the inventory information for a particular partId. It returns a SparePartInventory **(entity)** instance.

```
public SparePartInventory findByPrimaryKey(int partId)
  throws Exception {
    SparePartInventory inv = null;
    Statement stmt = null;
    ResultSet rs = null;
    StringBuffer sql = new StringBuffer();
    sql.append("SELECT * FROM SPAREPARTINVENTORY where PARTID=");
    sql.append(String.valueOf(partId));
    try {
      stmt = conn.createStatement();
      rs = stmt.executeQuery(sql.toString());
      if (rs.next()) {
        inv = new SparePartInventory();
        inv.setPartId(rs.getInt("PARTID"));
        inv.setQtyOnHand(rs.getInt("QTYONHAND"));
        inv.setReorderLevel(rs.getInt("REORDERLEVEL"));
        inv.setMinOrderQty(rs.getInt("MINORDERQTY"));
        return inv;
      }
      else {
          throw new Exception("SPAREPART INVENTORY RECORD IS NOT"
                              + "PRESENT IN DATABASE");
      }
    }
    catch (Exception e) {
        throw e;
    }
    finally {
      try {
        if (rs != null) rs.close();
        if (stmt != null) stmt.close();
      }
```

```
            catch (Exception e) {
                throw e;
            }
        }
    }
}
```

The Business class is shown below. The business class is essentially a **façade** to
the DAO classes. Each of the business class methods uses an appropriate DAO
class to retrieve the information. If you recollect, each of the DAO classes has a
constructor that takes the `java.sql.Connection` object as a parameter. This is
an important parameter as it helps to identity the connection to the correct
database. In order not to clutter up the code inside of the Business classes with
loading of JDBC classes, etc., we have decided to write a separate utility class
called the `com.dealer1.utils.DBConnection` class as shown below:

DBConnection.java

This class has a static method named `getConnection()` that will return an
instance of the `java.sql.Connection` object.

```
package com.dealer1.utils;

import java.util.*;
import java.io.*;
import java.sql.*;

public class DBConnection {

    private Connection conn = null;

    /** Creates new DBConnection */
    public DBConnection() throws Exception {}

    public static Connection getConnection() throws Exception {
```

This case study uses the MySQL database. The statements shown below load the
MySQL JDBC Driver. It then sets up the correct **Database URL** for **dealer1** database
and MySQL database **username/password** and calls the `getConnection()`
method on the `java.sql.DriverManager` class to get the connection.

```
        Class.forName("org.gjt.mm.mysql.Driver");

        String DBURL    = "jdbc:mysql://localhost:3306/dealer1";
        String UserName = "rirani";
        String Password = "rirani";

        return DriverManager.getConnection(DBURL, UserName, Password);
    }
}
```

You should change the username/password to reflect the values for your database installation. Even if you prefer to use a database other than MySQL, you should be able to change the database URL and username/password to the appropriate values for your database type and still get the java.sql.Connection object.

SparePartInventoryBO.java

```
package com.dealer1.bo;
import java.util.*;
import java.sql.*;
import com.dealer1.dao.SparePartInventoryDAO;
import com.dealer1.entity.SparePartInventory;
import com.dealer1.utils.DBConnection;

public class SparePartInventoryBO {

  public SparePartInventoryBO() {
  }
```

The findAll() method invokes the SparePartInventoryDAO class to retrieve the ArrayList containing the SparePartInventory(**entity**) instances.

```
public ArrayList findAll() throws Exception {
  connection conn = null;
    try {
```

This is the static method call to the DBConnection object that we saw above. It will return the java.sql.Connection object for the **dealer1** database. Then we create an instance of the SparePartInventoryDAO class and pass this Connection object as a parameter to its constructor.

```
      conn = DBConnection.getConnection();

      SparePartInventoryDAO dao = new SparePartInventoryDAO(conn);
```

Finally we invoke the findAll() method on the SparePartInventoryDAO class instance, which will return a java.util.ArrayList of SparePartInventory entity objects.

```
      return dao.findAll();
    }
    catch (Exception e) {
      throw e;
    }
    finally {
      try {
        if (conn != null) conn.close();
      }
      catch (Exception e) {
```

```
        throw e;
      }
    }
  }
```

The getInventoryDetails() method calls the findByPrimaryKey() method of the SparePartInventoryDAO class. It returns an instance of the SparePartInventory (**entity**) class.

```
public SparePartInventory getInventoryDetails(int partId)
      throws Exception {
  Connection conn = null;
  try {
    conn = DBConnection.getConnection();
    SparePartInventoryDAO dao = new SparePartInventoryDAO(conn);
    return dao.findByPrimaryKey(partId);
  }
  catch (Exception e) {
    throw e;
  }
  finally {
    try {
      if (conn != null) conn.close();
    }
    catch (Exception e) {
      throw e;
    }
  }
}
```

To expose the SparePartInventoryBO as a web service, what we really need to do is expose certain (not necessarily all) functionality of the Business Java class. Such a design helps the development team to introduce new data access or persistence mechanisms in the DAO and entity classes respectively, without affecting the interface that the clients will be invoking.

We will expose the findAll() method and the getInventoryDetails() method of the SparePartInventoryBO class. The AXIS WSDD for this is shown below. It should be pretty easy to understand it.

SparePartInventoryService.wsdd

```
<deployment name="SparePartInventoryService"
        xmlns="http://xml.apache.org/axis/wsdd/"
        xmlns:java="http://xml.apache.org/axis/wsdd/providers/java"
        xmlns:xsi="http://www.w3.org/2000/10/XMLSchema-instance">
  <service name="SparePartInventoryService" provider="java:RPC">
    <parameter name="className"
```

```
                value="com.dealer1.bo.SparePartInventoryBO"/>
    <parameter name="allowedMethods"
                value="getInventoryDetails findAll"/>
    <beanMapping qname="myNS:SparePartInventory"
                xmlns:myNS="SparePartInventoryService"
    languageSpecificType="java:com.dealer1.entity.SparePartInventory"/>
    </service>
</deployment>
```

Finally, to complete the cycle, here is the Java class that accesses the
SparePartInventoryService. For instructional purposes, we have shown a
sample invocation in the main() method. Note that this is the same class that will
be used by the Dealer Intranet Application. The client code shown below is almost
identical to the AXIS client code that we have seen so far in the book.

SparePartInventoryServiceClient.java

```java
package com.dealer1.wsclient;
import java.net.URL;
import org.apache.axis.client.Service;
import org.apache.axis.client.Call;
import org.apache.axis.encoding.XMLType;

import javax.xml.rpc.ParameterMode;
import javax.xml.rpc.namespace.QName;
import org.apache.axis.encoding.ser.BeanSerializerFactory;
import org.apache.axis.encoding.ser.BeanDeserializerFactory;

import com.dealer1.entity.SparePartInventory;

public class SparePartInventoryServiceClient {

    public SparePartInventoryServiceClient() {
    }

    public SparePartInventory getInventoryDetails(int partId)
        throws Exception {
        try {
```

The SparePartInventoryService URL for Dealer 1 is set below. Note that if
you decide to deploy these services on a separate machine, you will have to
change its value accordingly.

```java
        String endpointURL = "http://localhost:5080/"
                    + "dealer1/services/SparePartInventoryService";
        String methodName  = "getInventoryDetails";

        // Create the Service call
```

```
        Service service = new Service();
        Call call = (Call) service.createCall();
        call.setTargetEndpointAddress(new java.net.URL(endpointURL));
        call.setOperationName(new QName("SparePartInventoryService",
                                    methodName));
        call.addParameter("partid",XMLType.XSD_INT,
                        ParameterMode.PARAM_MODE_IN);

        QName qname = new QName("SparePartInventoryService",
                            "SparePartInventory");
        Class cls = com.dealer1.entity.SparePartInventory.class;
        call.registerTypeMapping(cls, qname,
                                BeanSerializerFactory.class,
                                BeanDeserializerFactory.class);
        call.setReturnType(qname);

        //Integer partId = new Integer(partId);
        Object[] params = new Object[] { new Integer(partId) };

        //Invoke the SparePartPrice Web Service
        SparePartInventory InvBean =
          (SparePartInventory) call.invoke(params);
        return InvBean;

    }
    catch (Exception e) {
      throw e;
    }
}
```

```
public static void main(String[] args) throws Exception {
    SparePartInventoryServiceClient client =
      new SparePartInventoryServiceClient();
    SparePartInventory inv = client.getInventoryDetails(1);
    System.out.println(inv.getPartId() + "-" + inv.getQtyOnHand());
}
}
```

Case Study Application Setup

In this section, we will go through the details of setting up the entire application. We will first identify the software that you will need to run the application.

Software Requirements

We will assume that you already have a working installation of Apache AXIS. We need the following software in addition to that:

❑ **MySQL Database version 3.23.**
The opensource MySQL Database is downloadable from
http://www.mysql.org/downloads/mysql-3.23.html. Install the program in
`<root-dir>\mysql` directory if you have not installed it already. You will
also need the JDBC Driver for MySQL (`mm.mysql-2.0.4-bin.jar`). This file
is packaged with the source code distribution for this chapter.

Source Code structure

The entire application has been packaged for you so that you can run the case
study with minimum of set-up. Shown below is the directory structure for
DEALER1:

```
%AXIS_DEVHOME%\
        chapter8\
                dealer1\
                        AppointmentServiceDeploy.wsdd
                        dealer-DDL.sql    [DEALER DATABASE DDL]
                        dealer1-DML.sql [DEALER1 DATABASE DML]
                        InventoryServiceDeploy.wsdd

                        src\com\dealer1\
                                bo\*.java [BUSINESS(BO) CLASSES]
                                dao\*.java [DAO CLASSES]
                                entity\*.java [ENTITY CLASSES]
                                utils\DBConnection.java
                                wsclient\
                                SparePartOrderServiceClient.java
                                wsclient\
                                SparePartInventoryServiceClient.java
                        \Dealer1\*.jsp [WEBSITE Files]
                        \images\*.gif/*.jpg
                        \WEB-INF\
                                perms.lst
                                server-config.wsdd
                                users.lst
                                web.xml
                                \classes\
                                        com\dealer1\bo\*.class
                                        com\dealer1\dao\*.class
                                        com\dealer1\entity\*.class
                                        com\dealer1\utils\*.class
```

```
                           com\dealer1\wsclient\*.class
                           \lib\  [CONTAINS AXIS JARS]
                                  axis.jar
                                  clutil.jar
                                  commons-logging.jar
                                  log4j.jar
                                  tools.jar
                                  tt-bytecode.jar
                                  wsdl4j.jar
```

In the `dealer1` directory, we have the DDL and DML files that will be used to create the database for DEALER1. We also have the `AppointmentServiceDeploy.wsdd` and `SparePartInventoryServiceDeploy.wsdd`, which are used to deploy the web services using the `Admin` utility of AXIS. However, we have already packaged a `server-config.wsdd` file for you so that you have these web services already configured in it. So, unless you decide to change the package structure, etc. you do not need to deploy these services in AXIS. We have the source files that are appropriately present under the `com.dealer.*` packages.

The intranet web site for Dealer 1 is present in the `/dealer1/` directory. This follows the normal J2EE Web Application structure with `WEB-INF` and the respective classes and lib directory under it. The lib directory contains all the necessary AXIS JAR files from the current AXIS distribution that you have on your machine. The classes directory will basically contains the `.class` files compiled from the sources present in the `src` directory.

For **DEALER2**, we have an identical source structure except that we now have a `/dealer2/` directory instead of `/dealer1/` and ofcourse appropriate `dealer2-DML.sql` file that is used to populate the Dealer2 database.

Similarly, the source directory structure for **UMW** is shown below:

```
%AXIS_DEVHOME%\
        chapter8\
                umw\
                        SparePartOrderServiceDeploy.wsdd
                        umw-DDL.sql  [UMW DATABASE DDL]
                        umw-DML.sql  [UMW DATABASE DML]
                        InventoryServiceDeploy.wsdd

                        src\com\umw\
                                bo\*.java [BUSINESS(BO) CLASSES]
                                dao\*.java [DAO CLASSES]
                                entity\*.java [ENTITY CLASSES]
                                utils\DBConnection.java
                                wsclient\AppointmentServiceClient.java
                                wsclient\SparePartInventoryServiceClient.java
```

```
                \UMW\*.jsp [WEBSITE Files]
                     \images\*.gif/*.jpg
                     \WEB-INF\
                             perms.lst
                             server-config.wsdd
                             users.lst
                             web.xml
                             \classes\
                                 com\umw\bo\*.class
                                 com\umw\dao\*.class
                                 com\umw\entity\*.class
                                 com\umw\utils\*.class
                                 com\umw\wsclient\*.class
                             \lib\  [CONTAINS AXIS JARS]
                                 axis.jar
                                 clutil.jar
                                 commons-logging.jar
                                 log4j.jar
                                 tools.jar
                                 tt-bytecode.jar
                                 wsdl4j.jar
```

So, at this stage we will assume that you have the got the above source directories for Dealer1, Dealer2 and UMW. You should have a directory structure on your drive, which looks like this:

```
%AXIS_DEVHOME%\
        chapter8\
                dealer1\...
                dealer2\...
                umw\...
```

Let us now move on to setting up the application. We will tackle this step-by-step beginning with the steps for Dealer1, then Dealer2, and finally UMW. Please make sure that you follow the instructions carefully, since our goal is to run three different systems on a single machine.

Tomcat Setup

First, we need to make sure that your Tomcat instance is set up correctly to run three server instances. We have provided a server.xml file in the %AXIS_DEVHOME%\chapter8 directory, that correctly sets up these three server instances for you. What you will need to do is copy this file to the %CATALINA_HOME%\conf directory. Make sure that you save your original server.xml file and replace it with this one. This server.xml file will setup the following three contexts for you:

Dealer1 : http://localhost:5080/Dealer1
Dealer2 : http://localhost:6080/Dealer2

UMW : `http://localhost:7080/UMW`

Then copy the MySQL JDBC Driver file, `mm.mysql-2.0.4-bin.jar` from the `%AXIS_DEVHOME%\chapter8` directory into the `%CATALINA_HOME%\common\lib` directory, so that it is available to all the contexts defined above.

Dealer 1 Setup

In the Dealer1 setup, we need to create the database for Dealer1 and finally copy the distribution for Dealer1 that we discussed in the previous section.

Create Database

1. Make sure that an instance of MySQL Server is running.

2. We have provided a script that will automatically set up the MySQL databases for this example. You will need to navigate to the `/dealer1/` folder and enter the following command. Use the **mysql** command as follows to create the **dealer1** database and generate the **dealer1**:

   ```
   %AXIS_DEVHOME%\chapter8\dealer1>mysql < dealer-DDL.sql
   ```

3. Finally run the `dealer1-DML.sql` file to populate the tables in the **dealer1** database as shown below:

   ```
   %AXIS_DEVHOME%\chapter8\dealer1>mysql < dealer1-DML.sql
   ```

4. Install the two services using the following commands. These commands assumes that the various JARS required for AXIS are on your classpath.

   ```
   %SYSTEM_ROOT%/wrox-axis/chapter8/dealer1>java
           org.apache.axis.client.AdminClient
               -l
   http://localhost:5080/axis/servlet/AxisServlet
           AppointmentServiceDeploy.wsdd
   ```

   ```
   %SYSTEM_ROOT%/wrox-axis/chapter8/dealer1>java
           org.apache.axis.client.AdminClient
               -l
   http://localhost:5080/axis/servlet/AxisServlet
           InventoryServiceDeploy.wsdd
   ```

In both these cases, you will have to make sure that `%mysql_installdir%/bin` is in your path, or that the `mysql.exe` program can be found by your system. Alternatively, you can replace the command `mysql` with the full path to the MySQL executable.

Deploy the Application

Copy `Dealer1` directory from `%AXIS_DEVHOME%\chapter8\dealer1` to the `%CATALINA_HOME%\webapps` directory. This will make sure that you have your web application, along with the web services all setup and ready.

Dealer 2 Setup

dealer2 takes exactly the same form as dealer1 but with the filenames updated to reflect the second application. Follow the steps outlined below.

Create Database

1. Make sure that an instance of MySQL Server is running.

2. Use the **mysql** command utility to create a MySQL database named **dealer2** by running the `dealer-DDL.sql` file, generating the dealer2 schema as shown below:

    ```
    %AXIS_DEVHOME%\chapter8\dealer2>mysql < dealer-DDL.sql
    ```

3. Finally run the `dealer2-DML.sql` file to populate the tables in the **dealer2** database as shown below:

    ```
    %AXIS_DEVHOME%\chapter8\dealer2>mysql < dealer2-DML.sql
    ```

4. Install the two services noting the change of port number for the server.

    ```
    %SYSTEM_ROOT%/wrox-axis/chapter8/dealer2>java
        org.apache.axis.client.AdminClient
            -1 http://localhost:6080/axis/servlet/AxisServlet
            AppointmentServiceDeploy.wsdd
    ```

    ```
    %SYSTEM_ROOT%/wrox-axis/chapter8/dealer2>java
        org.apache.axis.client.AdminClient
            -1 http://localhost:6080/axis/servlet/AxisServlet
            InventoryServiceDeploy.wsdd
    ```

Deploy the Application

Copy `Dealer2` directory from `%AXIS_DEVHOME%\chapter8\dealer2` to the `%CATALINA_HOME%\webapps` directory. This will make sure that you have your web application, along with the web services all setup and ready.

UMW Setup

Again, the setup for the UMW application is as before:

Create Database

1. Make sure that an instance of MySQL Server is running.

2. Create a database named **umw** and run the `umw-DDL.sql` file on this database to generate the **umw** schema as shown below:

    ```
    %AXIS_DEVHOME%\chapter8\umw> mysql < umw-DDL.sql
    ```

3. Finally run the `umw-DML.sql` file to populate the tables in the **umw** database as shown below:
    ```
    %AXIS_DEVHOME%\chapter8\umw>mysql < umw-DML.sql
    ```

3. Deploy the two services for the UMW application as follows:

```
%SYSTEM_ROOT%/wrox-axis/chapter8/umw>java
        org.apache.axis.client.AdminClient
        -l
http://localhost:7080/axis/servlet/AxisServlet
        InventoryServiceDeploy.wsdd

%SYSTEM_ROOT%/wrox-axis/chapter8/umw>java
        org.apache.axis.client.AdminClient
        -l
http://localhost:7080/axis/servlet/AxisServlet
        SparePartOrderServiceDeploy.wsdd
```

Deploy the Application

Copy UMW directory from %AXIS_DEVHOME%\chapter8\umw to the %CATALINA_HOME%\webapps directory.

Running the Application

We are now ready to run our application. Start your Tomcat instance. This will start up three Tomcat instances for Dealer1, Dealer2, and UMW, one after the other. The new few sections contain screenshots of the application. We have divided the screenshots based on functionality.

Spare Part Inventory

We can check the internal Spare Part Inventory web service, which is present for Dealer 1, Dealer 2, and UMW applications. We can check this for Dealer 1 as shown below:

1. Launch your browser and navigate to http://localhost:5080/Dealer1/index.jsp . You will get the screen shown below:

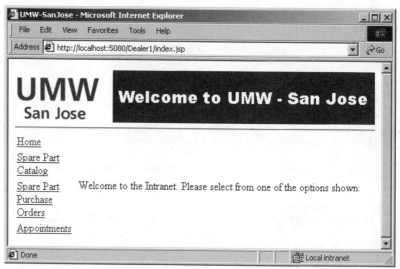

Case Study

8

2. Click on **Spare Part Catalog** link shown above. This will bring up the screen, which lists the spare parts present in the database. You will also find the Current Inventory column, which has been obtained from the `SparePartInventory` web service.

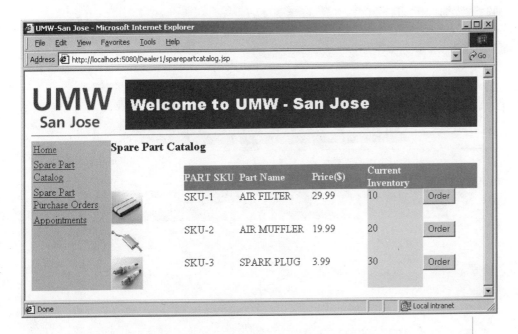

Spare Part Ordering

3. Click on the Order button for SKU-1 in the above screen. What we are doing here is essentially, placing an order for SKU-1. The Purchase Order will be sent to the `SparePartOrder` web service of UMW Application. After you click on **Order**, you will see the following screen:

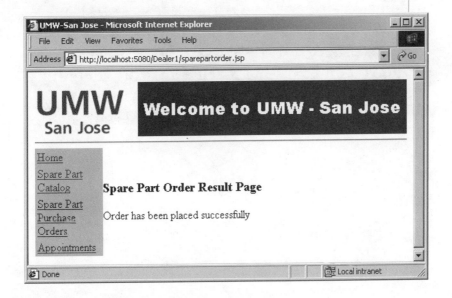

4. For Dealer 1, we can check the current list of purchase orders by clicking on the **Spare Part Purchase Orders** link. This will bring up the screen shown below:

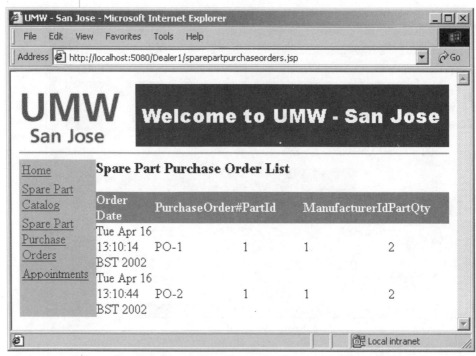

5. Now, let us launch another browser and navigate to the UMW application at. http://localhost:7080/UMW/index.jsp as shown below:

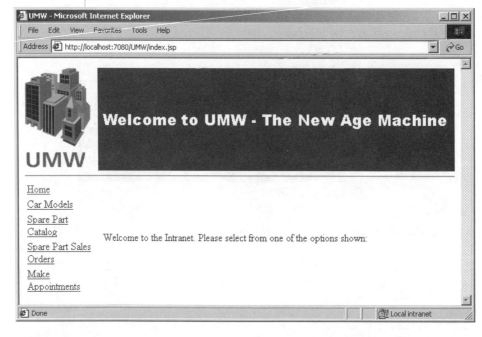

6. Click on the **Spare Part Sales Orders** link. This will display the list of purchase orders that have been received from the dealers. You will find the Dealer 1 purchase order that we just sent.

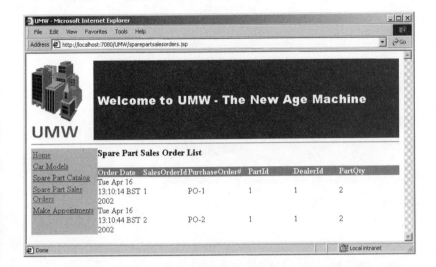

Car Appointment Service Reservation

While, you are in the UMW Application, click on **Make Appointments** Link. This will bring up the list of dealers that are accepting online reservations for Car Service.

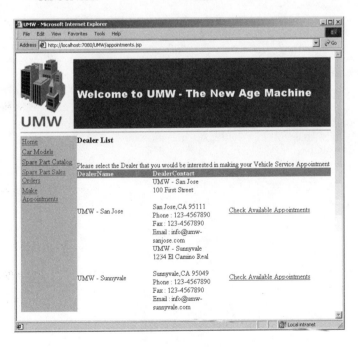

1. Click on **Check Available Appointments** list for Dealer 1; UMW – San Jose; this will bring up the link of appointment slots that are available, as shown below:

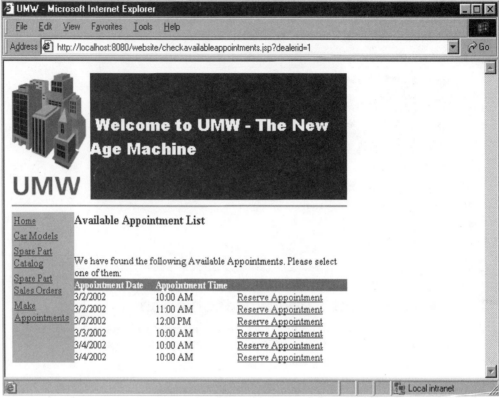

2. Select one of them, enter your name, and click **Submit**. It should give you a message that the reservation was made successfully. The UMW Web Application actually made a call to the Appointment web service of Dealer 1.

3. In the Dealer1 Application, if you click on **Appointments**, you will see the reservation that you just made. We are showing the result from the sample data that we ran.

Case Study

8

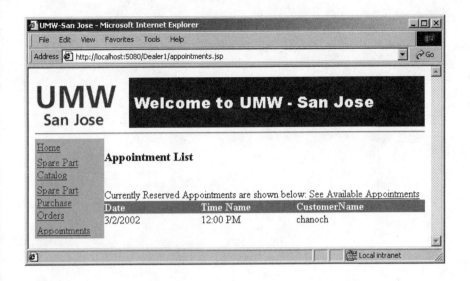

Conclusion

In this chapter, we demonstrated how to use AXIS within the context of a J2EE Web Application. We used a fictitious Car Manufacturing company, UMW, and its dealers. We saw how the IT Team was able to demonstrate the use of AXIS to develop and develop the web services; SparePartInventory, SparePartOrdering, and AppointmentService respectively.

Appendix A

AXIS TCP Monitor

If you have used the Apache Java SOAP implementation, then you might have used **TCPTunnelGui**, which is provided for monitoring TCP requests and responses. AXIS provides a similar utility class, tcpmon (org.apache.axis. utils.tcpmon), for monitoring requests and responses to any TCP port. You can also use tcpmon to act as a TCP router redirecting messages to any desired host and port. While it was obviously created with SOAP messages in mind tcpmon can used to monitor/redirect any traffic passing over TCP.

This utility really comes in to its own when trying to debug SOAP-based applications, as it enables you to see exactly what is being transmitted and received by different parts of the application with out having to write any extra logging code.

The tcpmon can be run as shown below:

```
> java org.apache.axis.utils.tcpmon
```

When you run tcpmon, you will see a window with the title **TCPMonitor**. By default, the **Listener** radio button is selected. The other option, **Proxy**, is used to specify the details of HTTP proxy server, which accepts the hostname and port of the proxy server; this is useful in HTTP tunneling scenarios.

Enter the values of **Listen Port#**, **Target Hostname**, and **Target Port#** for the listener as shown in the following screenshot.

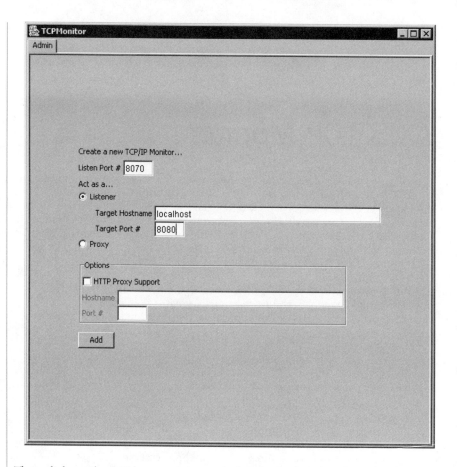

Then click on the **Add** button. A new window is displayed with a tab titled with the Listening Port number. Click on the tab and the following window appears showing the monitor listening for requests on the specified port. Only one application can listen on each port so if for instance you are running Tomcat on a its default port and try and listen with `tcpmon` on the same port a `java.net.BindException` exception will be displayed.

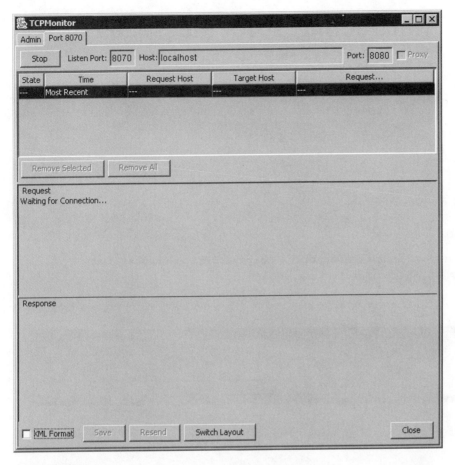

You could also come to this window directly by passing the values of listening port, target host name, and target port from the command prompt:

```
> java org.apache.axis.utils.tcpmon 8070 localhost 8080
```

At this point, the monitor is acting as an intermediary between the client and port 8080, waiting for incoming requests on port 8070. Once it receives a request, it will pass it on to the listener at port 8080. The request is displayed on the upper pane of the window. Since we are going to use Tomcat as the listener, all SOAP requests will be forwarded to the Tomcat engine on port 8080. You can also change the layout of panes by clicking on the **Switch Layout** button at the bottom. This shows the Request and Response panes side by side.

Redirecting SOAP Messages

We are going to test the monitor using `SparePartPriceServiceClient.java` from Chapter 2. However, before running the client application, we need to make a small change. The `endpointURL` points to `localhost` at port 8080. Since we want to direct all SOAP requests to `tcpmon`, we need to use port 8070, as specified in the `tcpmon` listening port, for sending all SOAP requests and receiving all SOAP responses from Tomcat through tcpmon. Hence, you need to change the `endpointURL` as shown below:

```
...
// EndPoint URL for the SparePartPrice  Web Service
String endpointURL =
            "http://localhost:8070/axis/services/SparePartPrice";
...
```

wrox-axis> **java wroxaxis.chapter2.SparePartPriceServiceClient**
The price is $10.99

You can see SOAP request and response messages in the `tcpmon` given below:

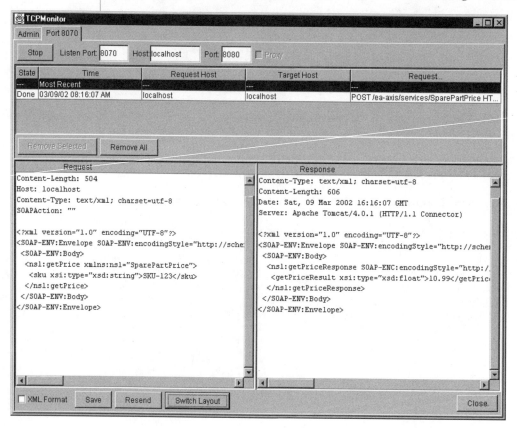

Now each time the client invokes the `SparePartPrice` web service, a connection to port 8070 on `localhost` is made. The request appears in the Request panel, and the response from the server in the Response Panel. `tcpmon` keeps a log of all request-response pairs, and allows you to view any particular pair by selecting an entry in the top panel. You may also remove selected, or all, entries by using **Remove Selected** and **Remove all** buttons respectively. You may also choose to save to a file for later viewing by using the **Save** button.

The **Request** panel shows the outgoing SOAP request comprising a standard HTTP header followed by an XML document that represents the client service invocation, and the **Response** panel shows the resulting SOAP response consisting of a standard HTTP header followed by an XML document that is the server response.

The **Resend** button will re-send the request you are currently viewing, and record a new response. You can edit the XML in the request window before re-sending the SOAP request, and we could use this feature for testing interoperability of SOAP requests generated by various other implementations.

Axis

Appendix B

J2EE Integration

Many organizations have already invested significant resources in developing and maintaining Java Enterprise Applications based on the J2EE standard. One key part of J2EE is the EJB Architecture – a distributed component model for developing enterprise-level server-side components that are scalable, secure, transactional, and multi-user. It is entirely possible to package your business logic into Java Beans and not worry about the EJB API. However, as your business logic becomes more complex and coupling it with enterprise functionality like transactions, resource management, the benefits of the EJB architecture rapidly become apparent. The EJB Container can provide all these system-level services (lifecycle management, connection pooling, transactions, etc.) leaving the developer to concentrate on developing the business logic.

In many cases, it would be useful to make at least some business logic already available in J2EE applications as a Web Service. It extends the reach of your service, as you can't directly access an EJB over the Internet. It also provides a level of abstraction so you could make only some of the functionality of the EJB available to external users or even change the implementation of the business logic without affecting external applications that rely on it.

It would be preferable to expose these EJB components as Web Services without too much extra work and using AXIS this is fairly simple.

We will:

❑   Discuss and develop a simple Stateless Session EJB - `SparePartPrice`

❑   Deploy the `SparePartPrice` EJB in **JBOSS 2.4.4**

❑   Demonstrate how we can access the `SparePartPrice` EJB using an AXIS Client

Note that the material here demonstrates how we can use AXIS with deployed EJB Components that are already deployed. It is not a tutorial on either EJBs or JBOSS. We will assume that readers of this book are comfortable with EJB fundamentals including writing a stateless Session EJB. Wrox Press' *Professional EJB* (ISBN 1-86100-508-3) provides extensive coverage on developing and deploying EJBs.

Note that the current version of AXIS (Beta 1) has no support for either Stateful Session Beans or Entity Beans. This is an often-requested feature and the developers are considering it for future versions.

J2EE Servers and AXIS

Let us look at a high-level architecture diagram that will demonstrate how we can use AXIS to invoke existing functionality that already resides within EJB components deployed in a J2EE Application Server.

Figure 1

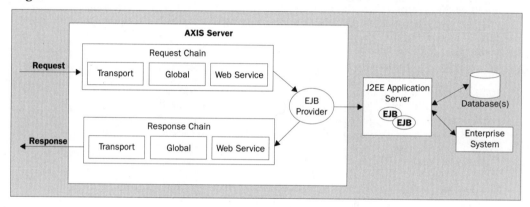

In the above diagram, some EJB's already deployed in a J2EE Application Server provide some useful functionality we want to access, for instance access to databases and enterprise systems. The aim is to retain this piece of the architecture EJB's residing in the Application Server – and invoke it via AXIS with minimal effort.

There are the now familiar Request Chain and Response Chain and we could provide our own hooks into the Transport, Global, and Web Service Chains respectively. AXIS provides a default Pivot Handler to invoke EJBs deployed in a J2EE Application Server, which is called EJBProvider (org.apache.axis.provider.EJBProvider). The EJBProvider is responsible for looking up the EJB Home Interface and retrieving the Remote Object, and then finally invoking the remote method on the EJB.

The WSDD configuration for a service in AXIS that uses the EJBProvider is shown below:

```
<service name="ServiceName" provider="java:EJB">
  <parameter name="beanJndiName" value="JNDIName"/>
  <parameter name="homeInterfaceName" value="homeInterfaceClassName"/>
  <parameter name="allowedMethods" value="methodName"/>
  <parameter name="jndiURL" value="NamingServiceProviderURL"/>
```

```
    <parameter name="jndiContextClass"
            value="InitialContextFactoryClassName"/>
</service>
```

To understand the above configuration, let us consider a very simple Stateless Session EJB, SparePartPrice that we will develop later. It has a single method named getSparePartPrice(). The EJB classes are shown below:

- ❑ SparePartPriceSessionHome.class [HOME INTERFACE] This is for the lifecycle operations associated with the EJB container's management of the bean.

- ❑ SparePartPriceSession.class [REMOTE INTERFACE] This defines the business methods that the bean implements and provides the external representation of the bean

- ❑ SparePartPriceSessionBean.class [BEAN IMPLEMENTATION] This contains the implementation of the bean.

Let us assume that we have this Session Bean deployed in JBOSS. The default JNDI values for accessing a JBOSS server are:

```
INITIAL_CONTEXT_FACTORY = org.jnp.interfaces.NamingContextFactory
PROVIDER_URL = jnp://localhost:1099
```

Finally, let us assume that the Java Naming and Directory Interface (JNDI) name for this EJB is SparePartPriceJNDIName.

Using the above values, if we had to define an AXIS Service named SparePartPriceEJBService, that accessed the above bean the WSDD details would be as follows:

```
<service name="SparePartPriceEJBService" provider="java:EJB">
  <parameter name="beanJndiName" value="SparePartPriceJNDIName"/>
  <parameter name="homeInterfaceName" value="SparePartPriceSessionHome"/>
  <parameter name="allowedMethods" value="getSparePartPrice"/>
  <parameter name="jndiURL" value=" jnp://localhost:1099"/>
  <parameter name="jndiContextClass"
            value=" org.jnp.interfaces.NamingContextFactory "/>
</service>
```

SparePartPrice EJB

The SparePartPrice EJB is a Stateless Session Bean. It has a single method named getSparePartPrice(), which can be used to get the price of a spare part.

SparePartPrice EJB Development

We have defined the SparePartPrice home interface, the remote interface, and the bean implementation. It should be straightforward for anyone with knowledge of simple EJB Session Beans.

SparePartPrice Home Interface

```
// SparePartPriceSessionHome.java

package wroxaxis.appendixb;

import javax.ejb.EJBHome;
import javax.ejb.CreateException;
import javax.ejb.EJBException;
import java.rmi.RemoteException;
import wroxaxis.appendixb.SparePartPriceSession;
import wroxaxis.appendixb.SparePartPriceSessionBean;
```

The `SparePartPriceSessionHome` interface extends the `javax.ejb.EJBHome` interface and has a single method `create()`, which is used to allow clients to access an instance of the bean. The `create()` method returns a reference to the remote interface of the bean, `SparePartPriceSession`.

```
public interface SparePartPriceSessionHome extends EJBHome {
  wroxaxis.appendixb.SparePartPriceSession create()
    throws CreateException, EJBException, RemoteException;
}
```

Remote Interface

```
// SparePartPriceSession.java

package wroxaxis.appendixb;

import javax.ejb.EJBObject;
import java.rmi.RemoteException;
import javax.ejb.EJBException;
import wroxaxis.appendixb.SparePartPriceSessionBean;
```

The remote interface of the bean defines the business methods that the bean exposes to the client. We have a single business method `getSparePartPrice()`, which takes a `String` parameter identifying the part we are interested in and returns a `Float` object containing the price of the item.

```
public interface SparePartPriceSession extends EJBObject {
    Float getSparePartPrice(String sku) throws RemoteException,
EJBException;
}
```

Bean Implementation

```
// SparePartPriceSessionBean.java

package wroxaxis.appendixb;
```

```
import javax.ejb.SessionBean;
import javax.ejb.SessionContext;
import java.rmi.RemoteException;
import javax.ejb.EJBException;
import javax.ejb.CreateException;
import wroxaxis.appendixb.SparePartPriceSessionHome;
import wroxaxis.appendixb.SparePartPriceSession;

public class SparePartPriceSessionBean implements SessionBean {
```

Shown below are the lifecycle methods of the bean; for this simple example we will be providing empty implementations for each of the lifecycle methods. The setSessionContext() method is called by the container just before the create() method. It is provided with a SessionContext object that can be used by the bean to introspect the environment under which it is running. We could store an instance of the context in an instance variable for later reference.

```
public void setSessionContext(SessionContext context)
    throws RemoteException, EJBException {
}
```

The ejbCreate() method is called by the EJB Container to create an instance of the bean. It is called right after the setSessionContext() method shown above. We could do some initialization or allocation of resources in this method. However, since we don't need anything like that, we provide an empty implementation.

```
public void ejbCreate()
    throws CreateException, EJBException, RemoteException {
}
```

The EJB Container invokes the ejbRemove() method when it needs to remove an instance of this bean from its instance pool. The bean can then free up resources that are allocated.

```
public void ejbRemove() throws RemoteException, EJBException {
}
```

If the client does not use the bean for a long time or if the server decides to free up resources, then it is possible that the Container will passivate the bean. It does that by invoking the ejbPassivate() method shown below, in which you could free up allocated resources. Similarly, the Container can re-activate this instance by calling the ejbActivate() method. Again, we provide empty implementations since we are not doing anything here.

```
public void ejbActivate() throws RemoteException, EJBException {
}

public void ejbPassivate() throws RemoteException, EJBException {
}
```

The getSparePartPrice() method, which was defined in the remote interface, is implemented here. To keep our implementation simple, we will be returning a hard-coded value of **$10.95**.

```
public Float getSparePartPrice(String sku){
  return new Float((float)10.95);
}
}
```

Deployment Descriptor

This is the standard ejb-jar.xml deployment descriptor. It defines the SparePartPrice EJB as a <session> bean and references the correct <home>, <remote> and <ejb-class> (bean implementation) classes. It also specifies the bean as Stateless.

```xml
<?xml version="1.0"?>
<!DOCTYPE ejb-jar PUBLIC '-//Sun Microsystems, Inc.//DTD Enterprise
JavaBeans
 2.0//EN' 'http://java.sun.com/j2ee/dtds/ejb-jar_2_0.dtd'>
<ejb-jar>
  <description>SparePartPrice Session EJB</description>
  <display-name>SparePartPriceSessionBean</display-name>
  <enterprise-beans>
    <session>
      <ejb-name>SparePartPriceSessionBean</ejb-name>
      <home> wroxaxis.appendixb.SparePartPriceSessionHome</home>
      <remote> wroxaxis.appendixb.SparePartPriceSession</remote>
      <ejb-class>wroxaxis.appendixb.SparePartPriceSessionBean</ejb-class>
      <session-type>Stateless</session-type>
      <transaction-type>Container</transaction-type>
    </session>
  </enterprise-beans>
  <assembly-descriptor>
    <container-transaction>
      <method>
        <ejb-name>SparePartPriceSessionBean</ejb-name>
        <method-intf>Remote</method-intf>
        <method-name>*</method-name>
      </method>
      <method>
        <ejb-name>SparePartPriceSessionBean</ejb-name>
        <method-name>*</method-name>
      </method>
      <method>
        <ejb-name>SparePartPriceSessionBean</ejb-name>
        <method-intf>Home</method-intf>
```

```
        <method-name>*</method-name>
      </method>
      <trans-attribute>NotSupported</trans-attribute>
    </container-transaction>
  </assembly-descriptor>
</ejb-jar>
```

Now that we have developed the `SparePartPrice` EJB, we will deploy it in JBOSS 2.4.4. At the same time, we will cover how to invoke it via AXIS.

First, let's create the directory structure for our development,

```
%AXIS_DEVHOME%\wroxaxis\appendixb\SparePartPriceSessionHome.java
%AXIS_DEVHOME%\wroxaxis\appendixb\SparePartPriceSession.java
%AXIS_DEVHOME%\wroxaxis\appendixb\SparePartPriceSessionBean.java
%AXIS_DEVHOME%\wroxaxis\appendixb\META-INF\ejb-jar.xml
```

JBOSS 2.4.4

In this section, we will be using the JBOSS 2.4.4 Application Server. This is free and can be downloaded from http://www.jboss.org/binary.jsp; (you just need the basic version not one that includes Tomcat or Jetty). Installation is simple, just unzipping the download to an appropriate directory – the default on Windows is `c:\jboss-2.4.4`. Start the application server, using `run.bat` (or `run.sh` if your running on UNIX), which is located in the `bin` subdirectory of the JBOSS installation directory.

JBOSS-specific Deployment Descriptor

JBOSS also has its own deployment descriptor. The JBOSS-specific deployment descriptor is called `jboss.xml`. The main point to note is the `<jndi-name>` of the `SparePartPriceSessionBean`. This JNDI name will be the same name that we shall use when we deploy our service in AXIS. Copy this file to `%AXIS_DEVHOME%\wroxaxis\appendixb\META-INF` directory.

```xml
<?xml version="1.0" encoding="UTF-8"?>
<jboss>
  <enterprise-beans>
    <session>
      <ejb-name>SparePartPriceSessionBean</ejb-name>
      <jndi-name>SparePartPriceJNDIName</jndi-name>
    </session>
  </enterprise-beans>
</jboss>
```

Deploying the SparePartPrice Session EJB in JBOSS

We now have everything we need to deploy our `SparePartPrice` EJB into JBOSS. To make things simple, we provide a batch file (`buildJBOSS.cmd`) that will do the following:

1. Compile the `SparePartPrice` EJB Source files. Note that the required JAR Files from JBOSS are included in the CLASSPATH.

2. Package the class files generated in Step 1, along with `ejb-jar.xml` and `jboss.xml` file into `SparePartPriceEJB.jar`. WebLogic, JBOSS does not need any additional processing of the JAR file.

3. Compile the AXIS SOAP Client program `JBOSSServiceClient.java` file that we will use to test the deployed EJB in JBOSS.

```
@REM buildJBOSS.cmd
SET JBOSS_DIST=d:\JBoss-2.4.4

@REM Create the build directory, and copy the deployment descriptors into
it
mkdir JBOSSBuild JBOSSBuild\META-INF
copy META-INF\ejb-jar.xml JBOSSBuild\META-INF
copy META-INF\jboss.xml JBOSSBuild\META-INF
cd ..\..

@REM Compile EJB classes into the build directory (jar preparation)

javac -classpath
.;%JBOSS_DIST%\lib\ext\jboss.jar;%JBOSS_DIST%\lib\ext\jboss-
j2ee.jar;%JBOSS_DIST%\lib\ext\jnpserver.jar;%JBOSS_DIST%\lib\ext\jndi.jar;%
CLASSPATH% -d wroxaxis/appendixb /JBOSSBuild
wroxaxis/appendixb/SparePartPriceSessionHome.java

javac -classpath
.;%JBOSS_DIST%\lib\ext\jboss.jar;%JBOSS_DIST%\lib\ext\jboss-
j2ee.jar;%JBOSS_DIST%\lib\ext\jnpserver.jar;%JBOSS_DIST%\lib\ext\jndi.jar;%
CLASSPATH% -d wroxaxis/appendixb /JBOSSBuild
wroxaxis/appendixb/SparePartPriceSession.java

javac -classpath
.;%JBOSS_DIST%\lib\ext\jboss.jar;%JBOSS_DIST%\lib\ext\jboss-
j2ee.jar;%JBOSS_DIST%\lib\ext\jnpserver.jar;%JBOSS_DIST%\lib\ext\jndi.jar;%
CLASSPATH% -d wroxaxis/appendixb/JBOSSBuild
wroxaxis/appendixb/SparePartPriceSessionBean.java
```

```
@REM Make a EJB jar file, including XML deployment descriptors

cd wroxaxis\appendixb\JBOSSBuild
jar cv0f SparePartPriceEJB.jar META-INF
wroxaxis/appendixb/SparePartPriceSessionHome.class
wroxaxis/appendixb/SparePartPriceSession.class
wroxaxis/appendixb/SparePartPriceSessionBean.class
cd ..
```

For UNIX users a shell script will be provided in the code download.

To build the `SparePartPriceEJB.jar` for JBOSS, perform the following steps:

1. Copy the file shown above, `buildJBOSS.cmd` into the
    `%AXIS_DEVHOME%\wroxaxis\appendixb` directory.

2. Open a console window and go to the
    `%AXIS_DEVHOME%\wroxaxis\appendixb` directory and run the
    `buildJBOSS.cmd` file. This will create a sub-directory named `JBOSSBuild`,
    which will contain the `SparePartPriceEJB.jar` file.

3. Make sure that JBOSS Server is running. Assuming that the environment
    variable `JBOSS_DIST` points to `c:\jboss-2.4.4`, copy the
    `SparePartPriceEJB.jar` file to the `c:\jboss-2.4.4\deploy` directory.
    JBOSS will automatically deploy the EJB.

Now that we have the `SparePartPriceEJB` deployed in JBOSS, we need to
move to the next step: to deploy the Service in AXIS. The WSDD file for this same
is shown below.

WSDD for the SparePartPrice Session Bean

The WSDD file is shown below. We will name our service
`SparePartPriceJBOSSEJB` to distinguish it from the WebLogic Service
(`SparePartPriceWLEJB`). The `beanJNDIName` is the same as the JNDI name
used in the `jboss.xml` file. The JNDI Context Factory and Provider URL are the
ones specific to JBOSS.

```
<deployment xmlns="http://xml.apache.org/axis/wsdd/"
            xmlns:java="http://xml.apache.org/axis/wsdd/providers/java"
            xmlns:xsi="http://www.w3.org/2000/10/XMLSchema-instance">
```

We will call this service **SparePartPriceWLEJB** as shown below. Notice that the
provider is **java:EJB,** which is the `EJBProvider` in AXIS.

```
<service name="SparePartPriceJBOSSEJB" provider="java:EJB">
```

Then we define the <parameter> elements as we discussed before. We need to be careful that the beanJNDIName is the same as the one that we specified in the jboss.xml file. The homeInterfaceName is the Home Interface class file, wroxaxis.appendixb.SparePartPriceSessionHome. The allowedMethods is getSparePartPrice(), which is the only method that was there in the Remote Interface of our EJB. Finally the JNDI Provider and Context are JBOSS specific values.

```
    <parameter name="beanJndiName" value="SparePartPriceJNDIName"/>
    <parameter name="homeInterfaceName"
      value="wroxaxis.appendixb.SparePartPriceSessionHome"/>
    <parameter name="allowedMethods" value="getSparePartPrice"/>
    <parameter name="jndiURL" value="jnp://localhost:1099"/>
    <parameter name="jndiContextClass"
            value="org.jnp.interfaces.NamingContextFactory"/>
  </service>
</deployment>
```

To deploy the SparePartPriceJBOSSEJB Service in AXIS, we will be using the **AdminClient** of AXIS. Follow the steps shown below:

1. Copy the deployJBOSSService.wsdd file to the %AXIS_DEVHOME%\wroxaxis\appendixb directory

2. Make sure that Tomcat Server is running (default port 8080)

3. Open a console window and give the following command:

```
%AXIS_DEVHOME%\wroxaxis\appendixb > java org.apache.axis.client.AdminClient -l
http://localhost:8080/axis/services/AdminService deployJBOSSService.wsdd
```

4. In order for AXIS to lookup the Home Interface and get the Remote Object, we need to make sure that the following files are present in the %AXIS_DEPLOYHOME%\WEB-INF\classes\wroxaxis\appendixb directory:
    *   SparePartPriceSessionHome.class
    *   SparePartPriceSession.class

    These files were generated by the buildJBOSS.cmd file and will be available in the %AXIS_DEVHOME%\wroxaxis\appendixb\JBOSSBuild\wroxaxis\appendixb directory

5. Also, copy the following JBOSS specific JAR files from the %JBOSS_DIST%\lib\ext directory into the %AXIS_DEPLOYHOME%\WEB-INF\lib directory:
    *   jboss.jar
    *   jboss-j2ee.jar
    *   jnpserver.jar

SOAP Client

Here is a simple AXIS SOAP Client that accesses the `SparePartPriceJBOSSEJB` service we have deployed in AXIS. The `JBOSSServiceClient.java` file is shown below. You should be able to follow it quite easily by now.

```java
// JBOSSServiceClient.java
package wroxaxis.appendixb;

import java.net.URL;
import org.apache.axis.client.Service;
import org.apache.axis.client.Call;
import org.apache.axis.encoding.XMLType;

import javax.xml.rpc.ParameterMode;
import javax.xml.rpc.namespace.QName;

public class JBOSSServiceClient {

  public JBOSSServiceClient() {
  }

  public static void main (String args[]) {
    try {

      String endpointURL =
        "http://localhost:8080/axis/services/SparePartPriceJBOSSEJB";
      // Method Name in the EJB
      String methodName  = "getSparePartPrice";
      // Create the Service call
      Service service = new Service();
      Call call = (Call) service.createCall();
      call.setTargetEndpointAddress(new java.net.URL(endpointURL));
      call.setOperationName(new QName("SparePartPriceJBOSSEJB",
                                      methodName));
      call.addParameter("name",XMLType.XSD_STRING,
                        ParameterMode.PARAM_MODE_IN);
      call.setReturnType(XMLType.XSD_FLOAT);

      Object[] params = new Object[] {"SKU-123"};
      Float price = (Float) call.invoke(params);

      //Print out the result
      System.out.println("The price is : " + price.floatValue());
    }
    catch (Exception e) {
```

```
        System.err.println(e.toString());
    }
  }
}
```

Running the SOAP Client

To run the `JBOSSServiceClient` program, follow the steps shown below:

1. Compile `JBOSSServiceClient.java`.

2. Make sure that both JBOSS and Tomcat are running.

3. Open a console window and navigate to `%AXIS_DEVHOME%` directory and run the program as shown below. You should get back the result as shown.

```
%AXIS_DEVHOME%> java wroxaxis.appendixb.JBOSSServiceClient
The price is : 10.95
```

Conclusion

The steps required to expose existing business functionality in EJB's as a Web Service are:

Make sure that your Application Server (JBOSS, etc.) is set up correctly and that the EJBs that you wish to expose are deployed.

Create the AXIS WSDD file to enable AXIS to look up the EJB.

Deploy the WSDD in AXIS to ensure that the EJB Interfaces are now available as a Web Service.

Utilizing existing applications is the key in an enterprise scenario. It is important that existing business functionality in EJB Components within the J2EE Application can be invoked in a seamless fashion. We have seen how easy it was to use the existing EJB Provider in AXIS to invoke the `SparePartPrice` Session EJB as a Web Service.

AXIS

Appendix C

JAX-RPC

In its effort to keep up with and keep in sync with the web services technology, Sun Microsystems has released a few specifications bundled in the so called "JAX Pack". In the JAX Pack, the specification that addresses the mechanism for making a Remote Procedure Call (RPC) and receiving responses using an XML protocol is known as **Java API for XML-based RPC** (JAX-RPC). The JAX-RPC specification is currently being developed as JSP-101 (http://jcp.org/jsr/detail/101.jsp), which is being worked on under the Java Community Process (JCP) and may be subjected to changes in the next releases.

Though JAX-RPC is still in its infancy, it's worth having a look at it for the following two reasons:

❑   Since JAX-RPC is from Sun, sooner or later all the Java vendors will be supporting it

❑   AXIS has already started supporting JAX-RPC though not fully at the moment, and this support will probably be extended

Since we are more interested in the second point, we will discuss JAX-RPC briefly and then look at AXIS support for JAX-RPC.

Introduction to JAX-RPC

We know that the RPC mechanism enables a remote procedure call from a client to be communicated to a remote server. In XML-based RPC, this remote procedure call is represented using an XML-based protocol, such as SOAP 1.1. The JAX-RPC specification defines a model and Java based APIs for deploying web services, making remote procedure calls to the web service, and receiving responses. Though the current version of the specification defines RPC calls over SOAP 1.1, JAX-RPC has a modular design that should enable it to support other XML based protocols in future. In a nutshell, the JAX-RPC addresses the following:

❑   An API for invoking services

❑   The requirements for implementing a run-time system to provide services

Since covering the JAX-RPC specification completely is beyond the scope of this appendix, we will just walk through the main features and concepts.

API for Invoking a Service

JAX-RPC defines client-side APIs required for dynamic invocation of a service. The core interfaces are listed below:

❑ `javax.xml.rpc.Call` – This interface provides support for dynamic invocation of an operation on the target service. An instance of a `Call` object is configured with the name of the specific operation (method), URI for the service endpoint, name, type, and mode (IN, OUT, or INOUT) of the parameters, and the return type of the method. The `Call` interface also supports request-response and one-way invocation modes.

❑ `javax.xml.rpc.Service` – This interface acts as a factory for the creation of `Call` instances.

❑ `javax.xml.rpc.ServiceFactory` – This is an abstract class that provides a factory for the creation of instances of type `java.xml.rpc.Service`. This enables a J2SE-based client to create a `Service` instance in a portable manner.

❑ `javax.xml.rpc.Stub` – This interface represents the client-side proxy for the target service.

❑ `javax.xml.rpc.JAXRPCException` – This class is thrown by the core APIs to indicate exceptions related to the JAX-RPC run-time mechanisms.

WSDL/XML to Java Mapping

The JAX-RPC specification defines a standard mapping of the WSDL definitions to Java and the mapping of XML data types to Java types. The WSDL/XML to Java mapping specification includes the following:

❑ Mapping of XML data types to the Java types

❑ Mapping the abstract definition of port type, operations, and messages to Java interfaces and classes

❑ Java representation of a `wsdl:port` address specification

❑ Java representation of a `wsdl:service` definition

Java to WSDL/XML Mapping

The specification also contains a standard mapping from Java definitions to XML and WSDL definitions that includes the following:

❑ Definition of a JAX-RPC supported-Java type

❑ Service definition interface for a JAX-RPC service

❑ Mapping from a Java service definition to WSDL definitions

❑ Mapping from the Java types to the XML data types

Message Handlers

JAX-RPC also defines Handlers for plugging in additional RPC processing behavior and enhancing the functionality of the runtime message processing system. The JAX-RPC specification defines an API for the handlers, chain and message context, and the interaction between them. The following diagram shows the main classes of the handler API. This is similar to the handler class API defined in AXIS. The chain is defined as `javax.xml.rpc.handler.HandlerChain` and it contains a generic `javax.xml.rpc.handler.MessageContext` class and the SOAP specific message context known as `javax.xml.rpc.handler.soap.SOAPMessageContext` that contains the SOAP request/response message wrapped inside an object of type `javax.xml.soap.SOAPMessage` as shown below: The `SOAPMessageHandler` is a handler class to be implemented for use in a message processing system.

Figure 1

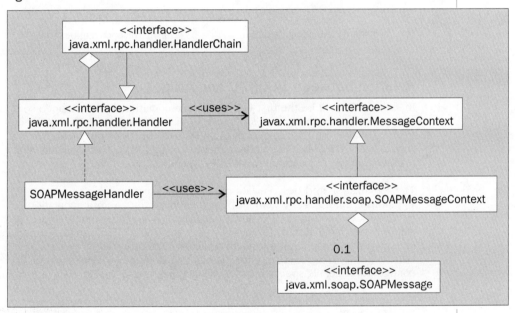

Type Mapping

The JAX-RPC specification defines a standard mapping between XML data types and Java types. The standard type mapping supports a set of XML data types defined in SOAP 1.1 encoding and XML schema specification like built-in data types (int, float, double, etc.), enumerations, arrays of bytes, `Structs`, `xsd:all`, `xsd:sequence` and `xsd:complexType` etc.

The JAX-RPC specification defines APIs to support an extensible type-mapping framework. These APIs enable development of pluggable serializers and deserializers to support extensible mapping between any Java type and XML data type.

Figure 2

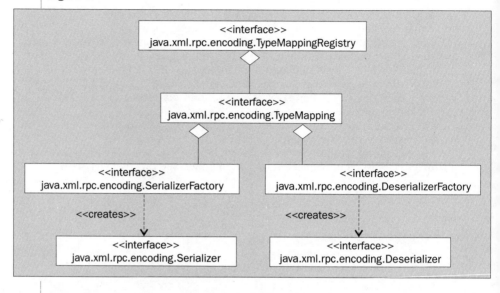

Relation between JAX-RPC and AXIS

In short, AXIS will be the first JAX-RPC implementation from any open source community. Apart from Sun's Reference Implementation (RI), AXIS is the only freely available implementation of JAX-RPC. But this does not mean that we should see AXIS only as an implementation of JAX-RPC. AXIS contains many features that are not defined in JAX-RPC specification.

The serialization and deserialization framework including the TypeMappingRegistry defined by AXIS is basically an implementation of the framework defined in the JAX-RPC specification with some extra features. For example, we have already discussed earlier that the AXIS deserializer interface is extended by a CallBack interface. Similarly AXIS uses WSDDTypeMappingRegistry for maintaining in-memory representation of configuration details specified in the WSDD file.

The framework for deployable items such as handlers and chains is based on JAX-RPC. But AXIS apart from implementing the JAX-RPC Handler and HandlerChain (JAX-RPC counterpart of AXIS Chain) AXIS also defines a TargetedChain with a specialized pivot handler.

AXIS implements the client-side APIs like Stub, Call, Service, ServiceFactory, and JAXRPCException all from the package, javax.xml.rpc that are defined in JAX-RPC specification. AXIS also implements the framework defined for the mapping for Java to XML/WSDL and vice versa.

Axis

Appendix D

Support and Code Download

We always value hearing from our readers, and we want to know what you think about this book: what you liked, what you didn't like, and what you think we can do better next time. You can send us your comments, either by returning the reply card in the back of the book, or by e-mailing us at feedback@wrox.com. Please be sure to mention the book title in your message.

Downloading the Code for this Book

When you log on to the Wrox site, http://www.wrox.com/, simply locate the title through our fast code download finder facility or by using one of the title lists. Click on Download in the Code column or on Download Code on the book's detail page.

The files that are available for download from our site have been archived using WinZip. When you have saved the archive to a folder on your hard-drive, you may need to extract the files using WinZip or a compatible tool (such as the `jar` utility that ships with the Java SDK). Inside the zip file will be a folder structure and an HTML file that explains the structure and gives you further information.

Errata

We've made every effort to ensure that there are no errors in the text or in the code. However, no one is perfect and mistakes can occur. If you find an error in one of our books, like a spelling mistake or a faulty piece of code, we would be very grateful for feedback. By sending in errata, you may save another reader hours of frustration, and of course, you will be helping us provide even higher quality information. Simply e-mail the information to support@wrox.com; your information will be checked and, if correct, posted to the errata page for that title.

To find errata on the web site log on to http://www.wrox.com/earlyadopter and simply locate and click on the title on that page. Click on the Book Errata link on the book's detail page:

E-Mail Support

If you have a problem using any of the code or techniques shown in the book, and wish to discuss it with an expert who knows the book in detail, then e-mail support@wrox.com with the title of the book and the last four numbers of the ISBN in the subject field of the e-mail. A typical e-mail should include the following things:

wrox
Programmer to Programmer™

p2p.wrox.com
The programmer's resource centre

A unique free service from Wrox Press
With the aim of helping programmers to help each other

Wrox Press aims to provide timely and practical information to today's programmer. P2P is a list server offering a host of targeted mailing lists where you can share knowledge with four fellow programmers and find solutions to your problems. Whatever the level of your programming knowledge, and whatever technology you use P2P can provide you with the information you need.

ASP Support for beginners and professionals, including a resource page with hundreds of links, and a popular ASP.NET mailing list.

DATABASES For database programmers, offering support on SQL Server, mySQL, and Oracle.

MOBILE Software development for the mobile market is growing rapidly. We provide lists for the several current standards, including WAP, Windows CE, and Symbian.

JAVA A complete set of Java lists, covering beginners, professionals, and server-side programmers (including JSP, servlets and EJBs)

.NET Microsoft's new OS platform, covering topics such as ASP.NET, C#, and general .NET discussion.

VISUAL BASIC Covers all aspects of VB programming, from programming Office macros to creating components for the .NET platform.

WEB DESIGN As web page requirements become more complex, programmer's are taking a more important role in creating web sites. For these programmers, we offer lists covering technologies such as Flash, Coldfusion, and JavaScript.

XML Covering all aspects of XML, including XSLT and schemas.

OPEN SOURCE Many Open Source topics covered including PHP, Apache, Perl, Linux, Python and more.

FOREIGN LANGUAGE Several lists dedicated to Spanish and German speaking programmers, categories include. NET, Java, XML, PHP and XML

How to subscribe
Simply visit the P2P site, at http://p2p.wrox.com/